HOW NOVELS THINK

How Novels Think

The Limits of Individualism from 1719–1900

NANCY ARMSTRONG

COLUMBIA UNIVERSITY PRESS
NEW YORK

COLUMBIA UNIVERSITY PRESS
Publishers Since 1893
New York   Chichester, West Sussex

Library of Congress Cataloging-in-Publication Data

Armstrong, Nancy, 1938–
    How novels think : the limits of British individualism from 1719–1900 /
Nancy Armstrong.
        p.   cm.
    Includes bibliographical references and index.
    ISBN 0–231–13058–9 (cloth : alk. paper) —
    ISBN 0–231–13059–7 (pbk. : alk. paper) — ISBN 0–231–50387–3 (e-book)
    1. English fiction—19th century—History and criticism. 2. Individualism in
literature. 3. Literature and society—Great Britain—History—19th century.
4. Literature and society—Great Britain—History—18th century. 5. English
fiction—18th century. 6. Didactic fiction, English—History and criticism.
7. Ethics in literature. I. Title.

PR868.I615A76 2006
823'.809—dc22

                                                                2005053782

Columbia University Press books are printed on permanent and durable acid-free paper.

Printed in the United States of America

c 10 9 8 7 6 5 4 3 2 1
p 10 9 8 7 6 5 4 3 2

In memory of Homer Obed Brown

Contents

ACKNOWLEDGMENTS

My lifelong skepticism about the truth of individualism no doubt inspired this book, and writing it was far from an individual venture. It could not have happened without the generosity of Rey Chow, who sent me to Jennifer Crewe, the very best of editors. She in turn persuaded me to make a book-length argument out of a series of talks on the novel I was delivering at a number of universities during the period from 1999 to 2004.

These being precisely the years I served as chair of English at Brown University, I relied on conversations with my graduate students to figure out most of what I wanted to say. That I did come to understand the overarching argument of my research during this period is owing to the remarkable group of new scholars with whom I worked closely, including Carolyn Berman, Frank Christianson, Lois Cucullu, Nick Daly, Amanda Emerson, Jen Fleissner, Jonathan Goldman, Jared Green, Avak Hasratian, Cole Heinowitz, Ivan Kreilkamp, John Marx, Lisa O'Connell, Caroline Reitz, Jen Ruth, Jason Solinger, Ezra Tawil, Cynthia Tolentino, Annette Van, and Eugenia Zuroski. Without the persistent ingenuity of my research assistant, Sian Silyn Roberts, I would still be lost in the library, looking for the edition of a novel I cited or tracking down the exact title of an article I read a year or two ago.

I am equally indebted to the junior faculty hired and in three cases tenured during my years as chair: Timothy Bewes, Stuart Burrows, Jean

Feerick, Olakunle George, Arlene Keizer, Daniel Kim, Rolland Murray, and Ravit Reichman. The extraordinary diversity of their projects and the infectious energy with which they discuss ideas put the lie to those who would cast the future of the humanities in doubt. My kitchen cabinet—Mutlu Blasing, Jim Egan, Phil Gould, Bill Keach, Kevin McLaughlin, Ellen Rooney, and Barbara Herrnstein Smith—turned the ordinary trials of a chairmanship into a group triumph.

I am blessed with good friends. Of my kin group in the profession, those imaginary interlocutors who wrote this book along with me are too numerous to name. I must single out Dan Cottom, John Kucich, Deidre Lynch, Pam Morris, Kathy Psomiades, Cliff Siskin, and Jennifer Wicke for seeing me through moments of uncertainty in the production and publication of the manuscript.

Len and Maude sustain the illusion of my autonomy.

Oak Bluffs, Massachusetts
May 2005

HOW NOVELS THINK

INTRODUCTION

HOW NOVELS THINK

Painted in 1780 and 1781 by Sir Joshua Reynolds, the portrait reproduced on the cover and as the frontispiece of this book illustrates the paradox that I will spell out over the course of five chapters. This image of Master Bunbury was quickly enveloped in a fantasy that permanently pinned an identity to the distinctive image of an otherwise nondescript boy. Although art historians still quarrel over which of two Bunbury brothers he actually was, the older or younger, the kind of identity I have in mind for this individual has little to do with birth. The transformation that secured a new kind of identity for the subject of Reynolds's painting began as an anecdote and was repeated over the next two centuries. In order to account for the portrait's curious expression, the slightly open mouth and wide-eyed stare, the anecdote has it that Reynolds told stories as he painted the boy who sat listening—spellbound—on a grassy knoll in front of a tree. Here, in miniature, is the modern subject.

According to eighteenth-century epistemology and moral philosophy, the modern subject came into being as it took in sensations from the outside world and, of that material, composed first the ideas and then the judgment and moral sense that gave it a self-enclosed and internally coherent identity. Thus we see in this painting, as opposed to Reynolds's portraits of distinguished men and women, a decisive shift of the viewer's attention away from the surface of the subject's body, traditionally read as the sign of his position in the world. More than perhaps any other Reynolds portrait, the painting of young Bunbury invites the viewer to speculate on the interior life animating the individual whose motion has been arrested by storytelling. The debate over whether Reynolds painted the first or second Bunbury son has taken second place to the psychological question of what would produce such an expression on the child's face. With the help of an anecdotal explanation, that expression invites us to imagine ourselves in his place, wearing much the same expression.

The fact that Bunbury's image provided the outward and visible signs of a unique state of mind also called attention to the painter.[1] In 1781 the *Gazetteer* reported what soon became the salient facts of the portrait. Young Bunbury was "so vivacious that Sir Joshua could not have settled him in any steady posture if he had not told him an entertaining story, which fixed his attention."[2] This story traveled with the image to the Royal Academy exhibition of 1781, where poet and philosopher Dr. James Beattie declared it one of the two best portraits by England's most celebrated painter and described it as "a Boy, supposed to be listening to a wonderful story" (quoted in Dorment, *British Painting*, 294). Horace Walpole was reported to have found the portrait "charming" (quoted in ibid., 296). Nor has the deterioration of the bituminous paint over time diminished either the painting's power to recall the anecdote or the anecdote's power to reanimate the image. Offering modern testimony to the story's ability to shift the source of the boy's uniqueness back onto the painter is Richard Dorment's speculation that "it may not be fanciful to see in the woods darkening behind Henry and the (gnarled?) tree trunk to the left, an evocation of the slightly scary settings usual in fairy stories" (ibid., 294). Given that Henry Fuseli, the well-known painter of nightmares, was Reynolds's contemporary and occasional interlocutor, it strikes me as entirely plausible that Reynolds did in fact coax this expression from the lad by telling him frightening stories. True to the gothic sensibility, the sensations to which the boy's facial expression is attributed did not arise from actual objects. Born of stories, these sensations came from somewhere in the foreground—already charged with emotion—to arrest the movement captured in his rumpled clothes and open shirt.

Let us assume that stories did move the subject of Reynolds's painting, even while they fixed his body to a place. For the purposes of this book, I would also ask you to assume that the well-lit natural landscape to the left of the tree trunk, where objects behave as objects should—a world in continuity with our own—as no less fictional than the dark and apparently phantasmagorical background on the right. I plan to read the familiar terrain of realism as the other side of the gothic, as if the two existed in a mutually defining relationship. In so enclosing painter, subject, and spectator entirely within a world of fiction where each exists as an individual to others, this way of reading the image provides what I consider a useful model for the mutually constitutive relationship between novelists and their protagonists during the period when Reynolds painted this portrait, a period when novels were acquiring the power to endow their readers with individuality as well.

This book argues that the history of the novel and the history of the modern subject are, quite literally, one and the same. The British novel provides the test case. It came into being, I believe, as writers sought to formulate a kind of subject that had not yet existed in writing. Once formulated in fiction, however, this subject proved uniquely capable of reproducing itself not only in authors but also in readers, in other novels, and across British culture in law, medicine, moral and political philosophy, biography, history, and other forms of writing that took the individual as their most basic unit. Simply put, this class- and culture-specific subject is what we mean by "the individual." To produce an individual, novels had to think as if there already were one, that such an individual was not only the narrating subject and source of writing but also the object of narration and referent of writing. To produce an individual, it was also necessary to invalidate competing notions of the subject—often proposed by other novels—as idiosyncratic, less than fully human, fantastic, or dangerous. The result was a cultural category and a bundle of rhetorical figures that were extremely fragile and always on the defensive yet notably flexible and ever ready to adapt to new cultural-historical conditions.[3]

THINKING UP THE INDIVIDUAL

To put conceptual flesh on this hypothesis, we might think of the human body much as John Locke thought of the human mind: as a "cabinet" or "storehouse" emptied of all innate qualities and waiting to be furnished with information from the world.[4] This evacuation of the body's intrinsic value raises the question of how and under what conditions such a body could accrue social and economic value. Much as the mind, in Locke's theory, acquired information through sensations of the world and then converted those sensations into ideas against which it measured subsequent sensations, so the body, in the fiction of Daniel Defoe and other eighteenth-century novelists, acquired social experience and converted those encounters with the world at large into self-restraint and good manners. The appearance and behavior of the body consequently came to serve as outward and visible signs of the knowledge acquired and judgment developed from firsthand experience. By midcentury, the same body displayed the individual's capacity for sympathy as well.

But not all fictional characters could become the protagonists of a novel. In order to qualify, a character had to harbor an acute dissatisfaction with his or her assigned position in the social world and feel compelled to find a better one. In contrast to the subject of his painting, Sir Joshua Reynolds was just such a person. The eleventh son of an improvident schoolmaster, he became the first president of the Royal Academy of Arts and gained a knighthood. Indeed, I would go so far as to say that Reynolds marked the difference between painter and subject by capturing the boy's restless energy in the stationary pose of a genre reserved for people of distinction. Reynolds then reanimated the portrait with a kind of life that called attention to the painter, as if to say that the painting added the elements of individuality to its traditional subject matter.[5] Novelists had to figure out the rhetorical means of generating dissatisfaction with the available social possibilities before they could create a human subject with the restlessness to grow—over time and in successive stages—both more complete as an individual and more worthy in social terms.[6] Novels thus gave tangible form to a desire that set the body on a collision course with limits that the old society had placed on the individual's options for self-fulfillment, transforming the body from an indicator of rank to the container of a unique subjectivity.

To put it another way, the novels to which I want first to call attention add something new to the attributes that tradition had attached to the positions composing eighteenth-century British society. This rhetorical additive—whether it manifests itself as restlessness, ambition, or eroticism—effectively dislodges the protagonist from an assigned position, pitching him or her into a field of possibilities where, as Defoe's *Robinson Crusoe* (1719) frequently reminds us, one runs the risk of becoming nothing at all. In that it strives to resolve a discrepancy between the individual's idea of, say, love or justice and the material conditions that he or she encounters, this supplement behaves in the manner Locke ascribes to "desire" when he writes: "The uneasiness a Man finds in himself upon the absence of any thing, whose present enjoyment carries the *Idea* of Delight with it, is that we call *Desire*, which is greater or less, as that uneasiness is more or less vehement."[7] In theory, this is all well and good, but how, one must ask, did such "uneasiness" change the way one understood the relationship between one's self and a world that initially failed to provide the conditions for happiness?

It was at this point that Enlightenment philosophy left off and fiction took over. We find the eighteenth-century novel characteristically unwilling to adjust the subject completely to the social world into which he or she was born. On the other hand, Defoe was clearly in the majority when he assumed that one could not simply adjust the world to accommodate the individual, not if that individual came from the same rung of the social ladder as either Crusoe or Moll Flanders (1722). Defoe found his answer in the picaresque form, which allows protagonists to move out of the hierarchy that initially defines them and into a new field of social possibilities, where they can find a place that accommodates their needs and abilities. Of course, only individuals whose wit, will, ability, and desire exceed those appropriate to the position to which they were born can achieve such mobility. Their exception to the social rule at once individuates these protagonists and makes them exemplary of individuals in general.

Where Samuel Richardson also drew on the picaresque tradition for the literary means of moving his protagonists from one position to another within the social order, he could not very well allow his morally scrupulous heroines anywhere near the same physical mobility that Defoe gave Crusoe and Moll. Pamela (1740) is imprisoned in her seducer's country estate, and Clarissa's (1747–48) movements are choreographed by Lovelace to put her in increasingly compromising positions until she lands in Mrs. Sinclair's establishment. To generate the kind of dissatisfaction essential to making a modern protagonist, Richardson came up with another way of driving a wedge between interiority and social position. Pamela's letters reveal her genuine displeasure with Mr. B's sexual advances, her determination to resist him so long as he tries to turn her into a kept woman, and thus her possession of a sensibility befitting a lady. It is literacy alone that transforms her from an object he can forcibly possess into a self-possessed subject who can consent to his offer of marriage. Embodying the core fantasy of the early novel—that writing makes the individual—Pamela writes herself into existence as the wife of a wealthy landowner. Looking back from Pamela at Crusoe and Moll, we can see that their extraordinary adventures could have done little to make them exemplary had they not possessed the means of authoring their respective stories. They were in this sense alone truly exceptional. Each could inscribe him or herself in writing as an object, or body, separate and apart from the subject that inhabited that body, and put that body through a sequence of moves to enhance its social value. Thus they perform what the Lockeans could only theorize: the possibility that a new form of literacy could provide something on the order of a supplement capable of turning an early modern subject into a self-governing individual.

If the novels of Jane Austen (1811–18) represent the perfect synthesis of desiring individual and self-governing citizen, they also mark the moment when that synthesis crumbled under the threat of social rebellion, the rioting of dislocated farm workers, the amassing of unemployed laborers in the industrial centers of England, and any number of social factors that sorely challenged the fantasy of a society composed of self-governing individuals. The first two decades of the nineteenth century also saw the first attempts at canonizing a tradition of fiction, as Anna Laetitia Barbauld, William Mudford, and Sir Walter Scott went to work compiling editions of English novels and writing critical introductions to justify their selections. That his project authorized his generation of novelists becomes evident as Scott calls special attention to the fact that, with Austen, "a style has arisen, within the last fifteen or twenty years, differing from the former [styles of all previous novels] in the points upon which interest hinges; neither alarming our credulity nor amusing our imagination by wild variety of incident, or by those pictures of romantic affection and sensibility, which were formerly as certain attributes of fictitious characters as they are of rare occurrence among those who actually live or die."[8] The novelist who relied on exotic situations and extravagant emotionalism for audience appeal would be found lacking under the new standard. At the same time, Scott is quick to add, the novelist who presumed to follow in Austen's footsteps and try his hand at "the art of copying from nature as she really exists in the common walks of life" would necessarily place "his composition within that extensive range of criticism which general experience offers to every reader" (231). There was now a generic standard by which to measure novels past and future.

As Homer O. Brown points out, the distinction Scott makes between Austen and her predecessors is the very same distinction that he makes between the novel and "romance."[9] Austen's novels mark the simultaneous modernization of the individual and maturation of the novel. Her protagonists whose changes of heart make small but important differences within a circumscribed community of country gentry, their hangers-on, and their dependents were being read alongside the protagonists of Scott. As the author of historical novels that were shaped by and helped to shape a British nation, he found it necessary to distinguish his own novels from "romance." In so doing, Scott no doubt was also interested in distancing himself from gothic fiction. During the period between 1788 and 1807, according to Robert Miles, the gothic represented about 30 percent of the market share.[10] Precisely when its conventions were being consolidated, then, the novel was again heading off in at least two directions, and the figure of the individual appeared to be still very much up for grabs. There was tension both within the tradition Scott sought to establish and between that tradition and the fiction he sought to exclude. Given this double pressure on his generic standard, the novels that reveal the formal exigencies of this moment are not Austen's so much as those novels that could not perform her magical reconciliation of individual demands with those of the larger community.

Scott's *Waverley* (1814) and Mary Shelley's *Frankenstein* (1818) are equally intent on defending the norms of citizenship from the encroachments of individual desire. Waverley's "desultory" education in his uncle's library encourages him to see the violence of the Highlanders through the heroic lens of romance. The monster's encounter with Milton's Satan and Goethe's Werther gives him the means of aggrandizing his assault on the innocent members of Frankenstein's family. As shaped by eighteenth-century novelists, the novel had a very different task in mind when it exploited the supplementary potential of writing. Indeed, education in both *Waverley* and *Frankenstein* cultivates forms of individualism so extravagant that they must be destroyed in the name of humanity. But such a renunciation of its signature trope is not something that novels, being novels, could perform without a serious struggle. Both works consequently bear the scars of their moment in history, as they transform extraordinary forms of individualism into subhuman forms, a threat at once to family and nation. There is no question that the world is much better off once Fergus MacIvor and Frankenstein's monster have been relegated to romance and gothic literature, respectively. Nevertheless, such figures do not pass quietly into historical oblivion. Having invested affect and aesthetic value in qualities of the human subject that exceed the limits of any modern social position, Scott and Shelley leave us in a world that borders on the lifeless when emptied of the grandiose individuality their novels must condemn.

Victorian novels make the turn against expressive individualism a mandatory component of the subject's growth and development. To create an individual, however, still requires the novel to offer an interiority in excess of the social position that individual is supposed to occupy. In the novels that appear during the second half of the nineteenth century, the desire to adjust the dynamic of the community to one's notion of it disrupts the community as a whole. Accordingly, signs of excess have to be disciplined, that is, observed, contained, sublimated, and redirected toward a socially acceptable goal. To become an individual under these circumstances, the subject must still surmount the limits of an assigned social position. This is only the first step on the path to individuality, however, and a false step at that. In a novel like Dickens's *Great Expectations* (1860), we find that individualism is by nature aggressive and expresses itself in cruelty toward the very people whom one should cherish. Cruelty becomes productive in this scenario, as it serves to wear away the protagonist's desire, reconcile him or her to a substitute, and channel the energy of individualism toward socially productive ends. I plan to read the sequence of transformations constituting such novels as a series of displacements driven not by the individual's restless energy so much as by an imperative to close the gap between self and social position without disturbing what appears to be a dangerously fragile social order. The result is a radical reformulation of the individual as a subject layered by successive displacements. This subject is necessarily divided against itself, as the desire essential to that subject's growth and development comes to pose a threat to its individuality. The protagonist of Victorian fiction does not become an individual on the basis of what and how intensely he or she desires; individuality depends on how he or she chooses to displace what is a fundamentally asocial desire onto a socially appropriate object. This process yields the internally conflicted subject produced by the novels that F. R. Leavis celebrates as constituting "the great tradition."[11] Something very much like this process also yields the multilayered consciousness of psychoanalysis.

Indeed, an argument can be made that Freud transformed the figures that I will use to distinguish various epochs in the history of the modern novel—excess, ambivalence, displacement, and repetition—into the tropes through which the unconscious expresses itself. Writing during the early twentieth century alongside the modernists, Freud set out to discover inside the individual many of the same turns of cultural thought that at once brought the individual into being and limited its existence in the interest of a community composed of similar subjects. What would be the point of psychoanalysis without the tropes of supplementation (an unconscious self in excess of one's self), of ambivalence (a love-hate relationship with that self), of displacement (the sequence of disguises, substitutes, and transfers by which we learn to get along with this self in a complex social world), and of repetition (which at once compels and rejects such accommodations)? In so relocating the outside on the inside, it is fair to say, Freud not only transformed the individual from a novel-made discourse into a self-perpetuating one; he also ensured that the subject's personal history would reproduce that of the novel. With Freud, therefore, the individual comes, in theory, to recapitulate the history of the novel, as it rethought its youthful aggression in light of the increasing responsibilities of adulthood and empire.

Over the course of the twentieth century, national traditions of the novel emerged throughout the anglophone world, as they did during the nineteenth century in the United States. I regard this kind of plurality as a later phenomenon. These novels—variously classified as international modernism, postcolonial fiction, and world literature—constitute a unique moment that emerged genealogically out of the consolidation of novelistic conventions and the proliferation of subgenres that characterize the nineteenth-century British novel, which in turn took shape in the open debate over the nature and limits of individualism that organizes the field of eighteenth-century British letters. While I am confining this claim to novels written in English, I suspect this generalization holds true for novels in other national languages as well, so that wherever novels are written and read they are, in all likelihood, reproducing the modern individual in both fiction and fact.[12] If there is any truth to what must remain, for purposes of this book, an unsupported claim, then studies of postcolonial fiction and, more recently, global literature in English have to question whether new national traditions of the novel produced by successive generations of international intellectuals actually challenge rather than perpetuate the hegemony of the British novel by appropriating its formal conventions and making them speak for suppressed or marginalized groups.

I cannot quite believe that any novel can reach in and modify the ideological core of the genre and still remain a novel. In saying this, I am not endorsing the claim that it is impossible to give voice to an emergent nation in the language of the colonial oppressor. What I mean by "the ideological core" is not the British, the European, or even the Western features of the novel but the presupposition that novels think like individuals about the difficulties of fulfilling oneself as an individual under specific cultural historical conditions. Whether this involves resistance, complicity, mimicry, or hybridity does not alter the basic fact that new generations of novels in English produced in different countries are by definition reproducing modern individuals wherever novels are written and read. To be sure, the global spread of the novel changes in wonderful new ways the formal strategies of a genre that sought to distinguish the modern middle class from a people of different ethnic practices, especially different literacies. At the same time, new varieties of novel cannot help taking up the project of universalizing the individual subject. That, simply put, is what novels do.

THE POSSIBILITY OF THINKING OTHERWISE

To this point in my argument, I have depicted the formal growth and development of individualism novelistically: namely, as a more or less inevitable consequence of the concept of the subject that was taking shape in philosophy and science as well as fiction. As I also implied at the outset, I seriously doubt that individualism could have taken shape and spread throughout the West as fast and decisively as it did unless and until the novel had transformed the concept into narrative form. Having described the British novel in novelistic terms, I want to emphasize my subsidiary point that certain novels did not rise to cultural dominance uncontested.[13] What we now call "the novel" won its title in a field of argumentation as it figured out how to adjust to, incorporate, and abject competing ways of thinking about the individual. Indeed, I must insist, the novel represented such opposition in terms that ensured the hegemony of its kind of individual. Although the space of one book does not allow me to do justice to the forms of fiction that novelistic thinking had to keep at bay in order to maintain its authority, I believe that they were very much at work wherever British culture felt compelled to render alternatives to individualism in phobic terms and relegate them to dreams, hallucinations, uncanny experiences, orientalism, exoticism, and tales of horror. In the pages to follow, I will go so far as to attribute the longevity of liberal individualism to its skill at defending the very concept of the individual against assaults on its universality that came from other modes of subject formation.

To get a handle on the relationship between thinking that produces an individual and thinking that calls into question the individual's autonomy, it is helpful to return to the model first put forth by Locke. His 1690 account of how the mind acquires and exercises reason allowed him to explain how men ideally developed into individuals capable of self-government and therefore capable of governing others. To acquire reason, as he tells the story, one fills "the yet empty Cabinet" of the mind with information gathered through encounters with the outside world that enters the mind via the physical senses (I.ii.15). The world supplies raw content in the form of objects, and the mind transforms sensations of those objects into ideas. Once filled with a certain number of sensations, Locke contends, the mind will begin to perceive its own operations. It will reflect on the material it has accumulated by way of the senses and determine how those sensations should be differentiated, arranged, assessed, and generalized. This capacity for judgment is, in Locke's words, one that "Man has wholly in himself" (II.i.4). Never mind that judgment cannot exist until the mind contains enough information for it to sort and classify; it is important for Locke and his followers to establish that judgment originates within the individual mind and is responsible for how we understand and ultimately how we feel about the things we see, hear, touch, taste, and smell.

In terms of its cultural logic, however, the Lockean concept of "sensation" proved to be a two-way street. The self-enclosure of the individual could be challenged on grounds that it was after all composed of information taken into the mind through the portals of the senses. If we begin with a mind that makes ideas as it brings the internal faculty of judgment to bear on the sensations received from things in the world, then the individual's growth and development could well proceed in a manner analogous to a state committed to the protection of personal property. Just as the subject mixes the labor of his body with the material world to convert that material into his very own property, so in mixing his judgment with sensations of the things of this world he accumulates intellectual property and acquires a mind of his own.[14] But if, by the same token, the knowledge one acquires—knowledge that the protagonist of *Robinson Crusoe* considers a major source of his self-worth—comes from outside, then who is to say that the subject is not permeable to sensations already packaged as ideas, invested with value, and charged with feeling? Who is to say that either our ideas or feelings are in fact our own?

In 1777 David Hume took issue with Locke's claim that our emotions are products of the ideas of pleasure and pain, good and evil, all of which are inferred from our sensations, but he did not part ways with Locke on the basic issue of self-enclosure. Hume simply shifted the emphasis to "our more lively perceptions, when we hear, or see, or feel, or love, or hate, or desire, or will" over and above "the less lively perceptions, of which we are conscious, when we reflect on any of those sensations or movements above mentioned."[15] We do not arrive at ideas through reasoning, in Hume's opinion, much less at the sentiments that move us to action. Quite the contrary, he contends, it is from "the constant conjunction of two objects—heat and flame"—that we learn to "expect the one from the appearance of the other" (43). Our knowledge that flames will be hot "is the necessary result of placing the mind in such circumstances" (46). So, too, when we feel "love, or hate, or desire, or will," we draw on previous occasions for such feeling and imagine ourselves back in those same circumstances. Thus, when we receive benefits, we automatically feel the passion of love, and we feel hatred, conversely, when we meet with injuries. Hume sends the individual back to primary sensations in order to insist that both ideas and feelings are shaped by "custom" rather than logical inference. If our emotional reactions seem to arise directly from some object, it is only because we have grown accustomed to responding with a particular emotion to that stimulus.

The claim that feelings come from within the individual inevitably gives rise to the question of how individuals share their feelings with one another. That they must do so without compromising their individuality is essential to the notion of a society made of individuals. In his revision of a grisly passage from Mandeville, Rousseau makes it absolutely clear that it is in man's nature to sympathize with his fellow human beings.[16] Refuting the notorious claim that human nature is void of the social virtues, Rousseau revels in the fact that Mandeville himself

> is forced to recognize man as a compassionate and sensitive Being and abandon ... his cold and subtle style, to offer us the pathetic picture of a man locked up, who outside sees a ferocious Beast tearing a Child from his Mother's breast, breaking his weak limbs with murderous fangs, and tearing the Child's throbbing entrails with its claws. What a dreadful agitation must not this witness to an event in which he takes no personal interest whatsoever experience? What anguish must he not suffer at this sight, unable to give any help to the fainted Mother or the dying Child?[17]

In order to show that man is by nature predisposed to share another's anguish, the scene Rousseau serves up is deliberately overdone. We can, I think, chalk up the durability of this example—found not only in Bernard Mandeville's *Fable of the Bees* (1714) and Rousseau's *Discourse on the Origins of Inequality* (1755) but also in Adam Smith's *Theory of Moral Sentiments* (1759) and many others—to its hyperbolic demonstration of the principle that one individual comes to know how another feels by witnessing the spectacle of the other's suffering.

According to Adam Smith, such emotions sometimes appear "to arise merely from the view of a certain emotion in another person." Emotions, he admits, "may seem to be transfused from one man to another, instantaneously, and antecedent to any knowledge in the person principally concerned."[18] But neither Rousseau nor Smith wants to think that our apparent ability to share emotions is owing to the spontaneous spread of feeling from one individual to another. Once we know the cause of emotion—say, a mother's anguish on witnessing her child's injury—we automatically use our imaginations, Smith contends, to "place ourselves in [her] situation, we conceive ourselves enduring all the same torments, we enter as it were into [her] body, and become in some measure the same person with [her], and thence form some idea of [her] sensations, and even feel something which, though weaker in degree, is not altogether unlike them" (4). As individuals, in other words, we can never actually feel what another person feels except as "something which, though weaker in degree, is not altogether unlike" those feelings. The fact the spectacle of the mother's grief includes her dismembered child makes Rousseau's imprisoned man so graphically aware of the cause of her anguish that he cannot help imagining himself experiencing it. It is significant that his pain, like the mother's, is that not of the victim but of a witness or spectator to an awful mauling. Where Rousseau compounds the anguish of his exemplary individual by rendering him helpless to alleviate its cause, Smith is curiously unconcerned with the victim's pain. A child "feels only the uneasiness of the present moment, which can never be very great," thanks to the "thoughtlessness and lack of foresight" that serve children as "an antidote against fear and anxiety" (8). The spectator occupies the position of subject in relation to the victim as object.

For Smith, as for Rousseau, it is important that sympathy be something that one feels rather than something that one does. To make this point, Rousseau puts his prisoner in a cage. Smith further distances the sympathetic viewer from the spectacle of pain and grief by replacing the cage that comes between the viewer and the scene of human suffering in Rousseau's image with the self-enclosure of the individual mind as it confronts an external object. Through repeated experiences as a spectator, Smith claims, the individual is divided, "as it were, into two persons": "The first is the spectator, whose sentiment with regard to my own conduct I endeavor to enter into, by placing myself in his situation, and by considering how it would appear to me, when seen from that particular point of view. The second is the agent, the person whom I properly call myself, and of whose conduct, under the character of the spectator, I was endeavoring to form some opinion" (164). In this scenario, spectator and agent take shape and carry out their respective roles strictly within the self and in relation to one another. As we witness repeated scenes of the joy and suffering of others, we not only learn to weigh the character and intensity of any spectacle of emotion against its cause; we also gain a progressively clearer sense of how our own emotions should look to other people. What this does is to double our inner spectator, so that the one who responds with inappropriate feeling and would impetuously spring to action is tempered by a contrastingly "impartial spectator" who looks on the scene with indifference and responds sympathetically in proportion to the cause of joy or pain. Especially when someone does us ill, according to Smith, we need to call on the idealized spectator within us to view the situation "from the place and with the eyes of a third person, who has no particular connection with either, and who judges impartially between us" (192). To imagine a collective made of individuals, in other words, Smith has even the most normative public sentiments originate from a source within the individual.[19]

The possibility that our most compelling feelings might have a source external to ourselves becomes especially apparent in writing associated with "sensibility," which critics and cultural historians mistakenly collapse into "sympathy" under the umbrella of sentimental literature. To the degree that the operations of sensibility violate the logic of sympathy, they question the autonomy of the individual as it developed in the tradition of Locke, Hume, and Smith. Sensibility assumes that sensations do not come directly from external objects, as Locke understood them, for objects can be loaded with meaning and charged with feeling well before we set eyes on them. As if to flaunt this possibility, Horace Walpole introduces such an object into *The Castle of Otranto* (1764), just as a royal wedding is about to begin. Annoyed with the delay of the ceremony, the father of the groom hurries to the scene of confusion, where he "beheld his child dashed to pieces, and almost buried under an enormous helmet, an hundred times more large than any casque ever made for human being, and shaded with a proportional quantity of black feathers."[20] This intrusive object simultaneously robs Manfred of an heir and announces the illegitimacy of his own claim to the principality, which becomes evident when a young man present at the scene "observes that the miraculous helmet was exactly like that on the figure in black marble of Alfonso the Good, one of their former princes" (18). The object not only embodies emblematically the story of usurpation and murder that is about to overturn the house of Manfred but also sets that narrative in motion. Those are the terms in which Manfred sees the helmet, as he starts "from his trance in a tempest of rage, and seizing the young man by the collar, [cries]: How darest thou utter such treason? Thy life shall pay for it" (20).

Where Walpole deliberately introduces a magical object into a world of more or less ordinary people in order to revitalize emotions long buried and empower them to override individual emotions, Henry Mackenzie's equally curious narrative, *The Man of Feeling* (1771), shows that even relatively ordinary objects can acquire the power to convey emotion directly from one individual to another. Witness the trail of affect that follows "the little garnet ring" from the finger of a madwoman as it passes from her hand to Harley's and gathers emotional steam:

"I love you for resembling my Billy; but I shall never love any man like him."—She stretched out her hand to Harley; he pressed it between both of his and bathed it with tears.—"Nay, that is Billy's ring," said she, "you cannot have it indeed; but here is another, look here, which I plated to-day of some gold-thread from this bit of stuff; will you keep if for my sake?... Harley looked on his ring.—He put a couple of guineas into the man's hand: "Be kind to that unfortunate"—he burst into tears and left.[21]

The very appearance of these words on the page indicates that feelings have ceased to observe the logic of sympathetic exchange and flow directly back and forth between the pair, making it difficult to tell where one leaves off and the other begins. The breakdown of the difference between subject and object accompanies the breakdown between spectator and spectacle of grief. It is difficult to say whether human emotion endows the ring with its emotive power or whether the object is responsible for generating all this emotion, so unstable is the boundary between subject and object, and thus the identity of each. Indeed, the object in this case proves capable of doubling on the spot and heading off in two directions. The extreme states of sensibility Harley encounters in Bedlam erode his self-enclosure, as emotion enters the individual from outside and then spreads of its own volition among people and things.

Any way of thinking that opposes individualism, as I believe much of the literature of sensibility does, would therefore challenge the novelistic proposition that feelings well up from within the subject in response to sensations and acquire the form of ideas that enrich that subject's personal storehouse of knowledge, as they do in the case of Smith's exemplary citizen. The novel could incorporate any number of sentimental arguments so long as they amplified the individual, rounding it out, so to speak, without eroding its self-enclosure. Jane Austen never fails to test these limits.

Into the world of country gentry, where each thing expresses its owner with similar precision, intrudes a new kind of object that— not unlike Walpole's helmet—casts the customary language of objects in doubt. One evening, Emma learns that a visitor to Miss Bates, widow of the local vicar and low on the community totem pole, was "struck by the sight of a pianoforté—a very elegant looking instrument—not a grand, but a large-sized pianoforté." The gift had come "from Broadwood's the day before ... entirely unexpected."[22] The arrival of such a gift, lacking the name of a sender, sets off numerous speculations as to who sent it and why. In contrast with Poe's purloined letter, Austen's errant object continues to disrupt the social order until its secret is fully disclosed. His grandmother's death allows the dashing and duplicitous Frank Churchill to claim the recipient of the pianoforte as his beloved and name himself as the sender of the erotic message. To Emma, who had fancied Churchill in love with her, he excuses himself on the grounds that he in turn fancied her "to have fathomed his secret. Natural enough!—his own mind full of intrigue, that he should suspect it in others" (404). So says the less-than-impartial spectator Mr. Knightley. By incorporating the pianoforte in the system of objects that maintains traditional Highbury society, Austen divests this object of its erotic mystery. In doing so, however, she makes the reader understand that an object is never just an object, especially where objects exist in a comfortable relation to their owners. Should a foreign object enter this picture, it soon becomes apparent that objects do not inhabit a dimension on the other side of language but are completely in and of it.

The pianoforte embodies this paradox. As the sign of Jane Fairfax's value as a woman and thus her capacity for upward mobility, the object in circulation not only troubles the traditional language of objects but sets the people whom they mediate in motion as well. Austen was clearly willing to countenance such mobility. At the same time, she was also concerned that if elegant objects were to be purchased on a whim and shipped from London in a day, then how could one determine an individual's identity and where he or she belonged in the finely gradated hierarchy that constituted the ideal society? A concerted effort at reenchantment was evidently called for. We can certainly read Emma's education as a process of demystification whereby she discovers, sometimes to her extreme embarrassment, that objects are *not* extensions of the subject. In contrast, Walpole's "miraculous helmet" and Mackenzie's "little garnet ring" do convey an emotional message directly from one individual to another; such objects work according to the principle of "contagion" (Smith, *Theory of Moral Sentiments*, 219). But we may also read this account of how the pianoforte got its meaning as a contrary process of reenchantment that establishes an elaborate sumptuary code that does for modern individuals what an earlier code had done for aristocratic bloodlines.

Emma (1816) demonstrates that there is indeed no such thing as an object that doesn't convey emotion along with sensation. Each object places its owner in the intricately differentiated classification system that is Highbury society. Consider, for example, what Emma sees when she looks from Donwell Abbey to the residence of Mr. Knightley: "The house was larger than Hartfield [home to the Woodhouses], and totally unlike it, covering a good deal of ground, rambling and irregular, with many comfortable and one or two handsome rooms.—It was just what it ought to be, and it looked what it was—and Emma felt an increasing respect for it, as the residence of a family of such true gentility, untainted in blood and understanding" (123). Those conversant in the language of objects sometimes called "taste" can distinguish good object relations from bad in another person on the basis of whether they display moderation, taste, concern for others, and a reluctance to deceive. Austen's heroines speak through objects and are granted subject status on the basis of what those objects say. Used in this way, objects are no longer objects pure and simple but become part objects, tokens of individual interiority. But whenever the emotional charge entering the individual from external objects through the senses overwhelm those genuine feelings that well up from within the individual, Austen's novels draw a line, as if to say, "sensibility, thou shalt go no farther." Thus, for every one of her heroines, she offers a "bad" sister driven by sensibility across that line to jeopardize the family's future.

If we say that before Austen the eighteenth-century novel was no more a fully consolidated and naturalized entity than the individual but participated in a many-faceted debate about individualism and whether it was fact or fiction, then how do we read any novel as one and entire? Short of mapping out the entire field of argumentation, we can detect the contours of these "outside" arguments on the inside of novels that make up the tradition of the novel. The presence of such a counterargument is nowhere more evident perhaps than in Austen's first mature novel. Written between 1794 and 1799 and published in 1818, the year after Austen's death, *Northanger Abbey* announces itself as such by declaring its difference from gothic novels on the grounds that Ann Radcliffe offers a false guide to life as it is lived in England: "Charming as were all Mrs Radcliffe's works, and charming even as were the works of all her imitators, it was not in them perhaps that human nature, at least in the midland counties of England, was to be looked for. Of the Alps and Pyrenees, with their pine forests and their vices, they might give a faithful delineation; and Italy, Switzer-land, and the South of France, might be as fruitful in horrors as they were there represented." This passage concludes a process by which the heroine takes in Radcliffe's depictions of a degenerate European aristocracy and uses them to read "human nature ... in the midland counties of England."[23]

Radcliffe's fiction induces Austen's heroine to defamiliarize what should be familiar, lending the things and people of the abbey some of the same aura of excitement she experiences in reading *The Mysteries of Udolpho* (1794). To recast this statement in Lockean terms, we might say that because of Radcliffe, Catherine Morland cannot see what is actually before her eyes, namely, "human nature" as it exists "in the midland counties of England." To authorize information that comes directly from the world outside the individual, Locke went to great lengths to distinguish that information from information that did not have a source in material objects.[24] Austen, too, regards information that is not at some point anchored to a referent as potentially bad information. When it succeeds in passing itself off as truth, such information observes what might be called the mimetic fallacy. Where this fallacy is in force, mediation—whether words or images—creates or distorts rather than accurately reflecting its object, as I suggested the Reynolds painting did when it put that rapt expression on little Bunbury's face. That is to say, where this fallacy prevails, such objects as the facial expression of the boy, which should be the source of in-formation, are themselves displaced by the story of how Reynolds cap-tured the boy's attention, a story that may or may not describe what Reynolds actually saw. Thus Austen attacks gothic fiction not only for making one invest meaning in objects that do not justify that invest-ment: "nothing could shortly be clearer, than that it had been all a voluntary, self-created delusion, each trifling circumstance receiving importance from an imagination resolved on alarm, and every thing forced to bend to one purpose by a mind which, before she entered the Abbey, had been craving to be frightened" (146). She also objects to readers who crave emotional stimulation at the cost of individu-al judgment and sympathy. Why in each of her novels does Austen insist on drawing this line? Why use something like the gothic—a situation where things and people do not stay fixed in their assigned categories—to do it?

Let us assume that the logic of sympathy was subject to a reversal. In that case, for us to share the feelings of another person would not be to imagine ourselves in that person's place and experience his or her emotions at one remove. Quite the contrary, to put ourselves in another's place would be to project our own emotions onto his or her body.[25] If such a reversal could happen, then what was to stop feelings from flowing in the opposite direction from spectacle to spectator, making us the ones to be infused with another's feelings? In this event, the radically individualistic logic of sympathy would capitulate to the antagonistic logic of contagion. Smith, like Rousseau, associated such spontaneous and collective emotional responses with the threat of factionalism that, during the first half of the eighteenth century, served as a code word for the Hobbesian body politic composed of warring religious sects and combative political groups controlled only by a powerful monarch. During the second half of the century, unruly mobs of displaced agrarian laborers and a growing number of urban poor assumed the role of chief antagonist to civil society.[26] In that it redefined the body politic as a corporate body of self-governing individuals, individualism offered a symbolic resolution to the problem posed by factionalism in both these senses.

Austen uses the appearance of a new novel at the lending library to demonstrate what happens when individual judgment is suspended and people begin to feel and act in the manner of a faction. Hearing talk of politics, Catherine Morland reports having "heard that something very shocking indeed, will soon come out in London" (81). Infected by her mistake, her friend and future sister-in-law rushes to the conclusion that this "something" can only be "a riot" (82). This reference causes the entire conversation to veer sharply away from actual objects—they were discussing the landscape surrounding the abbey— by means of associational logic. The hero brings the inflammatory discourse to a stop with this critique: "You talked of expected horrors in London, and instead of instantly conceiving, as any rational creature would have done, that such words could relate only to a circulating library, she immediately pictured to herself a mob of three thousand men assembling in St. George's Fields; the Bank attacked, the Tower threatened, the streets of London flowing with blood, a detachment of the 12th Light Dragoons ... called up from Northampton to quell the insurgents" (82). Here we have what might be called a cultural event (the arrival of a new book at a circulating library) rendered as a political event (a violent rebellion requiring military action). The great irony of this passage is that in demonstrating her heroine's folly in responding to a cultural event as if it were a political event, Austen effectively translates the imminent possibility of political conflict into a cultural debate in which words grounded in the object world invariably win the day.[27] Henry Tilney accuses his companions of ignoring the tranquil English countryside around them in order to hurry along a chain of associations that can only end in violence. Once translated onto this plane, Austen can solve the problem caused by the intrusion of London politics by introducing language that correctly names its referent as "a circulating library." This act of translation, I would argue, reinstates the definition of the public sphere as an arena of debate where individual viewpoints contended vigorously with one another in the form of novels as well as treatises and essays. If we tend *not* to think of the eighteenth century in terms of the bitterness of its religious disputes, the volatility of the British economy, and the violence engendered by a factionalized government, it is quite possibly because so many authors performed the act of translation that Austen carries out in this passage from *Northanger Abbey*.

THE LEGACY OF SENSIBILITY

Moving further into the nineteenth century, we find a number of prominent literary commentators and editors intent on bringing order to this snarl of literary arguments. Barbauld's *British Novelists, with an Essay, and Prefaces Biographical and Critical* appeared in fifty volumes in 1810. She devoted the first twenty-one volumes to the works of Richardson, Defoe, and Fielding. In the remaining volumes of her collection, however, Barbauld included works by Walpole, Henry Mackenzie, Oliver Goldsmith, Clara Reeve, Elizabeth Inchbald, Ann Radcliffe, Frances Burney, Charlotte Smith, Maria Edgeworth, and others. Homer O. Brown argues persuasively that today's histories of the novel began in the first two decades of the nineteenth century, when editors retrospectively imposed a tradition on the eighteenth century. But, as he also points out, these authors did not simply line up of their own accord (*Institutions of the Novel*, 52–82). No sooner was Barbauld's edition in print, as Brown tells the story, than Mudford's British Novelists came out in cheap editions (1810–17), to be followed by Scott's *Ballantyne's Novelist's Library* (1821–24). These early-nineteenth-century canonizers established novels celebrating the individual as central to the tradition of the novel, as they repeatedly included certain novels front and center in their collections and commentaries. Other novels were clearly designated peripheral, as they appeared rarely or toward the end of the series. Of the gothic, these collected editions reprinted relatively few. The editors created the spine for a history of the novel out of what had been largely an open-ended political debate about the nature of the individual. The tradition of the eighteenth-century novel consequently came to resemble the individual produced by the novels composing that tradition, one compelled by its own energy repeatedly to exceed itself and grow as it absorbed new information and remodeled the world as well as the individual who encountered it. What happened to those narratives that play out the contrary logic of sensibility?

First of all, I would argue, after Austen no novel could claim to offer an accurate view of "nature as she actually exists in the common walks of life" without including gothic elements. Thornfield Hall in *Jane Eyre* (1847), Miss Havisham's house in *Great Expectations* (1860), and the ghosts in *Wuthering Heights* (1847), *Villette* (1853), and *The Woman in White* (1860) are obvious cases in point. These novels incorporate anti-individualistic elements of the gothic, as virtually every important Victorian novel does, only to naturalize those elements as components in an all-encompassing narrative of growth and development. If, as Freud claims, the appearance of the uncanny in literature represented the surfacing of so-called primitive thought modes in modern adults who believed they had outgrown them, then Victorian realism implied that one became a modern adult as he or she surmounted such magical thinking. The Victorian novel was in this sense dependent on disruptions of the normative reality. Whenever they recast the subject's accumulation of knowledge as a process of detection, such novels were acknowledging their ties not only to the Enlightenment subject but also to the gothic sensibility. To produce what came to be known as British realism, the Victorians proceeded to rationalize the residual elements of sensibility by ascribing them to a protagonist's naïveté or neurosis, as well as to the deceptions perpetrated by those who were heartless, twisted, corrupt, malevolent, or just plain knavish. Despite their willingness to deal with this residual material, novels celebrating the individual maintained their cultural prestige by marginalizing challenges that they could not deal with by means of incorporation and subsumption. Thus during the very period when the novel was consolidating the formal conventions of the genre, there were periodic outbreaks of new and remarkable versions of the gothic, along with a proliferation of subgenres that include the romantic novel, the sensation novel, the imperial gothic novel, detective fiction, mummy stories, children's literature celebrating fairyland, boys' adventure stories, and so forth, offering models of subject formation that could not be placed in a tradition that itself resembles a novel. It was on this basis that most novels failed to qualify for a place in such twentieth-century histories of the novel as F. R. Leavis's *The Great Tradition* (1948) and Ian Watt's *The Rise of the English Novel* (1957).[28]

Having argued that the nineteenth-century subject was ultimately incapable of incorporating the contradiction posed by desires that arise from within, on the one hand, and those that invade the individual from without, on the other, in the last two chapters of this book I shall consider two popular romances written in the last two decades of the century. My reading of H. Rider Haggard's *She* (1887) and Bram Stoker's *Dracula* (1897) should explain why novels could not contain these materials without removing themselves from the mainstream. Both novels play out the logic of sensibility at the cost of the modern individual and a society composed of citizen-subjects. I like to think that this body of popular fiction began with the question raised when Victor Frankenstein contemplated what would happen to humankind were he to fashion a female counterpart for his monstrous experiment, allowing the pair to multiply their kind. It was as if Mary Shelley raised this question only to demonstrate that a novel could not follow that line of thinking so early in the nineteenth century and still make it as a popular novel. In the last decades of the century, however, fiction spelled out the conflict between the individual and some form of collectivity that obliterated individualism became novels many times over and to the delight of readers. By then, apparently, English readers had grown accustomed to the idea of living as modern individuals in the shadow of a collective that they could no longer imagine to be made of individuals like themselves.[29] The figure of mass man loomed large as the means both of conceptualizing the populations accumulating within their empire and of posing a threat to modern individualism. Novels made the double impact of this way of figuring humanity absolutely clear by giving it the features of the cannibal.

In *She*, Rider Haggard transports his British protagonists to northern Africa, where the protection of an ancient yet glorious woman is the only thing that keeps them from stewing in pots according to the custom of the Amahaggar people. The story approaches its nadir as the narrator explores the bowels of an extinct mountain kingdom and descends from the tombs of carefully preserved individuals to its lowest level. There he comes to the edge of a pit through which individual bodies have passed to form a mass, as in a gigantic privy:

> So far as I could judge, this pit was about the size of the dome of St. Paul's in London, and when the lamps were held up I saw that it was nothing but one vast charnel-house, being literally full of thousands of human skeletons, which lay piled up in an enormous gleaming pyramid, formed by the slipping down of the bodies at the apex as fresh ones were dropped in from above. Anything more appalling than this jumbled mass of the remains of a departed race I cannot imagine, and what had made it even more dreadful was that in this dry air a considerable number of the bodies had simply become desiccated with the skin still on them, and now, fixed in every conceivable position, stared at us out of the mountain of white bones, grotesquely horrible caricatures of humanity.[30]

Where this nightmare version of collective humanity consumes and dismembers the individual to convert its parts into a completely different organism, Stoker's vampire invites us to think of this relationship the other way around.[31] Dracula infects the individual with his blood, which robs that person of individuality. Here the individual's private storehouse of ideas is not only infiltrated but also transformed by an alien desire that overwhelms the internal faculty of judgment. Even so, as I argue, Haggard's cannibals and Stoker's vampires observe a cultural logic more alike than different. Both overturn the social contract by obliterating the boundary that it came into being to protect: by joining these bodies, one forsakes all claim to individuality based on the premise that there is one mind per body and one body per mind.[32]

Anachronistic though it may seem, I want to suggest that the peculiar threat posed by these versions of collective man comes from a residual strand of sensibility that gathered an ominous energy against the background of a growing mass of urban poor, the uprising of colonial populations, and the steady encroachment of the new mass media on traditional British culture.[33] Mass man is distinguished by the fact that its psychic energy exceeds the sum total of individual desires composing such a group, were that group indeed composed of individuals. In the late-nineteenth-century romance, something like this transindividual desire sends a current through the human aggregate, welding any and all individuals into a single body without regard for differences of race, gender, class, and nation. Although novels that participated in the "romance revival" questioned whether we are in fact individuals for whom interiority is destiny, those novels nevertheless rejoined the mainstream in defending the individual against external assaults, which they portrayed as an assault on humanity itself.

I will conclude by explaining why these phobic representations of the human aggregate made it difficult for future novelists, their critics, and readers to imagine a society in which individuals can freely pursue their desires without encroaching on the rights of others. It remains one of the more glaring contradictions of Western cultural history that at a time when individualism had clearly achieved hegemony within a nation intent on spreading itself around the globe, that model of individualism went on the defensive, as if to say that the modern individual could only define him- or herself as such in opposition to an engulfing otherness, or mass, that obliterated individuality. If mainstream novels offered readers the fantasy of domestic plenitude or wholeness of being within the household, then popular romances rendered all alternatives to such a household as a monstrous life form capable of transforming the individual from a self-governing citizen into an instrument of group desire. We shall be able to abandon this defensive position, in my opinion, only when novels begin to think of a genuine alternative to the individual, one that does not inspire phobia and yet is grounded in the world we now inhabit. The novel of course was not made to think beyond the individual, but neither, on the other hand, was it made to reproduce the status quo.

I

How the Misfit Became a Moral Protagonist

Contrary to prevailing critical opinion, modern secular morality did not draw the extraordinary power it exercises to this day from any institutional religion, the Bible, or even a general sense of Judeo-Christian ethics. Its power, I believe, comes from and authorizes those works of fiction where morality appears to emanate from the very core of an individual, as that individual confronts and opposes socially inculcated systems of value. From this perspective, what I call bourgeois morality cannot be considered a value in and of itself so much as a way of reading, assessing, and revising both the prevailing categories of identity and whatever cultural apparatus may authorize them.[1] Often suspicious of pleasure, unconcerned with profit, and heedless of life's little necessities, this peculiarly modern form of morality appears to be nothing more nor less than the assertion of individuality itself, the objects one desires, and the means by which one pursues them. In opposing the values sustaining a blood-based hierarchy, bourgeois morality lends value to qualities within an individual that entitle him or her to a social position more gratifying than any station in life defined by wealth or rank alone. Indeed, we might see bourgeois morality as a rhetorical device that exists for the purpose of convincing us that such an alternative source of value is already there in the individual, waiting to be recognized by modern authors and readers. For it to be missing in some, the moral sense has to be present in most. This was not always true.[2]

To work with this notion of the term "morality," however, I want to push it two steps further. For one thing, I see the novel's apparent discovery of a source of value already there within an individual as a means of adding something distinctively modern to the very notion of the individual. Contemporary critical theory uses the figure of the supplement to describe an additive so different from and culturally so incompatible with its host category that it cannot be incorporated without a thoroughgoing reorganization of that category.[3] No matter how many features the entity so supplemented seems to share with its earlier form and rhetorical behavior, the supplement in this aggressive sense changes the character to which it has been added into something with new and different properties and potentialities. I believe that it took this "something" in the form of a rhetorical additive to convince a readership that ordinary individuals were capable of acting and, if capable of acting, then also capable of refusing to act on desires independent of their social position, desires that presumably came strictly from within the individual. This chapter shows how the misfit incorporated the rhetorical power of the supplement to transform the British subject from a state of being, or position, into a process of becoming, or performance, whereby that subject could achieve a place commensurate to its desires and abilities.

While we cannot regard this additive as "material" in any conventional sense of the term, I nevertheless insist that bourgeois morality inflects the material wealth of a modern nation and its ruling elite just as powerfully as the elements of birth and rank gave meaning to the wealth of an earlier agrarian economy and aristocratic culture. This is precisely its point. Bourgeois morality sets itself up in opposition to the shallow devotion to objects and concern for surfaces that it invariably attributes, however indirectly, to an earlier and less deserving ruling class. What we now call materialism in the loose sense of the term—concern for property, the things of this world (especially things that can be bought), and the health of the body and its biological reproduction—consequently becomes the yardstick for bourgeois morality. In pursuing these universally desirable objects, an individual is either mindful or heedless of the common good. Provided they are not acquired at another's expense (which would fly in the face of modern morality), these goods serve as the reward for that individual's self-restraint and even self-sacrifice and as such become signs of his or her morality.[4] Though not with anything approaching the consistency of novels, other kinds of writing—including travel writing, treatises on taste and moral philosophy, essays on morals and manners at home and around the world, anything dealing with self-improvement, indeed, anything dealing with improvement—used this additive to think about the individual's relation to the given social order. Our own reading habits are the result.

THE BAD SUBJECT

The assumption that the modern subject is the product rather than the source of fiction is of course a version of the signature move of all the major strains of poststructuralism. What Louis Althusser calls the "ideological state apparatus," for example, performs a similar reversal of individual identity and linguistic attribution. According to his account, the early modern church gave the individual freedom only to submit to external forms of authority, authority as different from that individual as day is from night. By contrast, the educational institutions of the modern secular state stress the freedom of subjectivity and conceptualize the individual, in the words of Althusser, as "a centre of initiatives author of and responsible for its actions." For Althusser, a modern society depends for coherence on the education of individuals to locate them within sociocultural categories and to induce them to observe—without threat of force—the constraints defining their respective positions. Thus the modern state creates a contradiction within the subject between the ideology of free subjectivity and the fact of social subjection. No ideological apparatus is ever foolproof, and this mechanism of "hailing," or "interpellation," however expertly and repetitively performed, occasionally fails. What Althusser calls "bad subjects" are individuals who take the ideology of free subjectivity too much to heart and do not freely consent to their subjection. Bad subjects, he explains, on occasion provoke the intervention of the army or police.[5]

Between the subject who freely accepts his or her subjection and the criminal or heretic, the novel introduced a whole world of possibilities without which, I believe, a modern secular state ruled chiefly by ideology could not have emerged when and how it did. The shift from a culture dominated by the church, which also maintained itself by physical force, to a culture that relies primarily on ideology to keep people in place required no less than a political revolution in many countries. Curiously enough, although many people anticipated a revolution in Great Britain during the turbulent period between 1776 and 1848, it was not one of the countries to undergo a radical change in political government.[6] Yet Britain eventually became the very example of the modern nation-state. Thus the emergence of a modern nation during the late eighteenth century raises an important question. When he characterizes modern states as states that displace violence with ideology as the means of controlling a population, Althusser does not address how, short of political revolution, ideology might have usurped the power formerly exercised by the military and the police to govern a population during turbulent times. Another essay by Althusser sets us on the path to an answer.

In examining exactly how early modern European culture rethought government in Enlightenment terms, Althusser focuses on how the social contract produces a logical contradiction within the old notion of the subject and then proceeds to conceal that contradiction behind a narrative of individual development.[7] Such duplicity was not Rousseau's aim, as Althusser reads it, so much as a by-product of the materials with which he worked. To imagine a state that did not put free subjectivity at odds with political subjection, a state in which free subjectivity and political subjection were indeed one and the same, Rousseau rejects an early modern solution and tries to imagine a purely secular government authorized by something more than its subjects' consent to be governed. The individual can preserve his freedom, in Rousseau's view, only if that individual consents to be governed by no one other than himself. To perform this grand equivocation, Rousseau comes up with a political body to which the individual's subjection is not subjection so much as the guarantee of his freedom, because that political body forms only as the individual himself acquires the very authority to which he submits.[8]

For Althusser, this is the point in Rousseau's argument where the author abandons the logic of contractual exchange and resorts to figuration in order to rethink the two parties to that exchange.[9] To convert the early modern state into an aggregate of freely consenting individuals, he has to conceptualize an entirely new kind of individual, one endowed with the natural ability to understand the advantages of becoming a citizen. This new man gives Rousseau a fresh starting point from which to rethink the state as a political elite composed of individuals much like himself. But where does this social additive come from? What can the conceptual architects of the modern state use as their foundational category? It is in answer to these questions that Althusser's notion of the bad subject, an individual who simply does not fit any available social category, suddenly becomes extremely important. The modern individual is not only a novelistic rendering of Rousseau's new man, by nature inclined to self-government, but also the embodiment of Althusser's bad subject, by nature incapable of being "hailed."

By the 1740s, men of English letters were roundly dismissing Rousseau's social contract as politically improbable, but that did not prevent them from thinking in contractual terms.[10] In his essay "Of the Original Contract," for example, David Hume points out the near-complete lack of historical evidence that any such promise provided the inaugural moment and foundation for government. There are, in his estimation, only two sources for the idea that men feel obligated to serve the general good and so submit voluntarily to government. "The first," as he explains, "are those to which men are impelled by a natural instinct..., independent of all ideas of obligation, and of all views, either to public or private utility." These obligations include "love of children, gratitude to benefactors, pity to the unfortunate" and occur before any reflection on the general good, which nevertheless results when one responds to these natural instincts. But Hume is more interested in a second kind of moral duty that is "not supported by any original instinct."[11] "If the reason be asked of that obedience, which we are bound to pay to government," Hume would "readily" supply this answer: because without such predisposition to obedience, *society could not otherwise exist* (italics his). He concludes his essay with what initially looks like a dismissal of the social contract on grounds that it is more fiction than historical truth: "The only passage I meet with in antiquity, where the obligation of obedience to government is ascribed to a promise, is in PLATO's *Crito*, where SOCRATES refuses to escape from prison, because he had tacitly promised to obey the laws" (201). In explaining, however, why men nevertheless obey the state even when there is no threat of force or monarch to disobey at risk of treason, Hume reveals his debt to the very logic he seems intent on dismissing. People, he claims, are perfectly aware of the fact that they "could not live at all in society, at least in a civilized society, without laws and magistrates and judges, to prevent the encroachments of the strong upon the weak, of the violent upon the just and equitable" (197).[12] While he dismisses Rousseau's claim for the natural origin of the contract, then, Hume accepts as common sense the principle that one has to limit one's desires in order to live within a peaceable community.

CONTRACTUAL MORALITY

If Daniel Defoe can be called the first novelist and exponent of possessive individualism, it is primarily because his *Robinson Crusoe* identified individualism with the expression of certain qualities of mind, qualities worthy of written expression. I will not dwell on how the eponymous hero rationalizes repeated acts of disobedience toward various forms of social authority, from his father to the traditional Christian god. Let me simply assert that in making such gestures, Crusoe—quite without irony—defines himself in terms of what I have been calling the bad subject: "In the relating what is already past of my Story, this will be the more easily believ'd, when I shall add, that thro' all the Variety of Miseries that had to this Day befallen me, I have never had so much as one Thought of it being the Hand of God, or that it was a just Punishment for my Sin; my rebellious Behaviour against my Father, or my present Sins which were great; or so much as a punishment for the Course of my wicked Life."[13] It is important that Crusoe does not see himself as sinful so much as naturally disinclined to respond to traditional forms of authority. "I never had so much as one Thought of what would become of me," he explains, but was completely "thoughtless of a God, or a Providence; acted like a meer Brute from the Principles of Nature and by the Dictates of common Sense only, and indeed hardly that" (65). I am less interested in how this protagonist initially identifies what prompts him to reject the place assigned him within the middle ranks than I am in the rhetorical consequences of his refusal to fit in. Accordingly, I focus on what happens to the category of the bad subject in the new model of government that emerges as Crusoe discovers other men on his island. To coexist with these people, he must hold one and all to the same code of conduct that he brought to bear on himself, a code that implicitly acknowledges its philosophical debt to the English version of the social contract. As he explains to the ship's captain who has escaped mutineers, "My *Conditions are but two*. 1. That while you stay on this Island with me, you will not pretend to any Authority here; and if I put Arms into your Hands, you will upon all Occasions give them up to me, and do not Prejudice to me or mine, upon this Island,

and in the mean time be govern'ed by my Orders. 2. That if the Ship is, or may be recover'd, you will carry me and my Man to *England* Passage free" (184). This is not merely an exchange of services but an agreement on the part of each to respect and defend both the other's autonomy and his mobility.

According to John Locke's *Second Treatise of Government*, a son does not simply step into his father's position but earns his citizenship as he comes to understand the law. To understand the law is to obey it and thus to fulfill the precondition for governing others.[14] Citizenship therefore depends entirely on one's ability to harness the very aggression by means of which one expresses one's individuality. In this respect, the modern state can, from its very inception, be understood as a defensive formation, a collective dedicated to protecting both its citizens and those unfit to be citizens from any aggression that would encroach on their respective rights to property and personal autonomy. The modern state is justified, in other words, by the need to defend individualism against forms of aggression that often bear uncanny resemblance to expressions of that very same individualism. Under these circumstances, how can the bad subject become a good citizen? Bourgeois morality accomplishes this sleight of hand. This peculiar code of conduct opposes self-expression that springs straight from the heart to those expressions of feeling crafted to flatter, cajole, deceive, coerce, or corrupt those for whom they are performed. At the same time, bourgeois morality also distinguishes those passions and drives that serve the general good from those more likely to disrupt the social order. For the expressive individual to become a good subject, his desires must not only be strictly his; they must ultimately serve the general interest as well.

When Crusoe is alone, there is no discernible difference between his particular interest and the general interest. Thus the first half of the story reads as an unfolding of the supplement, whereby Crusoe accrues to himself first knowledge of the land around him and then the land itself in the form of property. This accumulation of information in the form of property transforms him from laborer to landowner. To put Locke's twin principles of mind and property into narrative form, in other words, Defoe adds something to Crusoe that exceeds the limits of his assigned social position. This something exerts itself implicitly in and through the "I" offering this explanation, as well as in the influence of his "rambling Thoughts": "Being the third Son of the Family, and not bred to any Trade, my Head began to be fill'd very early with rambling Thoughts: My Father, who was very ancient, had given me a competent Share of Learning, as far as House-Education and a Country Free-School generally goes, and design'd me for the Law; but I would be satisfied with nothing but going to Sea" (4). Besides overturning the Lockean model whereby the son would become a citizen as he reproduced the father's understanding of the law, Crusoe's stubborn insistence on mobility affords him a setting in which that excess can spill over onto the landscape and convert what had at home been completely mapped and classified into a new form of property that expressed his own will and desire:

> You are to understand, that now I had, as I may call it, two Plantations on the Island; one my little Fortification or Tent, with the Wall about it under the Rock, with the Cave behind me, which by this time I had enlarg'd into several Apartments, or Caves, one within another.... Besides this, I had my Country Seat, and I had now a tolerable Plantation there also; for first, I had my little Bower, as I call'd it, ... *that is to say*, I kept the Hedge which circled it in, constantly fitted up to its usual Height, the Ladder standing always on the Inside. (110–11)

One cannot help noting that the desire for self-expansion would simply expand desire were it not for the fact that it is ever accompanied by fear that is assuaged only by mechanisms of self-enclosure. Crusoe's "Ladder" tips us off to the fact that this subject is inclined to feel vulnerable with each expansion of property: vulnerable, ever anxious to preserve the autonomy of his body and its provisions, and thus extremely defensive, even though he is clearly the intruder.

That this process of expansion and self-enclosure dominates more than half the novel is rather self-evident, and generations of illustrious commentators, none more so perhaps than Rousseau and Marx, have provided a rich legacy of readings that testify to Defoe's accomplishment. Less interesting to the majority of readers is the process by which Defoe transforms Crusoe into the governor of a peaceful cosmopolitan nation. By means of this transformation, his protagonist no longer plays the role of supplement, at least not so overtly, and acts in the name of a disparate assortment of individuals so as to make them cohere as a group. He exacts a sacrifice of individualism in return for protection of life, limb, and property. From the perspective of such a government, an individual's willingness to stay in his place is what gives him moral value.

The apparent contradiction posed by the two halves of Crusoe's stay on the island is one and the same as the contradiction enacted by the social contract itself, which demands that an individual restrain his or her individuality in exchange for the state's protection of that individuality against other forms of self-expression. To constrain his fellow individuals, Crusoe must cease to be a bad subject himself. Defoe prepares us to regard Crusoe's shift from self-expression to self-constraint as an act of self-preservation by representing Crusoe's insatiable desire for property as a sequence of defensive maneuvers designed to preserve his life and belongings from imaginary predators. Moreover, Crusoe's rise to leadership takes the form of a sequence of conflicts whereby he rescues other individuals from overt forms of barbarism. Against the physical brutality of cannibals and mutineers, Defoe pits Crusoe's literacy, which includes his ability to count, map, measure, classify, and disseminate fictitious accounts of the island and its inhabitants to those who lack his intellectual mastery. The manual labor that he eventually delegates to Friday is what created the property that he proceeds to defend by means of intellectual labor after others arrive on the scene.[15] That those who share his distinctive form of literacy also readily agree to play by his rules of government becomes apparent as Crusoe instructs the captain whose crew has mutinied "that we must divide the prisoners."

This is how Defoe's protagonist deals with the difference in sheer numbers that would give the mutineers supremacy in a world where authority goes to the faction that can establish a monopoly on violence: "I told [the captain] he should go back again, and choose out those [potentially compliant] five and tell them . . . that he would take out those five to be his Assistants, and that the Governour would keep the other two, and the three that we sent Prisoners to the Castle (my Cave) as Hostages, for the Fidelity of those five; and that if they prov'd unfaithful in the Execution, the five Hostages would be hang'd in Chairs alive upon the Shore" (194). While Defoe does use the fear of punishment to found his new community, he translates government by violence into a fiction that he disseminates to the mutineers. In a sense, then, one could say that he governs by fear rather than the fact of violence. Crusoe crafts his fiction so as to make those naturally prone to violence believe that violence will befall them. More important to establishing his authority is his ability to convince five potential citizens that their failure to conform will hurt their fellow sailors and thereby damage the community. Thus he assumes these chosen five capable of understanding that it is in their interest to submit to the law because they serve the collective interest by doing so. If it is by individuating the old community of mutineers that he contains their capacity for violence, then it is in terms of their degree of individuation that he represents the new community that will sail forth for England: "Our Strength was now thus ordered for Expedition: 1, The Captain, his Mate, and Passenger, 2. Then the two Prisoners of the first Gang, to whom having their Characters from the Captain, I had given their Liberty, and trusted them with Arms, 3. The other two I had kept till now, in my Bower, pinion'd; but upon the Captain's Motion, had now releas'd. 4. These five releas'd at last: So that they were twelve in all, besides five we kept Prisoners in the Cave, for Hostages" (195). Initially describing these men in terms of their national identities and religious affiliations, the novel here reclassifies them on the basis of how well they observe the minimalist norms of social behavior embodied in the aboriginal Friday.

Crusoe also squirrels the five recalcitrant individuals away from public view the better to represent the threat of a return of violence: not only the threat of the violence these five individuals might do to others but the threat of the violence that the government might do to them as well. In this way, the emergent form of government relegates violence to the domain of imagination and fear. With this move, we might be tempted to say, Crusoe has solved the problem implicit in the logic of the social contract, namely, how to produce individuals who want to submit to the state. But such are the wages of his success in crossing over from the one category to the other that Crusoe loses the moral energy of the misfit as he becomes the exemplary citizen, so that his successful negotiation of contractual logic is his downfall in rhetorical terms. After identifying ourselves with his excesses as an individual, it is difficult for modern readers to wish for the kind of homogeneity required of members in the new community.

SEXUAL MORALITY

By means of labor, at first manual but increasingly devoted to observation, information gathering, and classification, Crusoe transforms himself from a lone castaway into a reproducible model of the self-governing subject. Moll Flanders and Roxana are as industrious as he. But rather than converting land into property and so elevating their respective stations in life, Crusoe's female counterparts marry up and out of the places assigned to them as they trade in sexual favors with those in positions of authority over them. Where early modern cultures would have it be their father's, brother's, guardian's, or owner's prerogative to offer them in marriage, Moll and Roxana seize the opportunity to exchange themselves with men. In doing so, they identify the entrepreneurial energy of the bad subject with sexual energy: the power both to attract and to satisfy customers. In making themselves something other than docile bodies, however, these women set themselves on a course that leads not to citizenship but in the other direction, to criminality and social exclusion. If Defoe cannot bring himself to sanction their sexual behavior, then we must wonder why he nevertheless authorizes these women to tell their own stories. To begin dealing with this question, we have to assess the relative advantages to be gained and the drawbacks to be suffered by translating the social contract into sexual terms.

Robinson Crusoe's story suggests that to become an exemplary citizen subject it is not enough for the bad subject to forgo the practices that put him at odds with his father's culture; he must also reconstitute himself from the ground up. Thus Crusoe not only expresses himself through the acquisition of property; he also learns to curtail his acquisitive impulses and share the island with other equally acquisitive individuals. The parallels between Crusoe's apotheosis as the governor and the process by which Defoe's women similarly attempt to cross over the ontological gulf separating the bad subject from the exemplary citizen is instructive. In removing themselves from the trade among men, Moll and Roxana cease to be docile bodies and become loose women. Such looseness disrupts the exchange of women among men of the same rank and allows marriage alliances to form that observe the limits of person and property. As they assume positions within a social body composed of such alliances, Moll and Roxana acquire the ability to survey and evaluate their former behavior, thereby displaying, as Crusoe does, a capacity for self-government. Moll explains her conversion to bourgeois respectability in just such terms: "I took possession of a House well Furnish'd, and a Husband in very good Circumstances, so that I had the prospect of a very happy Life, if I knew how to manage it; and I had leisure to consider of the real Value of the

Life I was likely to live; how different it was from the loose ungovern'd part I had acted before, and how much happier a Life of Virtue and Sobriety is, than that which we call a Life of Pleasure."[16] In this role, Defoe's female protagonists neither encroach on the sanctity of other households nor brook any encroachment on their own.

But while trading in sexual favors seems to be the only way for Roxana and Moll to move out of unsatisfactory positions in what they portray as a predatory social order and into positions that are both gratifying and morally sanctioned, their achievement is notably unstable. Any respectability they may have won is already jeopardized by a form of behavior that is among the few expressions of individualism with the power to eradicate any basis for moral value. In Moll's case, desire for her husband's brother poses that threat. In reflecting on "the unhappy consequences of too great Freedoms between Persons, stated as we were, upon the pretence of innocent intentions, Love of Friendship, *and the like*," she observes, "the Flesh has generally so great a share in those Friendships, that it is at great odds but inclination prevails at last over the most solemn Resolutions; and ... Vice breaks in at the breaches of Decency" (99). Why is individualism something that cannot be expressed in sexual terms without incurring moral disapproval and ultimately, therefore, jeopardizing one's eligibility for membership in the social body? The answer rests on the difference between the social contract, as Crusoe enacts it, and the marriage contract available to women.[17]

In the wake of late-twentieth-century feminism, we tend to stress the downside of defining men's relation to the body politic in terms of a social contract and women's in terms of a sexual contract. But there was and, in some respects, still is something potentially positive to be gained through the exchange implicit in the sexual contract. The man who coerces sexual favors from a woman without agreeing to provide for her implicitly violates the ideal relationship between a householder and his dependents. According to Locke, each householder is responsible for reproducing his own form of self-government in each of his offspring and servants. An individual reared in such a household would respect other households, just as he respected each and every member of his own, simply because he understood such reverence for the autonomy of others as necessary to the preservation and prosperity of each. To coerce sexual favors either from a woman who, like Moll, was born into the servant class or from a woman fallen in social position, as Roxana is, would be to invert this principle. Victims of this predatory behavior become aggressors, which is, after all, what the term "loose woman" implies.

Because they rise by means of such corruption, these misfits give us no sense that the world is one scintilla better because they have found positions of respectability within it. Moll unwittingly enters into an opportunistic marriage with her own brother and, until she knows her next advantageous move, remains in that relationship even after learning of its incestuous nature. Roxana reproduces her own sexual licentiousness in her servant Amy. In trading up to positions of respectability, both trade up to positions they cannot fully occupy. That the household Locke imagined as the basic unit of a new contractual state is simply unable to incorporate and transform the very qualities that made these women successful is demonstrated by the fact that they must tell their stories under fictitious names.[18] Defoe titles this pair of novels with pseudonyms—"Moll" and "Roxana"— behind which his protagonists can conceal the unscrupulous means by which they acquired the moral authority to make an object lesson of themselves in print. In fictionalizing their names, paradoxically, he lends these characters the life that accompanies excess, life implied by their being larger than fiction, making it clear that most of the novel remains outside and in excess of any self-governing subject.

To indicate more explicitly that Roxana's behavior is simply too hostile to respectable society for her to remain there, Defoe concludes her story by reversing her fortunes: "after some few Years of flourishing, and outwardly happy Circumstances, I fell into a dreadful Course of Calamities, and *Amy* also: the very Reverse of our former Good Days; the Blast of Heaven seem'd to follow the Injury done to the poor Girl [her daughter], by us both; and I was brought so low again, that my Repentance seem'd to be only the consequence of my Misery, as my Misery was of my Crime" (329–30). Moll and Roxana have the advantage of having property wholly in and of themselves. As a result, Defoe can send Moll to America rather than to a desert island and see what she can do for herself with nothing but her native beauty and wit for property. He sets Roxana loose on the same terms in England. But in trying to imagine how the household might be transformed from within and on English soil, he produces households that incorporate many of the features that created bad subjects to begin with, households whose appearance of respectability masks a sexual scandal.

Defoe died in 1731. Fourteen years later, a version of *Roxana* revised by one of his editors responded to the problem created by the relationship between the heroine, her servant Amy, and the daughter who threatened to expose their past promiscuity. This edition included a second volume that expanded Roxana's reversal of fortune to include a protracted account of her repentance and budding parental concern. Yet another revised edition published in 1775 proved equally popular with late-eighteenth- and nineteenth-century readers. In this edition, in the words of a modern editor, "the narrator's very vocabulary becomes more respectable, and her actions, while still to be repented, are considerably less criminal. In particular, that strangest and most disturbing part of the plot, the relentless pursuit of the narrator by her discarded daughter, is entirely omitted. Instead, in lengthy additions to Defoe's text, 'Roxana' discovers the joys of being a good wife and mother."[19]

Does this sequence of revisions of *Roxana* indicate that later readers failed to grasp Defoe's irony and thus the ruthlessness with which he exposes the hypocrisy of people who display respectability but fail to practice it in private? Or, on the other hand, does Defoe's failure to condemn his heroines for their lack of genuine familial affection simply place his fiction at an earlier moment in time, when moral judgments of common women were not so tightly bound to sexual conduct? I would agree that Roxana's frank acceptance of the conditions of her existence, which all but guarantee that the contracts into which she enters are mutually exploitive, gives her the power to question the honesty of those who cloak their private lives in respectability. I would also be inclined to say that material circumstances rather than emotional tendencies would have determined a heroine's morality in the period before Samuel Richardson's *Pamela*. This might well mean that in the estimation of early-eighteenth-century readers Roxana adequately acquitted her parental obligations by paying a couple to give her children a relatively wholesome upbringing. But while I am willing to grant an element of truth to both alternatives, I am convinced that the best explanation lies elsewhere.

I do not believe that Defoe was as concerned with the morality of his heroines nearly so much as he was interested in devising the means of turning a social misfit into the kind of citizen to whom he would willingly submit. Indeed, I like to think that Defoe was especially interested in these women because they most fully embodied the supplement, their property being solely in themselves in the form of their sexual labor. At the same time, their sexuality so directly assaults the autonomy of others that it cannot be incorporated within the social body charged with protecting individual autonomy. Once taken into that body, Moll and Roxana must either be ejected or else continue to expose the moral hypocrisy of the whole. That Defoe was fully cognizant of the problem posed by a woman's marketing of her sexuality becomes crystal clear as his heroines achieve respectability by means so incompatible with such respectability that those means must be attributed to someone else. His reader is consequently hard-pressed to say which is the false and which the true Moll or Roxana, the teller or the heroine of the tale. To ensure Moll's respectability, Defoe must join her two identities by uniting her with the first man for whom she feels genuine affection, her only free object choice. As later editions of *Roxana* suggest, that protagonist remains insecure even after the novel's conclusion. Because neither heroine can incorporate the very features that got her to the point where she can offer the reader such a retrospective, neither achieves the wholeness and autonomy of a citizen subject. In each case, the narrative subject, or desirous individual, is completely at odds with the narrating subject, or citizen subject. Such a resolution would not work for a man but only for a woman for whom the sexual contract at once displaces the social contract and safeguards her under the protections accorded to property.

Not so, however, for their writing, which reads like a more honest exposé of the sexual practices of the time than any that Samuel Richardson produced. Moll recounts, for example, how much she "lov'd the company indeed of Men of Mirth and Wit, Men of Gallantry and Figure, and was often entertain'd with such, as I was also with others; but I found by just Observation, that the brightest Men came upon the dullest Errand, *that is to say*, the Dullest as to what I aim'ed at; on the other Hand, those who came with the best Proposals were the Dullest and most disagreeable Part of the World" (48). If we think of her sexuality as the additive that allows her to thrive in social terms, we must simultaneously admire her honesty and condemn her narrow mercenary interests. No one comes out the better for this exchange. But if, instead of sexuality, we think of writing as the additive that transforms her from a docile body into a misfit whose upward mobility, as marked by literacy, we can admire, then it suddenly becomes possible to imagine turning such a misfit into a self-governing subject. Writing can serve both purposes: to express the aspects of individuality that an unsatisfactory social position would suppress and to limit those excesses once they have found a satisfactory situation. From this perspective, the pseudonymous titles of *Moll Flanders* and *Roxana* display writing's power to express and to limit the excesses of individualism at one and the same time.

In his first two novels, Richardson can indeed be accused of exploiting the advantages of both the male and the female picaresque, as Defoe had formulated them. Defoe set Moll and Roxana in motion in situations where their sexual precocity was certain to violate the autonomy of other households. To avoid this problem, he had Crusoe unleash his ambition on an island where no one would be the poorer for his gain. Let us but imagine Crusoe in a petticoat and using personal letter writing to fend off nearly constant sexual assaults, and we have Pamela, whose body is nothing if not her own property. While her sexuality is, as Henry Fielding contended, the feature that initially attracts her libertine master, it is finally her writing that masters him. "It was not to your disadvantage," he explains to her, "that I did see the letter you hint at; for they gave me a very high opinion of you." Then, having suggested that her writing created the object of his admiration, Mr. B performs the novel's own sleight of hand and reverses the relation between object and representation: "If I had not [already] loved you, do you think I would have troubled myself about your letters?"[20] The answer, rhetorically speaking, has to be "no," even though in logical terms it can only be "yes." Having learned the lesson of Defoe's heroines, it would appear, Richardson uses Pamela's letter writing to convert excessive sexuality into a form of familial affection capable of reforming the libertine practices that he attributes to the ruling class. Let us next imagine Moll and Roxana resisting the blandishments of their masters with the same energy that drives Crusoe to resist his father, god, nature, and foreigners. To turn them into Clarissa, we need only strip Defoe's women of the anonymity characterizing servants and prostitutes and have them tell readers capable of similar indignation how they were forced to receive unwanted sexual advances on pain of losing their economic livelihood. As Clarissa responds to each sexual overture in writing, it is finally writing that ensures her a position of authority with a multinational readership. By converting Moll's and Roxana's sexual precocity into verbal aggression, Defoe sets the stage for discursively aggressive protagonists like Pamela and Clarissa.

Well before Defoe, the dissenting tradition had argued for a government that began at home and as a moral obligation. But during the early eighteenth century, the novel gave that old formula a new and decisive twist. The daughter's fate came to represent that of the individual and to place certain limits on self-expression. If the wayward daughter reflected poorly on her father to the point of threatening his position within a community of men, then the coercive father reflected badly on that community if he defined men as unfit to care for their dependents. The only way around this double bind, as Richardson saw it, was to create a situation that authorized the daughter to choose a husband for herself, a man of a class above hers but one who valued women more for their qualities of mind and heart than for their social position or physical charm. Pamela engineers this kind of marriage by writing letters, and she elevates her entire family in the process. But still more compelling than Richardson's first attempt at fiction was *Clarissa*, an international best seller that put its stamp on the fiction of several European nations and their colonies.[21]

Between the epistolary prolixity of Richardson and Jane Austen's stylistic precision, the novel took a quantum leap. Henry Fielding's claim that it was not her writing but her withholding of sexual favors that enabled Richardson's otherwise unremarkable servant girl to entrap a wealthy suitor implied that his fiction, offering so many scenes of seduction while professing so many scruples, was nothing more than a tease in its own right.[22] Austen leaves no such room for readers to imagine that her heroines' reluctance to enter into relationships with men occupying a position above them is anything less than genuine. It is their restraint, their ability to reject not only unwanted sexual advances but advantageous marriage proposals as well that converts their otherwise docile bodies into those of bad subjects. By saying no, these heroines challenge the marriage rules that maintain the social hierarchy. To become exemplary citizens, they must translate their compulsion to perform such acts of defiance into an equally strong compulsion to repair any social ruptures they might have caused. Think of the acts of contrition that Austen has Emma perform, for example, after she has made the dependent Miss Bates the butt of her irony. Of all the means that protect her heroines from the kind of misinterpretation to which Richardson had left Pamela vulnerable, however, I insist that Austen's narrator is by far the most important.

With the appearance of this narrator, the British novel closes the gap between precocious heroine and morally judgmental narrator, resolving the formal problem that kept *Moll Flanders* and *Roxana* off the list of recommended reading until well into the twentieth century.[23] Austen's narrator knows even more about the heroine than the heroine knows about herself. At the same time, that narrator is neither limited to a specific body of experience nor therefore coerced, out of fear of personal exposure, to censor the truth with which she goes public. Obviously siding with the heroine of *Persuasion* over and against her well-meaning but too traditional adviser, Austen's narrator lets it be known that "Anne knew that Lady Russell must be suffering some pain in understanding and relinquishing Mr. Elliott, and be making some struggles to become truly acquainted with, and do justice to Captain Wentworth," with whom Anne has long been in love. It being socially awkward for that heroine to admit that her mentor has used the wrong criteria in initially assessing the worth of the man, the narrator continues,

> This however was what Lady Russell had now to do. She must learn to feel that she had been mistaken with regard to both; that she had been unduly influenced by appearances in each; that because Captain Wentworth's manners had not suited her own ideas, she had been too quick in suspecting them to indicate a character of dangerous impetuosity.... There was nothing less for Lady Russell to do, than to admit she had been pretty completely wrong, and to take up a new set of opinions and hopes.[24]

Rather than have the heroine tell her own story in the manner of memoir or epistolary writing, Austen's impersonal narrator records the process by which an individual's feelings, often feelings of which she herself is only half aware, turn into judgments and manifest themselves in words that divide or consolidate the community. Bridging the formal gulf between individual and aggregate, the narrator does not give voice to any one individual's thinking so much as to that of the culture setting a standard for protagonists and readers alike. In this case, writing still operates as the supplement, but writing lends the subject what she needs in order to fill her position, not what she needs in order to reject it. The closer the heroine's self-expression comes to achieving the forms established by the narrator's written standard, the closer she approaches the status of exemplary subject: one in whom self-expression and self-government exist in perfect accord. Let me pause briefly and suggest how writing provided the means to enlarge and modernize the old social order represented by Austen's country gentry and yet do so without challenging the hierarchical disposition of its members.

More than one Austen heroine turns down an offer of marriage that would give her a definitive move up the social ladder and a secure economic position for life. Such a refusal creates a minor scandal in *Pride and Prejudice*. Indeed, so incredible is Elizabeth Bennet's blunt refusal of Mr. Collins—to whom the Bennet's country residence has been entailed—that he dismisses her resistance as "usual with young ladies [who] reject the addresses of the man whom they secretly mean to accept, when he first applies for their favour."[25] To do away with any resemblance between her own motivations and the coyness of a heroine cast in the Richardsonian mold, Elizabeth wastes no time in assuring the presumptuous Collins, "I am not one of those young ladies (if such young ladies there are) who are so daring as to risk their happiness on the chance of being asked a second time. I am perfectly serious in my refusal.—You could not make *me* happy, and I am convinced that I am the last woman in the world who could make *you* so" (75). This signature move on the part of the Austen heroine marks the perfect realization of the bad subject as supplement. She puts at risk her father's position as head of household by refusing to secure his position among men of his own rank.

What is more, by refusing to consent to marriage in the terms it has been proposed, she becomes a rule breaker in the only way that can be morally authorized. Heedless of how she might be jeopardizing her economic security along with that of her family, she holds out for a contract based on a certain quality of feeling. This feeling arises directly from Elizabeth Bennet's resistance to Mr. Darcy's hauteur, his class-coded displays of superiority, and the disproportionate luxury of his friends and family when compared to her own precarious circumstances. This is not resistance that can be overcome in a wink or softened with money. Indeed, so intense is the antagonism between his rank and hers that her father, who would ordinarily be delighted to marry off a daughter to a man of Darcy's position, feels compelled to ask her, "What are you doing? Are you out of your senses, to be accepting this man? Have you not always hated him?" On hearing his daughter recant those feelings, Mr. Bennet continues to interrogate her, "He is rich, to be sure, and you may have more fine clothes and fine carriages than [your sister] Jane. But will they make you happy?" (259–60). To ensure this question elicits a resounding no from her readers, Austen has already provided the example of Charlotte Lucas, who consented to marry the otherwise unworthy Collins simply because he could provide her with a comfortable home. Elizabeth recalls that she "had always felt that Charlotte's opinion of matrimony was not exactly like her own. Even so, she continues, "she could not have supposed it possible that . . . [Charlotte] would have sacrificed every better feeling to worldly advantage. Charlotte the wife of Mr. Collins, was a most humiliating picture!" (88). In thus speaking Lizzie's unspoken thoughts, the narrator implies that the culture itself shares her indignation. This heroine—indeed, every Austen heroine—wants something from marriage that is significantly lacking in a marriage to Collins that offers nothing but social and economic security. If Charlotte Lucas's marriage is clearly *not* an example to follow, are we then to assume that *Pride and Prejudice* advocates a marriage contracted in defiance of those principles? Would the novel have us find Elizabeth's marriage superior to those of her sisters simply because they did not have to buck convention in making a match and can thus be assumed to bring nothing in excess of convention, nothing of themselves, to the match?

Quite possibly so, but there is much more to overcoming convention than at first meets the eye. Austen puts these questions to rest as her heroine conquers Mr. Bennet's incredulity "by [her] repeated assurances that Mr. Darcy was really the object of her choice, by explaining the gradual change which her estimation of him had undergone, relating her absolute certainty that his affection was not the work of a day, but had stood the test of many months suspense" (260). The episode where Elizabeth gazes at Darcy's miniature while his housekeeper sings her master's praises is the episode that scholars most often identify as the emotional turning point in the novel, the moment when the heroine falls in love with her only suitable match. Elizabeth indeed rereads the signs of the class above hers as anchored, in Darcy's case, to qualities within the man that allow her to recalculate his worth in terms of bourgeois morality. Indeed, of this encounter the narrator inquires, "What praise is more valuable than the praise of an intelligent servant? As a brother, a landlord, a master, she considered how many people's happiness were in his guardianship! . . . How much of good or evil must be done by him! Every idea that had been brought forward by the housekeeper was favourable to his character, and as she stood before the canvas, on which he was represented, . . . she thought of his regard with a deeper sentiment of gratitude than it had ever raised before" (170–71). Were this novel's purpose only to subordinate the upstart heroine by convincing her of Darcy's superiority in her terms as well as his, I do not believe that *Pride and Prejudice* would be considered the exemplary novel that it is. While it is true that Elizabeth is won over as the signs of Darcy's rank come to represent the virtues of the responsible head of household, the novel assigns him the task of further enlightening the heroine. "As a child I was taught what was *right*," he confesses, "but I was not taught to correct my temper. I was given good principles, but left to follow them in pride and conceit. . . . Unfortunately an only son, . . . I was spoilt by my parents, who though good themselves . . . , allowed, encouraged, almost taught me to be selfish and overbearing, to care for none beyond my own family circle, to think meanly of all the rest of the world, to *wish* at least to think meanly of their sense and worth compared with my own" (254). With this statement, Darcy reinscribes the signs of rank that spoke so eloquently to Elizabeth at Pemberly within the tradition of meaning that maintained the very status distinctions the novel has been calling into question.

With his next statement, however, Darcy lends new moral value to traditional rank by means of an economically coded explanation that identifies Elizabeth as the source of value added: "Such I was, from eight to eight and twenty; and such I might still have been but for you, dearest, loveliest Elizabeth!" First, he explains, she stripped away the value of his rank: "By you, I was properly humbled. I came to you without a doubt of my reception." He goes on to recall how she proved that rank, in and of itself, had very little value: "You shewed me how insufficient were all my pretensions to please a woman worthy of being pleased." In this way, he concludes, she made it possible for him to acquire value of a superior kind: "What do I not owe you! You taught me a lesson, hard indeed at first, but most advantageous" (254–55). Thus out of the mutual antagonism of the codes they respectively embody—he to her family and rank, she to his conviction that his family and superiority of rank mean moral superiority—a subtle synthesis emerges: a new "truth" that attaches traditional signs of class to the morality of the social contract. The novel itself affords access to this truth. For it simultaneously revises the basis of class superiority and teaches the reader, much as Darcy claims that Elizabeth taught him, to transform the signs of mere rank into a form of self-expression that improves both parties who enter into such an exchange. By increasing their value as individuals, we might say, the novel enhances the potential value of individuals in general.

MORALITY AS DISCIPLINE

As envisioned by the eighteenth century, the social contract exacted from individuals a promise to curb their individuality in order to secure its sanctity and protection. Enlightenment intellectuals—and I would certainly include Austen under this umbrella—saw this curb on selfish gratification as the first and best guarantee of full citizenship. To their way of thinking, such self-restraint entailed no loss of individuality but, quite the contrary, guaranteed an accretion to the self of individual rights. During the romantic era, however, fiction turned its attention from individual to aggregate, as novels sought to synthesize local cultural economies, on the one hand, and the practices of a cosmopolitan leisure class, on the other, and so produce a culture at once nationalist and novelistic. What happened to the bad subject as a result of this shift in focus? The figure could no longer generate expressions of excessive individualism that simultaneously detached the individual from a restrictive social category and made it possible for him or her to become more fully a citizen-subject, thus the judge and governor of others. Indeed, later fiction assumed individuals to be excessively individuated by nature, thus misfits *avant la lettre*, and, as such, threats to the autonomy of household and nation, a potential latent in Defoe's Moll and Roxana. My next chapter explains how fiction consequently abandoned the task of imagining an increasingly democratic nation during the early nineteenth century and reimagined the nation as one that required of its members progressively greater feats of sublimation.

This about-face in ideological direction transformed the rhetoric of fiction in the manner forecast when Robinson Crusoe achieved hegemonic authority over his island kingdom. In doing so, it created all the same rhetorical problems that accompanied that transformation of the novel form. Morality was for Victorians, as for readers of the previous century, something that appeared to come from within the protagonist as that individual resisted limits placed on self-expression by his or her position in society; morality had to be one's own rather than someone else's. During the period following the revolutions in the American colonies and in France, as well as widespread and often violent outbursts of popular discontent at home, the fiction that came to be established as "the novel" grew suspicious of individualism, much as Crusoe did, and sought a means other than overt, violent repression to harness its energy for collective purposes. Indeed, to push the analogy between the nineteenth-century novel and the closing chapters of Crusoe's story further, we might be tempted to say that fiction began to think of itself as the means of discipline rather than supplementation. As Crusoe imagines a fictional governor and assumes that role for the mutineers who populate his island, we find it increasingly difficult to value him for the plucky individualism that compelled him to resist father, overlord, and deity. Moreover, Defoe's replacement of subjection by violence with subjection by fictional violence is not only too transparent to make subjection appear as freedom but also too likely to descend the slippery slope to actual violence. At times, therefore, Crusoe seems to resemble the very forms of authority that he once sought to overcome. Despite the loss of appeal that accompanies his shift from representative individual to figure of discipline, however, it is important to recognize that Crusoe is no less shaped by the principle of supplementarity than before. He no longer manifests the presocial elements of individualism, but neither does he slide back into the position socially ordained for him at the novel's opening. By the end of his stay on the island, he enjoys certain attributes acquired strictly through words—namely, the rumor of an omniscient governor—that inscribe him in a position of authority.

Moving to the end of the eighteenth century, we can observe the gap between self-expressive and self-governing subjects disappearing into the narrowing gap between Austen's plucky heroine and the narrator whose collective wisdom she must embrace in order to become mistress of Pemberly. We can, I have suggested, understand the voice of such collective wisdom as a subtler form of the same writing that allowed Moll and Roxana to defend themselves against their former excesses. We can, in other words, understand Austen's narrator as the expression of Elizabeth Bennet's thoroughly acculturated self, a product of her negotiation of the culture more than a product of her nature, a form of self-expression that must address the reader from outside the heroine's consciousness until it is fully incorporated within.

Later fiction would transform bourgeois morality into something on the order of Crusoe's phantasmatic governor and Austen's equally phantasmatic narrator. Neither a function of individual desire nor a form of social authority, bourgeois morality comes to constitute a category that is separate from both and mediates between them. In his ingenious reading of Rousseau's social contract, Althusser calls attention to a discrepancy at the heart of contractual rhetoric on which its persuasive power depended. The contract represents itself as a voluntary act on the part of the presocial individual. That individual does not lose individual agency by submitting to the laws of the state, because he submits of his own volition, as Friday does when he places his head beneath Crusoe's foot. In submitting to a collective composed of individuals who have themselves similarly submitted, moreover, the presocial individual gains a freedom he did not enjoy in a state of nature in that he has submitted to no one else but himself. The presupposition is that any and all individuals will not only submit but, in so doing, come to understand themselves and their personal interests in much the same way.

This fantasy is not one that can ever be realized, as Althusser points out, without some third party to ensure that the exchange between individual and collective is in fact an exchange between an individual and an aggregate of more or less similar individuals. For the figure of exchange to become both psychological and sociopolitical reality, he insists, there has to be a cultural apparatus that sees to it that many different individuals imagine their relation to the real in approximately these terms. Embracing much the same realism, diverse individuals will assume that those who also embrace it are all much the same; this is of course the kernel of truth to be found in Benedict Anderson's *Imagined Communities*, which sees the appearance of a national tradition of the novel as the sure sign that a culture is emerging into modern nationhood.[26] As Rousseau contended, only education can supply this third mediating and subject-shaping component of the social contract. Before Michel Foucault's *History of Sexuality: An Introduction* and *Discipline and Punish*, Jeremy Bentham's *Theory of Fictions* is perhaps the most forthright political argument for the authority of fiction, thus the fiction of authority. It is surely the clearest statement of the paradox that inhabits that argument. Published in part in 1812 but not in its entirety until 1932, this work argues that one understands most of one's physical experience in terms of fictions of right, obligation, truth, or justice. "In theory," Bentham contends, these purely fictional phenomena "were assumed for axioms; and in practice they were observed as rules," axioms that existed chiefly in language and rules that were put into effect through speech acts. In order for language to exercise such power over people and property, however, it cannot appear to do so. Thus, at the moment of fiction's triumph, Bentham declares that "the season of *Fiction* is now over: insomuch that what formerly might have been tolerated and countenanced under the name, would, if now attempted to be set on foot, be censured *posture*."[27] If subjects are going to be regulated by the extraordinary web of fictions attending the social contract and giving it mind and objectivity, flesh and world, then fiction itself had to be regulated. Henceforth bad subjects would have to be forcibly restrained.

I believe that, from the first, fiction hid its considerable power to perform this function behind the apparently natural process of education by means of which fiction imagined transforming unleashed individualism into civil morality. It is through a series of what might be called lessons, after all, that novels transform signs of an individual's natural excess into the cultural wisdom of a citizen-subject. Rather than simply part of a curriculum that educates, we might more accurately identify the novel as the larger cultural framework within which education proper provides but one means of converting bad subjects into citizens. The novel in this larger sense cannot be pinned down to any individual novel, tradition, or institution of the novel. The novel is more like a ubiquitous cultural narrative that not only measures personal growth in terms of an individual's ability to locate him- or herself productively within the aggregate but also and simultaneously measures the aggregate in terms of its ability to accommodate the increasing heterogeneity of individuals. If the novel itself is the supplement that puts the modern individual in motion, then morality is the rhetoric by which the novel signals at different moments in history exactly where to draw the line that limits individualism so that a balance may be struck between these competing claims.

In contrast with both domestic culture and the official institutions of education, the nineteenth-century novel justified itself as a form of mediation that appeared to be no more than mediation, because it declared itself fiction rather than truth. Like Defoe's figure of the governor or Austen's narrator, however, nineteenth-century fiction acquired a peculiar power to constitute the two parties whose relationship it regulated. In this respect, fiction itself began to operate as the additive responsible for kicking the history of the modern subject into successive historical gears. In speaking for the collective, Defoe's governor and Austen's narrator reshaped in some irreversible way the authors who created them, much as Rousseau's presocial individual remade himself as a citizen in the act of agreeing to submit to the state. So too is the second party or aggregate of citizens changed each time another individual agrees to submit, any one of whom could provide the supplement that, when incorporated, would require a thoroughgoing organization of the group.

No other medium then available could have reconstituted the imagined relation between individual reader and national readership with the rhetorical dexterity of the novel. By means of the reading contract that it established, the novel not only revised the way that literate people imagined both parties of the social contract, it also put a moral stamp on exchanges that guaranteed the normalcy if not the homogeneity of its readership. To authorize cultural practices that relied, as Crusoe did, on a largely imaginary form of government, however, fiction had to change horses in midstream. It had to outlaw precisely the precocious individual who had such great appeal for eighteenth-century readers. The unmarried woman continued to embody the principle of expressive individualism in later fiction, but her ticket to happiness through an advantageous marriage would no longer rest on her power to refuse anything less than she deserved. Happiness came to depend instead on her ability to renounce desire and accept a position that initially seemed significantly beneath her. In this way, British fiction replaced self-expression with self-government as the key to social success.

WHEN NOVELS MADE NATIONS

Bounded on the one side by the traumatic upheaval in France of 1789 and on the other by the Peterloo Massacre of 1819, Jane Austen's career coincided with momentous changes in the material conditions under which readers could imagine anyone achieving individuality. The widespread mechanization of labor, massive appropriations of common lands, migrations of unskilled labor to the cities, and the shift from the gold standard to various paper currencies together created the conditions for what Karl Marx would describe as the classic form of capitalism.[1] In this chapter, I want to investigate another order of change occurring at the same time, one essential, I believe, to the success of those transformations underway in the socioeconomic realm. The change I have in mind enabled a British readership to understand itself as a stable aggregate of individuals, even as the new economy dispersed some of those individuals across the globe, redistributed other segments of the population within England itself, and brought in a steady flow of labor from Ireland. Inside the relatively prosperous household, a corresponding revolution was redefining the ideal English home as a field of objects that in part or whole came from elsewhere and were made by foreign hands. In the Highbury of Austen's *Emma*, the arrival of a pianoforte from London constitutes such a revolution at the micro level. To preserve a sense of cultural coherence under such conditions, the novel had to refigure the social body so that readers could imagine it remaining English while taking in foreigners and foreign objects and extending itself onto foreign soil. Those Englishmen residing in Great Britain came to consider their fellow Englishmen as more or less English according to how they met or failed to observe forms of self-containment aimed at maintaining a stable social order.[2] Being British consequently ceased to refer to one's place of birth, native language, or home and became instead a set of obligations and constraints that people could carry with them to other countries.

This was the moment when Austen achieved her delicate synthesis of individual self-expression and social subjection by at once introducing some flexibility into the hierarchical world inhabited by her county gentry and subordinating her upwardly mobile heroines to the cultural standard articulated by her narrators. Other novels anticipated the century to come in a rather different way, as they took up the task of transforming the notion of the social body from a group of benevolent landowners and their local dependents to a nation that had to incorporate a much more diverse range of social types and provide them with a livelihood. The novels I have in mind necessarily dissolved the Austen synthesis and created the terms for the dialectical relationship of subjectivity and subjection that shapes mainstream Victorian fiction. To remodel the genre for such a purpose, this fiction could no longer cast the bad subject as the protagonist without challenging the foundational principle that only self-governing subjects could become citizens. Yet this same fiction apparently needed the bad subject as much as ever before. Extravagant, even monstrous forms of individualism erupt in these transitional novels to demonstrate that fiction could not assimilate all that energy to a community of self-governing citizens, not without completely destroying the fantasy that such a community could emerge one individual at a time. Thus this fiction confronted the fact that it could no longer fulfill its generic commitment both to encourage expressive individualism and to imagine a more inclusionary social body. This fiction renounced individualism in the interests of social stability only with great reluctance, however, leaving the reader with a world that was not only monster free but also significantly diminished, as if missing some vital component precisely because family feeling and social duty had won the day.

Étienne Balibar's brief genealogy of the modern subject bears directly on the formal aspects of this transformation and locates it squarely in the decades immediately following the French Revolution. What I have identified as a significant change in the novel form, Balibar identifies with a new moment in the history of the European subject itself. Indeed, he poses a question in terms that allow me to clarify the change marking this moment at all levels of cultural production: "If freedom means freedom *of the subject*, or subjects, is it because there is, in 'subjectivity,' an originary source of spontaneity and autonomy, something irreducible to objective constraints and determinations? Or is it not rather because 'freedom' can only be the result and counterpart of liberation, emancipation, *becoming* free: a trajectory inscribed *in* the very texture of the individual, with all its contradictions, which starts with subjection and always maintains an inner or outer relation with it?"[3] The difference between these two questions may at first glance seem little more than a matter of emphasis. Each involves the negotiation by one entity ("the subject") of the difference between two states of being: free subjectivity, on the one hand, and subjection to some higher authority, on the other. The first question describes much the same relation between these two components of the modern subject as did novels that saw the bad subject as an "originary source of spontaneity and autonomy" in excess of and irreducible to an assigned social position. But the second question significantly modifies the eighteenth-century definition of the subject.

Rather than something that is first and foremost present in the presocial individual and compels him or her to overcome some social limitation standing in the way of an a priori need for gratification, this second definition of freedom insists that individuality emerges only as the subject psychologically overcomes the limits of his or her social position. In other words, this later subject has no self to express until he or she has acquired the cultural means of expressing it. The subject that seemed to preexist its social position in eighteenth-century fiction comes into being, in this reformulation, as it confronts the limits of that position and understands what aspects of his or her subjectivity cannot be socially enacted. In this case, we might say, the cultural limit becomes the supplement. A subtle change perhaps, but nevertheless a profound one: In refusing to settle for a position that does not afford gratification, the eighteenth-century subject asked the social order to relax its boundaries and include elements previously excluded from respectable society. In overcoming some external social limit, the nineteenth-century subject effects no such revision of the social classification system in which its seeks gratification. (It would be too dangerous to imagine such revision on a mass scale.) The nineteenth-century subject consequently undergoes an internal revolution that redirects presocial ambitions at socially acceptable goals. In effect, that subject adapts to a position more limited than its subjectivity, which constitutes an inner world apart and only partially expressed in social terms.

This chapter considers two novels that renounce the positive figuration of the bad subject and with it what Balibar calls an "originary source of spontaneity and autonomy, something irreducible to objective constraints and determinations."[4] Both Mary Shelley's *Frankenstein* and Sir Walter Scott's *Waverley* condemn the excesses of individualism that propelled earlier protagonists into respectable social positions. To acquire anything like free subjectivity, their protagonists must find a way of being themselves within the constraints that transform any diverse group of individuals into a coherent whole. Free subjectivity is something that develops with and in relation to citizenship rather than originating outside and prior to it. Yet both works of fiction also distinguish themselves from the novels that follow, novels that defined the mission of Victorian fiction, because both resist the new ideological imperative to make free subjectivity the result rather than the cause of a liberal society. Even as they throw their ethical weight behind the social stability that comes from harnessing individual energy, both novels invest aesthetic value in precisely what must be sacrificed for the greater good. It is as if the novel form itself were refusing to abandon either the bad subject it used to celebrate or the more inclusionary society that embraced such subjects as its citizens.

AMBIVALENT OBJECTS

I use the figure of ambivalence to describe both the distinctive affect that novels of this period communicate—a simultaneous desire for and disgust with grandiose forms of self-expression—and the rhetorical figure they use to generate it. Conventional wisdom links acute ambivalence to certain pathological states, as well as to jealousy and mourning, usually on the part of the author, that renders him or her unable to say either yes or no by compelling that individual to say both yes and no whenever he or she endeavors to say either. Alternatively, ambivalence can be characterized as an emotional state that both produces and is generated by a distinctive kind of object. Perfectly benevolent and fundamentally hostile, this object inspires both longing and loathing in the subject with a simultaneity that disallows any compromise or dialectic of these opposing affects. Finding it impossible to carry on a relationship with such an object, the individual generally resolves this problem by splitting that object in two, producing a good object and a bad object, each of which contains certain features of the other. Gilles Deleuze uses the concept of the "virtual object" to argue that the pleasure principle and the reality principle are complementary rather than contradictory. As such, the two principles cannot exist without each other but "borrow from and feed into one another." The two principles are kept on the same track by a "virtual object" composed of both halves of this object, which we encounter under such names "as Melanie Klein's good *and* bad objects, the 'transitional' object, the fetish object and above all Lacan's *objet a.* . . . These virtual objects are incorporated in the real objects," among which Deleuze includes parts of the subject's body, another person, or even "very special objects such as toys or fetishes." As he explains, "whatever the reality in which the virtual object is incorporated, it does not become integrated; it remains planted or stuck there, and does not find in the real object the half which completes it, but rather testifies to the other virtual half which the real continues to lack."[5] I am not suggesting that all objects that are either good or bad are formed according to the principle of ambivalence. On the contrary, the *good* object and the *bad* object in the sense I mean here are objects in which positive and negative elements are simultaneously present and inseparable one from the other. The presence of each in the other is what bonds the two as a single figure.

It should come as no surprise that the ambivalence shaping novels of the period under discussion generates rather clear and absolutely incompatible readings of excessive individualism. As my reading of *Robinson Crusoe* sought to demonstrate, the features that prevent an individual from fitting into the given social order are precisely what provide the narrative motor of the novel and the source of its appeal. That affective investment does not change as we move into the early nineteenth century. What does change is the moral investment that the novel asks its reader to make in figures of spontaneity and excess. Romantic-era fiction reinvests moral authority in a set of features associated with the social contract, thus with a regulatory body or collective norm. Again, Balibar is helpful, when he argues against the notion that in the decades following the French Revolution it became reasonable to think of the contract "as a mechanism that 'socializes' equals purely by virtue of their equality." Instead, he contends, we should think of the social contract as adding something to equality that "compensates for its 'excess' of universality."

In the century that followed, the dissatisfaction that was considered an "indispensable preliminary" to individual fulfillment was transformed into something altogether different through a dialectic "of animality and humanity in man." Citizenship was itself a kind of supplement as well as a limit on subjectivity. "The Declaration of 1789 gives this supplement its most economical form," Balibar observes, "that of a *de jure* fact: 'Men are born and remain'" individuals, but they require socialization before they can express that individuality in authoritative forms.[6] As he suggests, one's "preliminary" individualism—the stuff that bad subjects are made of—has to find social forms of expression before the individual can achieve the individuality distinguishing the citizen-subject; the raw energy of individualism is dangerously antisocial. Between 1789 and 1819, the novel accordingly shifts its moral investment to the supplementary qualities associated with citizenship and yet remains aesthetically bound and committed to those qualities associated with an earlier individualism it must now renounce. The result is a perfectly ambivalent text that represents the excesses of individualism as irresistibly attractive and utterly loathsome at the same time.

STRANGE BEDFELLOWS

In his classic study of the historical novel, Georg Lukács calls Walter Scott a "sober, conservative petty aristocrat," only to credit him in the next breath for giving "perfect artistic expression to the basic progressive tendency of this period, i.e., the historical defence of progress."[7] Lukács bases this claim largely on Scott's first novel, *Waverley*, published in 1814 but written in fits and starts over the preceding nine years. In the course of making a name for himself as a novelist, Scott also edited *The Novels of Daniel Defoe* in 1809 and the extremely influential *Ballantine's Novelist's Library* from 1821 to 1824.[8] By way of contrast, Mary Shelley was an elite cosmopolitan and the daughter of radical thinkers. She preferred the company of poets who also dabbled in radical politics. By her account, she stayed home one rainy day near Geneva and invented a ghost story for the amusement of her companions.[9] The result was *Frankenstein*, first published in

1818. It is only fair to acknowledge that *Waverley* and *Frankenstein* register all the differences in education, social background, taste, politics, gender, and national identity that make Scott and Shelley such an unlikely pair for purposes of specifying just how British fiction rethought the excesses of individualism for a nineteenth-century readership. Even so, I plan to read the two novels as working toward the same objective. After the second decade of the nineteenth century, thanks in part to their efforts, the British novel could no longer tell the story of subject formation without telling the story of nation formation as well. This mutually defining relationship between an individual and a collective body intent on achieving autonomy and coherence in its own right changed the way readers henceforth imagined both.

With the occasional exception of Austen, Scott tends to monopolize accounts of this moment in the history of the novel, while *Frankenstein*, like all of Shelley's fiction, is considered more or less *sui generis*. To understand fully the ambivalence shaping each and characterizing what is, for me, a distinct moment in the history of the modern subject, it is instructive to look, first, at Scott's historical landscape through the psychoanalytic lens more commonly brought to bear on Shelley's and then to reverse that course of action by reading *Frankenstein* as a historical novel in the manner that we usually reserve for reading *Waverley*. Criticism generally takes for granted that a gothic novel concerns itself primarily with the texture, contours, and objective of the wish that shapes it and only secondarily with the individual's engagement in national politics.[10] To grasp the libidinal economy of *Waverley*, one has to ask the sorts of questions usually asked of the often fantastic landscape of *Frankenstein*. How does the northern frontier to which Scott dispatches his protagonist resemble those liminal places of the mind in Shelley's novel where scientific reasoning both suspends common sense and exposes the reader to emotions beyond the normal intensities of human feeling? How does the protagonist who gets himself into such a state hold on to the elements of cultural identity that will allow him to return to homeland and family? What are the psychic costs of taking on a national identity, and how does the imaginary landscape ascribed to the nation register this act of reincorporation? In reading *Waverley* as we would *Frankenstein*, in other words, I want to assume that the so-called external world serves as the medium of self-expression, so that the world reveals the currents of thought at work reshaping it.

Extreme forms of self-expression invariably send us back to the conventions of realism as comfortably self-affirming in contrast to a world so thoroughly taken over by human desire that the difference between self and world disappears. In restoring the constraints of realism that tell us what we are reading is a normative view, however, fiction does not return us to the world as it was before it became the medium of individualism. Indeed, I suggest here and throughout that from time to time novels make radical departures from anything resembling their established terrain in order to adapt the range and contours of realism for new historical conditions. The moment during which both Scott and Shelley wrote was definitely one of those times. In turning to *Frankenstein*, then, I read Shelley's uncanny tale as a work of historical fiction by asking those questions of her novel that Scott's fiction invites us to ask of it: What happens to the autonomy of the nation when it opens its boundaries to strangers? What elements of the foreign culture can that nation incorporate and still retain its autonomy and continuity over time? What happens to social geography as a result of such acts of incorporation?

If the demands placed on members of a community destroy the sources of gratification that the hero pursues in *Waverley*, then *Frankenstein* goes in exactly the opposite direction and has its protagonist pursue a form of self-gratification that destroys the community that would place limits on him. Yet each novel in its own way destroys the equilibrium by which eighteenth-century fiction maintained the illusion that the subject in the two different senses established by the social contract could ultimately be represented as one. As envisioned by eighteenth-century intellectuals, the social contract exacted the promise of self-restraint from individuals who saw this limit to their individuality as the first and best guarantee of full citizenship. To their way of thinking, such self-restraint entailed no loss of individuality but, quite the contrary, secured their inherent individuality in the form of private property and individual rights. For Scott and Shelley, on the other hand, what had been represented as an exchange of something wholly negative, what Balibar means by "animality," for something wholly positive, in the form of property rights, those qualities that we equate with "civility" or even with humanity itself, came to be understood as a loss of some core element of individuality that connected men at once to their heroic past and to a competitive nature. That both Scott and Shelley had a serious problem representing individualism—its lack and its excess, respectively—tells me that the genre in which they wrote was simply unsuited to perform the reversal of ideological gears that British culture required of early-nineteenth-century novelists.

Yet, as I demonstrate, if eighteenth-century novels called the modern individual into being as an independent agent and measure of social change, then nineteenth-century novels succeeded in transforming that earlier way of formulating individualism into a force that threatened to disrupt a stable and internally coherent community. Writing at the precise moment of transition, Scott and Shelley demonstrate that what had been most individualistic about the individual was in fact simultaneously irresistible and loathsome: irresistible in that it expanded the range of human potential and loathsome in that those exceptional qualities necessarily destroyed what was mundane, necessary, normal, comfortable, and right. The rhetorical structure of chiasmus provides the formal strategy by which Shelley incorporated certain features of the good object into the bad and Scott incorporated certain elements of the bad object into the good. The two authors thereby entered into an unwitting partnership that transformed the novel into a perfectly ambivalent object. As it changed the relation between individual and collective body, now understood as the nation, this formal strategy revised both, creating an imaginary geography that made each—land and inhabitants—an essential component of the other.

Political History as Melancholia

To become fully individuated, the British subject had to possess some piece of presocial humanity in the form of desires that exceeded the limits of his or her social position, desires originating at the very core of himself that made it impossible for him to fit in. Moreover, this protagonist had to overcome the limits set by family, class, or nation without either destroying that collectivity or placing himself permanently outside it. Shelley and Scott perform this legerdemain by turning time into space. "Some favorable opportunities [for observing the] contrast [between premodern and modern] have been afforded me," Scott explains, "by the state of society in the northern part of the island at the period of my history, and may serve at once to vary and to illustrate the moral lessons which I would willingly consider as the most important part of my plan."[11] In direct contradiction to the qualities required of modern men and women, the honor code of the Highlanders calls for suicidal heroism in its men and nunlike devotion in its women. To the degree that he internalizes that code of honor and yearns for such a woman, Scott's Waverley acquires some of the qualities of Highland culture, but the novel also makes it very clear that he cannot throw in his lot with the Highlanders and retain his status as a modern individual and member in good standing of British society. That Scott must keep his protagonist from taking the ontological leap that would prevent him from returning south to England is no more in doubt than it is in the case of Shelley's icebound adventurer Walton. What is in question, however, is why Waverley must cross over into Highland culture in the first place. What lack in Scott's new man can be filled only if he incorporates certain features of this particularly barbarous form of early modern culture?

Most readers consider the wedding with which *Waverley* closes as Scott's way of resolving symbolically the conflict represented by the spatial juxtaposition of early modern Scotland and modern England.[12] These readers take the novel at its word when it promises to offer a glimpse of the British Isles a mere sixty years earlier. Rather than assume we are encountering such a political-historical landscape, however, I have promised to treat Scott's national geography as the very kind of psychological landscape that an early-nineteenth-century readership would expect to find in the gothic novels that were enjoying such popularity at about the same time.[13] Once we recognize the novel's conclusion as a purely artificial resolution, we can abandon the notion that Waverley pursues Lukács's middle way and mediates between an early modern social order that was clearly obsolete at the time the novel was written (if not sixty years before) and a modern bourgeois society.[14] We can also abandon the notion that the household formed by the protagonist's marriage to Rose dialectically resolves a historical struggle going on outside the household. Instead, we can attend to an affective undertow that defines both the struggle and its resolution as components of an emotional economy hostile to historical change. This change, as I describe it, pried emotional investments free of local kin groups and transferred their affect to the self-enclosed domestic units out of which modern nations were being made. It at once tolled the knell of expressive individualism and guaranteed the return of the bad subject, not as the misfit for whom a space must be cleared within the social order but as the compulsive violation of bourgeois sexuality that Victorian fiction had to sublimate or kill off.

To understand the marriage of Waverley and Rose as a way of coming to terms with a cultural historical change of such magnitude, it is quite possible to read the narrative that leads to this resolution as a successful mourning process. Here, the subject incorporates the lost object, integrates some of its more salient features, discards the remainder, and becomes whole, complex, and internally coherent by accepting the difference between self and other. Such a reading is consistent with Lukács's reasons for celebrating *Waverley* as the exemplary historical novel. But were we to stress the gothic qualities of the narrative, then a phase or variant of the mourning process known as melancholia would provide the more accurate guide to the emotional logic of Scott's novel. For purposes of such a reading, it makes sense to think of melancholia as an exact inversion of the process of incorporation and assimilation that allows the successful mourner to let go of the desired object while preserving its desirability. The melancholic individual refuses either to make peace with or to relegate the lost object to the past. To preserve the object of desire, the individual performs what might be called preventive mourning, or acts of memorialization that precede and anticipate the loss of that object.[15] In so doing, the individual reconstitutes a felt lack as a lost object external to himself, thereby substituting a memento or relic for the desired object even before that object has disappeared.[16] When we use this model to describe how a novel thinks, we are not of course excavating some psychoanalytic truth about the author, much less about his protagonist. On the contrary, we are examining the affective organization of the textual material itself, in this case, the wholesale desecration of an iconographic landscape that could be integrated neither with a modern social order nor with the fiction that defers to such an order as reality itself.

During the early nineteenth century, the novel offered up the national landscape as one in which individuals could become fully themselves. The novel extends this apparent invitation to expressive individualism, however, only to show that unrestrained individuality had to be contained, cut down to size, degraded, domesticated, or else subjected to some violent act of repression. Through this process of self-expansion, loss, and self-contraction, I am suggesting, fiction drained away desire from the bad subject in order to reinvest it in the imaginary nation. The reader is made to care about a future for which individual fulfillment is no longer the guarantee, a future that depends on the ability of the aggregate to maintain spatial coherence and reproduce its definitive cultural categories and values over time. If we emphasize Waverley's relationship with the Highland chieftain Fergus MacIvor, then Waverley's ability to survive the decisive Battle of Preston and return to England seems to fit the pattern associated with mourning, the pattern, that is, of incorporation, integration, separation, and acceptance of death. If we first focus on Waverley's relationship with Fergus's sister, Flora, however, an altogether different pattern emerges. In combination, both patterns balance optimism about the future against longing for the past, which the one must sacrifice and the other preserve in order to bring the story to a successful conclusion. The contrary emotional investments characterizing this fiction should not be read as a flaw in its thinking, however, but as the secret of its rhetorical success: namely, the formal equilibrium it achieves between equally necessary but absolutely incompatible components of the modern subject.

Waverley initially rejects Rose Bradwardine as "too frank, too confiding, too kind; amiable qualities undoubtedly, but destructive of the marvelous with which a youth of imagination delights to dress the empress of his affections" (66). That he must reject Rose in order to protect the literary ideal produced by his education becomes apparent when, on leaving the decidedly prosaic Rose, he immediately becomes enchanted with the more poetic Flora. The Highland home of Fergus and Flora MacIvor exceeds precisely where the Bradwardine estate falls short of Waverley's aesthetic standard. The illusion of complete gratification, the sense of a dream come true, is destined to perish, but not before Waverley falls deeply in love with the illusion of complete self-fulfillment embodied in the person of Flora: "Edward thought he had never, even in his wildest dreams, imagined a figure of such exquisite and interesting loveliness. The wild beauty of the retreat, bursting upon him as if by magic, augmented the mingled feeling of delight and awe with which he approached her, like a fair enchantress of Boiardo or Ariosto, by whose nod the scenery seemed to have been created, an Eden in the wilderness" (106). But when he tries to translate his wish for this magical object into the prosaic conventions of marriage, Waverley quickly learns that the beguiling heroine of an early modern romance could not love a man in the manner modern novels required of their more pedestrian heroines. As Flora explains to Waverley, "I have had but one wish—the restoration of my royal benefactors to their rightful throne.... Let me but live to see the day of that happy restoration, and a Highland cottage, a French convent, or an English palace, will be alike indifferent to me" (135).

The kind of household that has a Rose Bradwardine at its center is noticeably absent from this catalog. Indeed, anything like a companionate marriage is outside the realm of possibility for Flora, since the only environment she can inhabit belongs to a "wild" culture that was disappearing by the time Scott sat down to write his novel. She wisely explains to Waverley why they would be as divided in marriage as characters from different traditions of literature: "You, Mr Waverley, would for ever refer to the idea of domestic happiness which your imagination is capable of painting, and whatever fell short of that ideal representation would be construed into coldness and indifference, while you might consider the enthusiasm with which I regarded the success of the royal family, as defrauding your affection of its due return" (135). Here begins a process of deidealization in which Waverley seeks but fails to repair the damage to his literary representation of Scotland and its indigenous people. It is rather obvious why Scott cannot imagine the national future in terms of a match between Waverley and Flora. Not so obvious is why this prompts him to force a match between Waverley and Rose. By wedding English core to Scottish periphery, Scott appears to fulfill the progressive mission of the novel to imagine a more inclusive social body. But can we really say that Scott has done so if he predicates the wedding of Waverley and Rose on the destruction of Tully-Veolan, the Bradwardine's ancestral estate?

No, the novel never so much as hints at a return to a whole and internally coherent social world that would signal the successful conclusion of the mourning process. The description recounting Waverley's first glimpse of Tully-Veolan after the battle of Preston is choked with the debris of a psychic life that characterizes the landscape of melancholia. And what is this debris if not the bits and pieces of the literary culture Scott has systematically dismantled: "The battlements above the gate were broken and thrown down, and the carved Bears, which were said to have done sentinel's duty upon the top for centuries, now hurled from their posts, lay among the rubbish. The avenue was cruelly wasted. Several large trees were felled and left lying across the path; and the cattle of the villagers, and the more rude hoofs of dragoon horses, had poached into black mud the verdant turf which Waverley had so much admired" (296).

Rose's quarters are subject to similar violence, so that in her absence the novel can resurrect her as the embodiment of the lost aesthetic ideal. Indeed, there in the wreckage of her dismantled domicile, what does Waverley find but the same copy of Ariosto he had given Rose that appeared to materialize in the figure of Flora as "the fair enchantress": "Viewing the front of the building, thus wasted and defaced, [Waverley's] eyes naturally sought the little balcony which more properly belonged to Rose's apartment.... Several of her books were mingled with broken flower-pots and other remnants. Among these Waverley distinguished one of his own, a small copy of Ariosto, and gathered it like a treasure, though wasted by wind and rain" (297). Chosen rather than choosing, capable of being but not of doing, Rose constitutes a form of femininity that men do not necessarily desire but nevertheless invest with great moral value. While Scott has given Rose all the features that would eventually characterize the Victorian angel in the house, not all the ingenuity of his fiction can succeed in making us find this figure desirable before its historical moment is ripe. To make Waverley's marriage to Rose serve as an adequate representation of his fulfillment as a British citizen and modern individual, Scott must replace Flora with Rose. In constructing a plot that substitutes a novelistic heroine for the embodiment of Jacobite aspirations as the hero's object of desire, however, Scott cannot figure out how to transfer aesthetic value from the one to the other in a way that confirms his reinvestment of moral value. The two forms of value therefore part company and enter into opposition.

The novel found it all too easy to preserve the magic of art by bringing it to life in the person of Flora. When it comes to reversing the Pygmalion story and rendering those aesthetic qualities in a mundane object, the result is less satisfactory. As we can infer from the scene of her ruined apartment and copy of Ariosto, the novel is not really all that interested in Rose. While we catch only those glimpses of the girl herself that are absolutely required by the plot, we see a great deal of attention to her estate, both its grounds and its interior. It is the place rather than the woman in which Scott invests his concern: "[All] Bears whatsoever were replaced upon their stations, and renewed or repaired with so much care, that they bore no tokens of the violence which had so lately descended upon them.... The house itself had been thoroughly repaired as well as the gardens, with the strictest attention to maintain the original character of both, and to remove, as far as possible, all appearance of the ravage they had sustained (334).

The novel certainly tries to endow the Bradwardine estate with the qualities of a timeless work of art that outlasts historical change.[17] Precisely because it is so faithful to the original, however, the novel also encourages us to understand this place as something altogether new, a miniature of the original in which all the ancient parts have been stripped of their history, polished with personal affection, and offered up as a monument to a culture that is over and done. Against this background, Rose emerges as the morally superior woman, while Flora remains the locus of the novel's aesthetic investment.

This household cannot abide the presence of a Fergus MacIvor any more than it can tolerate Flora as the desired object, but it must deal with Fergus's masculinity in a quite different way. Supporter of Charles Stuart, scourge of the English military, and obstacle to the unification of Great Britain, Fergus must be executed before Tully-Veolan can provide the means of imagining a new British nation. Once the features of an ancient and now barbarous tradition have been banished in the flesh, however, they reappear within Tully-Veolan as the idealized traces of the exclusion enabling that place to maintain an illusion of wholeness: "It was a large and spirited painting, representing Fergus Mac-Ivor and Waverley in their Highland dress, the scene a wild, rocky, and mountainous pass, down which the clan were descending in the background" (338). By enclosing the wild Fergus within the respectable parlor, the social organization represented by the clan passes from the status of a residual social formation actively contesting English modernity to that of a relic of old Scotland and an ornament of modern British life. Has Scott extended the boundaries of England into Scotland so that he can establish a clear distinction between Scottishness and Englishness? Yes, one might be tempted to conclude that he has, were it not for the fact that such a reading would be no more faithful to the spirit of the text than would our easy acceptance of the Waverley-Bradwardine match as a resolution to the conflict between England and Scotland.

How we read the conclusion all depends on whether we think that the Bradwardine estate represents the more inclusive brand of Englishness called Britishness at the end of the novel and so consider it capable of containing the antinomies it presumes to mediate. Or, alternatively, in making the modern British household, might we say that Scott has whittled down the possibilities of group identity to a set within which all the ontological and ideological differences between England and Scotland exist as so many elements of interior decoration?

The ambivalent architecture of Tully-Veolan, a place simultaneously English and Scottish, old and new, both enlarged and miniaturized, at once the product of history and an ahistorical summation of the past, balances the positive and negative aspects of premodern Scotland too perfectly for us to come down on either side without undervaluing the other. To regard Tully-Veolan as a synthesis of any kind is to read this novel from a later-nineteenth-century perspective that could, unlike Scott, see Rose as Flora's aesthetic superior.

Waverley shows us how the conflict between an individual's inclinations and his rightful social position came to be defined not in contrary but in contradictory terms, so that to achieve one was by definition to put the other out of reach. As a result, Waverley seems to mature through the process of enacting desires that he must finally reject, and the community composed of individuals like himself seems relatively inclusive in contrast to the warring camps between which he wanders. Mary Shelley's novel appears to have an entirely different objective from Scott's. In *Frankenstein*, excessive individualism—those qualities that make it impossible for her protagonist to fit in—so threatens the social order that it cannot be tolerated.

MELANCHOLIA AS POLITICAL HISTORY

Despite the very different circumstances under which Mary Shelley produced her first novel, her husband, the poet Shelley, introduced *Frankenstein*, much as Scott did *Waverley*, by declaring it "exempt" from "the disadvantages of a mere tale of specters or enchantment."[18] He described her creation of situations "impossible as a physical fact" as a means of representing "human passions more comprehensive and commanding" than one can observe in "existing events" (5). She found it necessary, in her husband's view, to add something in excess of the individual to demonstrate what would happen to the human community were that individual to become fully himself. Where Scott eschewed gothic convention in order to situate his protagonist in the landscape of recent history, Mary Shelley renounced local geography for the vast Arctic seas, a *terra nullius* beyond the Highlands, which, as Walton's stalled expedition suggests, proves beyond the reach of the historical imagination as well.[19] Nevertheless, Shelley belongs as much to the moment when novels made nations as Scott does, indeed all the more so because her protagonist is a cosmopolite with no particular attachment to a specific geographical location.

Human beings are what count in *Frankenstein*, not their origins, or their means of economic livelihood, or even their language and social behavior. People acknowledge in each other familiar forms of humanity because, the novel suggests, they consider those forms beautiful, and they react with varying degrees of tolerance to difference. The Irish are the least assimilable in this regard, because they are the least cosmopolitan and thus least able to take the sympathetic leap of identification that characterizes both the extended Frankenstein family and the De Lacey household where the monster resides as a secret tenant.[20] The boundaries delineating nations are, in this novel, as permeable and thus potentially inclusive as the boundaries surrounding these two extended families. It is no accident that Switzerland is Frankenstein's homeland, the Alps that cut a swath across southern Europe his favorite landscape, and a young man who specializes in foreign languages his dearest companion. A narrative that wants to insist on the pan-European character of kinship must, however, first imagine the very social formation it challenges: an aggregate composed of self-contained individuals that looks very much like the compromise formation Scott offers the reader at the end of *Waverley*.

The story of *Frankenstein* comes to us as a letter written by the English Walton to his sister back home. Walton has commissioned a ship and crew to sail into Arctic waters so that he may "satiate my ardent curiosity with the sight of a part of the world never before visited, and may tread a land never before imprinted by the foot of man" (7). Shelley's narrator seeks a terrain, in other words, outside the limits of both self and nation. While icebound short of this objective and on the brink of perishing along with his captain and crew, Walton spots Frankenstein in pursuit of the monster. It is thus to the leader of an imperiled community that Frankenstein recounts the story of the monster's making and the subsequent destruction of the extended Frankenstein family. Surely this intersection of an English vessel with a figure straight out of Faustian legend is ripe with allegorical possibilities. Against the harmonious community, Shelley pits a double protagonist who embodies superior rationality poisoned by an insatiable will to knowledge. To what does Frankenstein give life as he produces a human being, if not to an object that puts a dreadful face on what exceeds the limits of his own collective identity? The monster embodies that which comes from within a human being but is not human, because, as a composite of individual human beings, it exceeds the limit of individualism. Even if we detect signs of Shelley's traumatic attempts at sexual reproduction in her fable of reproduction gone awry, we cannot ignore other signs indicating the pervasive turn against the individual as bad subject by means of which a number of works were rethinking the contractual relationship between individual and aggregate.[21]

To explain how Shelley revised the terms of the social contract for the century of Malthus, Darwin, and Marx, I read her novel together with Immanuel Kant's 1795 essay "Perpetual Peace." There, Kant contends that a representative republic is the only state capable of rule by law rather than violence. Any other form of government is despotic. States under monarchy are ruled by an individual who is not himself subject to the law and therefore perfectly free to command his subjects "to sacrifice themselves for something that does not concern them."[22] Such is the fate that Walton's captain and crew nearly share with the Frankenstein family. The civilized world must earn that distinction by becoming one all-inclusive world republic that can guarantee what Kant calls "the conditions of universal hospitality" (439). The cosmopolitan character of the Frankenstein and De Lacey families suggests a Europe on its way to becoming an all-encompassing state under which foreigners would be granted, in Kant's words, "a right of visit, a right of demanding of others that they admit one to their society. This right all men have by virtue of their common possession of the surface of the earth, where, as on a spherical surface, they cannot infinitely disperse and hence must finally tolerate the presence of each other" (439). What did Mary Shelley do to the possibility of such a transnational community when she introduced a monster to a community on its way to enjoying universal hospitality? There are two basic ways of answering this question.

The first has to do with the fact that the monster's education places him outside the law of hospitality. In what Scott regarded as one of the only two improbabilities in an otherwise probable tale, the monster's education begins with his vicarious participation in the lives of the De Laceys, where he hears their personal histories and listens as they read Volney's *The Ruin of Empires* to one another.[23] The monster characterizes this phase of his education in rather novelistic terms: "Such was the history of my beloved cottagers. It impressed me deeply. I learned, from the views of social life which it developed, to admire their virtues, and to deprecate the vices of mankind" (85). But his quite promising start on the road to humanity abruptly changes direction when he comes across a portmanteau containing three books. "I now continually studied and exercised my mind upon these histories," he explains to Frankenstein, "whilst my friends were employed in their ordinary occupations" (86). His solitary reading expands the monster's emotions to embrace extremes well outside the range of the literacy shared by the De Lacey household. From Plutarch, he acquires admiration for the high purpose of peaceable lawgivers as well as abhorrence for war, while Goethe's Werther and Milton's Satan give extravagant expression to the sense of bereavement that accompanies the recognition that he can never overcome his difference from human beings. "All, save I, were at rest or in enjoyment," he tells Frankenstein, "I, like the arch fiend, bore a hell within me; and, finding myself unsympathised with, wished to tear up the trees, spread havoc and destruction around me, and then to have sat down and enjoyed the ruin" (92). The monster wants to belong to a community that lives by the law of hospitality with an intensity that prompts him to destroy what he cannot join. Yet there is something about his very nature that eliminates all possibility of belonging, forcing him to stay outside the community of self-governing subjects and thus remain incompletely human.[24]

The second reason that Shelley introduced this figure into an otherwise idyllic community has everything to do with the monster's nature. To understand precisely how his monstrousness sets a limit on the inclusiveness of the novel's cosmopolitan community, let us recall the moment when Frankenstein first set eyes on the creature who perfectly objectifies his antisocial ambitions: "His limbs were in proportion, and I had selected his features as beautiful. Beautiful!—Great God! His yellow skin scarcely covered the work of muscles and arteries beneath; his hair was of a lustrous black, and flowing; his teeth of a pearly whiteness; but these luxuriances only formed a more horrid contrast with his watery eyes, that seemed almost of the same colour as the dun white sockets in which they were set, his shrivelled complexion, and straight black lips" (39). The monster gives objective visual form to those aspects of his creator's individualism that exceed limits set, it would seem, by nature itself. His physical appearance announces the monster's abject status by displaying on its skin and face signs of its own interior (i.e., "the work of muscles and arteries beneath," eyes that "seemed almost of the same colour as the dun white sockets in which they were set"). Add to this the mixed signs of life and death (pearly teeth and flowing hair with a shriveled complexion and straight black lips), and you have an amalgamation of disparate, anonymous, unnaturally revitalized parts whose appearance offers a disgusting parody of the natural body that encloses the individual subject. He is at once too much and not enough of an individual to belong to a community that considers the individual its basic unit.

When he cautiously approaches the blind father, De Lacey, and appeals for sanctuary in his house, the monster's speech strikes the stranger as that of a countryman: "'By your language, stranger, I suppose you are my countryman;—are you French?'" (90). When the monster explains how much he longs for human company, the old man reassures him, "Do not despair. To be friendless is indeed to be unfortunate; but the hearts of men, when unprejudiced by any obvious self-interest, are full of brotherly love and charity" (90). Engaging only the monster's voice, the old man is inclined to sympathize with the stranger: "I am blind, and cannot judge of your countenance, but there is something in your words which persuades me that you are sincere. I am poor, and an exile; but it will afford me true pleasure to be in any way serviceable to a human creature" (91). But while the monster's voice is not only human but humane as well, his physical appearance offers a spectacle of violence done to the human form. Just as the monster is about to reveal the many kind acts of service he has already performed for the De Lacey family, the children return. Understandably at a loss to imagine how the sighted members of the De Lacey family feel on seeing him conversing with their father in their home, the monster asks, "Who can describe their horror and consternation on beholding me?" (91). Given the graphically rendered melodramatic moments where the extremely positive features of the monster give way to negative features that are just as extreme, one might be tempted to consider this story a movie waiting to happen. We have to modify that supposition, however, in light of the fact that cinematic versions of the story invariably strip Shelley's monster of the eloquence that invites sympathetic identification. By eliminating the enormous disjunction between his voice, on the one hand, and his physical appearance, or spectacle, on the other hand, cinematic versions of the story also eliminate the amalgamation of extremely sympathetic features with those that are fundamentally disgusting, transforming the monster from a figure of ambivalence to one of pure abjection.[25] On the basis of the figure that the monster cuts in the novel, by contrast, it is difficult to think of another literary figure that so emphatically says at one and the same time "I am just like you" and "I am the last thing on earth that you could be."

The sequence of scenes in which Frankenstein agrees and then goes back on his promise to make a female companion for the monster repeats the monster's exchange with De Lacey and carries the logic of ambivalence yet one step further. Under the sway of the monster's eloquence, Frankenstein is momentarily persuaded that a female companion would assuage and humanize his tormentor. He cannot pursue this line of thinking for long, however, without confronting the problem posed by the monster's appearance. The monster may acquire the cultural attributes of the most educated human being, but his body will always look like a botched job. This recalcitrant fact gives his creator pause to consider the wisdom of making a female monster: "She . . . might turn with disgust from him to the superior beauty of man; she might quit him, and he be again alone, exasperated by the fresh provocation of being deserted by one of his own species" (114). If Frankenstein cannot imagine the monster joining humanity once he settles down with a mate, then neither can he quite grant that monster the status of another "species," the progenitor of beings capable of living with their own kind independently from man. In creating a female companion, Frankenstein concludes, he might well be creating not a species but a debased race of human beings with the power to destroy the normative prototype. In this case, the violence that might ensue from a troubled marriage between the monstrous pair would be nothing compared to the conflict within the human community that would certainly result from their happy union. "Even if they were to leave Europe, and inhabit the deserts of the new world," he reasons, "yet one of the first results of those sympathies for which the dæmon would thirst would be children, and *a race of devils* would be propagated upon the earth, who might make the very existence of the species of man a condition precarious and full of terror. Had I a right, for my own benefit, to inflict this curse upon everlasting generations?" (114, my emphasis). After considering only this side of the story, we might agree that Frankenstein was ethically compelled to destroy the monster's intended. How could the repetition of his initial excess undo the destruction to the human community produced by that excess? The category of the unhuman would only grow exponentially, these peculiar monsters being capable neither of successful incorporation nor of complete excorporation from the human.

Arriving at this conclusion on a wave of moral righteousness, Frankenstein proceeds to scatter the pieces of the female monster he has partially assembled, thereby dismantling a future household in a manner that not only repeats the monster's destruction of the De Lacey household but also recalls Scott's description of the English desecration of Tully-Veolan following the Battle of Preston. Guided by Kantian reasoning, we would have to read the intrusion of the monster in a way that is sharply critical of such violent behavior. Contending that even the most selfish and bellicose inclinations of a group call instead for rational forbearance, Kant advocates a plan "whereby the powers of each selfish inclination are so arranged in opposition that one moderates or destroys the ruinous effects of the other" (443). "The problem of so organizing a state," he continues, "however hard it may seem, can be solved even for *a race of devils*, if only they are intelligent" (443, my emphasis). Indeed, according to Kant, even such "a race" would eventually learn that warfare is a losing proposition, a conclusion the monster appears to have reached of his own accord. If given a mate, he promises to "go to the vast wilds of South America," as if in fulfillment of Locke's argument that one could make a home and ultimately a nation peaceably by appropriating for himself some of the resources that a seemingly inexhaustible America provides. Or so the monster reassures his maker: "My food is not that of man; I do not destroy the lamb and the kid, to glut my appetite; acorns and berries afford me sufficient nourishment. My companion will be of the same nature as myself, and will be content with the same fare. We shall make our bed of dried leaves; the sun will shine on us as on man, and will ripen our food. The picture I present to you is peaceful and human, and you must feel that you could deny it only in the wantonness of power and cruelty" (99). Frankenstein justifies his decision to destroy the monster's future companion on grounds that such creatures are aggressively selfish by nature, even though the novel pointedly demonstrates that the monster's propensity for violence stems from his familiarity with the literary models of Werther and Satan, as well as from the fact that no human who sees him can sufficiently tolerate his difference to perform the leap of sympathetic identification. Frankenstein's reading of the situation observes the principle of population put forth by Thomas Malthus (1798) to the effect that biological reproduction inevitably outstrips the food supply, setting groups of men against one another in a struggle for survival. His reading also looks ahead to Charles Darwin's principle of natural selection

(1859), which pits one species against another in a rivalry that ends only when one kills off the other: a perfect inversion, in other words, of the Kantian model based on toleration of difference. Still and all, as I have argued, although such natural rivalry would soon shape Victorian fiction, it was hardly the only game in town, or even the dominant one, when Shelley wrote her only famous novel.

Thus the novel supports two incompatible arguments, one claiming that Frankenstein is right to destroy the monster's mate and the other contending that he is wrong to do so. In the first case, the monster is responsible for the destruction of the Frankenstein family, and, in the second, Frankenstein himself is culpable. The narrative that bonds these arguments in a single story line produces a formal ambivalence that ultimately questions any modern definition of nationalism: Can a nation reach out to embrace universal humanity? Does one's claim to belong to such a community originate in culture—language, the observation of manners and morals, and literature—or are there forms of difference that cannot be assimilated without destroying the very basis of that community? Shelley's monster does not try to hang on to his difference, as Kant assumed that foreigners would. Through a literary education, he strives to overcome the limits of his origin and become European, only to discover that, much like the supplement, he cannot do so without radically transforming the very meaning of that term. The common ground established between man and monster through his conversation with the old man vanishes the moment other members of the De Lacey family behold his countenance. Indeed, his very presence in their midst transforms their cottage into unhallowed ground, as the De Lacey son explains to his landlord: "It is utterly useless . . . we can never again inhabit your cottage" (93). Responding in the manner of rebels and savages, the monster recalls "turn[ing] my fury towards inanimate objects. As night advanced, I placed a variety of combustibles around the cottage; and, after having destroyed every vestige of cultivation in the garden. . . . I lighted the dry branch of a tree, and danced with fury around the devoted cottage, . . . I waved my brand; [the sun] sunk, and, with a loud scream, I fired the straw, and heath, and bushes, which I had collected. The wind fanned the fire, and the cottage was quickly enveloped by the flames, which clung to it, and licked it with their forked and destroying tongues" (94). Thus either way, as that which cannot be tolerated or that which is itself intolerant, he exposes the limits of universal citizenship. In a nation composed of extended families, the truly one-of-a-kind individual must either make that community absolutely inclusive or else completely destroy it. At this moment in history, the novel will not pursue either option.

Shelley exposes the flaw in the logic of Kant's cosmopolitan community: it too depends on a foundational act of exclusion. To imagine a nation that rests on the toleration of difference, one must implicitly exclude those who lack a capacity for tolerance, the religiously committed, the racially prejudiced, anyone who defines him- or herself as pure in opposition to some pollutant. Kant uses the cannibal to represent the absolute intolerance for difference: "The chief difference between European and American savages lies in the fact that many tribes of the latter have been eaten up by their enemies, while the former know to make better use of their conquered enemies than to dine off them; they know better how to use them to increase the number of their subjects and thus the quality of instruments for even more extensive wars" (437). Ironically, the only difference between civilized and savage man in this comparison is the pragmatism of the European, which allows him to supersede his primitive counterpart in the efficiency with which self eradicates other, obliterating difference itself.[26] For Kant, individuality and community are two sides of the same conceptual coin, individual differences being the basis for a universality where each is himself precisely because of his difference from others, a universality that therefore depends on eliminating injustice and war. Where Kant invokes the cannibal, Shelley has her protagonist admit, "I considered the being whom I had cast among mankind, and endowed with the will and power to effect purposes of horror . . . nearly in the light of my own vampire, my own spirit let loose from the grave, and forced to destroy all that was dear to me" (49). In contrast with Kant, Shelley describes intolerance as vampirelike, something within the individual that compels him to see the community as that which prevents him from becoming fully himself. To become fully oneself is to become something in excess of the human in this novel: in effect, a monster. Thus Shelley creates a difference that works within the individual to expose the limit past which he cannot extend itself without canceling out his membership in the human community.

There are, we must conclude, different differences, one that separates individuals from one another, or difference within the order of same, and that difference which distinguishes humanity from all the rest of organic and inorganic life. The first preserves the fiction of consciousness, however highly developed, enclosed within the body to whose life and reproduction it is subsequently devoted. The second understands that human knowledge—in the form of language, especially print culture—comes from elsewhere and has little respect for the conventions that sustain and reproduce us. The modern state, as Kant describes it, translates all essential differences into cultural differences that cannot challenge the natural basis for universal humanness. But even in such a nation, Shelley responds, some difference would necessarily remain irreducible so as to mark the external limit of humanity. Thus the difference between cannibal and vampire describes the limits at which the community devours the individual, on the one hand, and where the individual destroys the community, on the other. The difference between cannibal and vampire describes the difference between mourning and melancholy as well. Mourning can incorporate the positive qualities of the lost object and let go of the rest, thereby revitalizing the mourner. Melancholy, in contrast, finds its resolution in the production of ambivalent objects, certain features of which refuse incorporation. In contrast with the mourner, the confirmed melancholic refuses to let go of the bad object and sustains himself by waging war against objectifications of that which the culture requires him to renounce.

Scott and Shelley may have had very different social groups in mind when they set their respective protagonists on the road to excess and potential exclusion. Scott extends Englishness into the lowlands of Scotland in order to formulate an imaginary Britishness that could include both nations—provided Highland culture were eliminated. Shelley, on the other hand, sets out to exceed the limits of the human itself and in that way imagine a transnational republic where virtually any individual could be represented. If in the resolution to *Waverley* we encounter a community that simultaneously expands and contracts as it embraces modern Britishness and excludes what were the prevailing kinship systems, then we can say that Shelley's novel transforms a pan-European community from an organically coherent whole to one made of many hostile parts that become coherent only through some monstrous act of violence. Both authors nevertheless set the unexpressed elements of their hero's individuality in opposition to the social roles those heroes must perform. Both pushed the individual beyond the limits of collective identity in order to expand that collective beyond the limits of the historical moment, in the one case, and the species, in the other, so as to include members of another group.

Waverley and *Frankenstein* open the floodgates of inclusion, how-ever, only to establish irreducible differences between cultural mate-rial that can be contained within the collective identity and material that cannot be so tolerated. To the degree that both authors use figures of romance and epic ontologically hostile to the novel for purposes of marking this limit, Scott's Highlanders perform the same function as Shelley's devilish race of monsters. Shelley shares Scott's ambivalence toward the very medium in which both authors happened to be work-ing. Although she represents the monstrous potential of unharnessed individuality in striking contrast to the overly domesticated interior where Scott locates the modern individual in *Waverley*, the two pro-vide equally eloquent testimony to an aesthetic loss. That is to say, both represent the loss of expressive individualism as a sacrifice of the heroic genres from an earlier literary tradition. In its place, both Shelley and Scott throw their moral weight behind such disappoint-ingly ordinary human beings as Walton and Waverley and the limited definition of community that ushers in the age of realism.

3

WHY A GOOD MAN IS HARD TO FIND IN VICTORIAN FICTION

The Victorian novel not only portrayed all women who expressed extreme forms of individualism as extremely unattractive but also punished them so harshly as to persuade a readership that the very excesses that once led to self-fulfillment and the illusion of a more flexible social order now yielded exactly the opposite results. Rather than acting out excesses that would qualify her to tell the story of how she became an individual, a woman was much better off internalizing those excesses, as Jane Eyre does. By having her heroine perform extravagant acts of self-abnegation, Brontë created what can only be described as an ontological gap between her most famous protagonist and Bertha Mason, a woman whose monstrous interiority disfigured her appearance and behavior to the point where they were no longer recognizably female, much less feminine. Elsewhere I have written extensively on the process by which Jane overcame the very qualities responsible for her survival and explain exactly how, in combination with her inheritance, such self-discipline empowered her to tell a story in which she alone set the standard for moral judgment and social behavior.[1] Where eighteenth-century heroines from Moll to Elizabeth Bennet stretched the limits of self-expression, I am suggesting, their Victorian counterparts contracted those limits so as to transform individualistic energy into forms of self-management and containment. The question is, why?

Contrary to what is still the prevailing critical attitude toward this moment in cultural history, I reject the assumption that the brutality this fiction often displays toward women reflects some deep and pervasive hostility toward women per se. Nor, on the other hand, do I think that the Victorian idea of femininity endangered women's physical and mental health any more than modern stereotypes do. I consider both assumptions products of our own moment in the history of the modern subject. Victorian women who embodied self-discipline—which required not only some extraordinary act of self-renunciation but also some extraordinary excess of self to renounce[2]—did so, I argue, in order to revise two important aspects of the individualism that had shaped the British novel from the start. What had been contrary behaviors now obviously posed a contradiction, and one character could no longer bridge the moral gulf separating Moll the adventuress from the Moll whom Defoe authorizes to tell her story. Better to finesse the contradiction by splitting the two. Thus we find Victorian fiction differentiating between what might be called femaleness (aggressive tendencies formerly celebrated as expressive of individualism) and femininity (the domestic virtues anchoring the new ruling-class home). Novelists used this dualism within the woman to avoid exposing the rather obvious contradiction within the ruling-class man between the qualities enabling socioeconomic success and those required for paternal authority.

Victorian heroines pale before the monstrous behaviors of Catherine Earnshaw, Bertha Mason, Edith Dombey, Lady Deadlock, Becky Sharp, Maggie Tulliver, Tess Durbeyfield, Lizzie Eustace, and the protagonists of sensation novels, and that is all to the good. The self-constrained, even tepid heroine survives to restore and perpetuate the domestic culture threatened by her unruly counterpart. By thus embodying the excesses of an earlier individualism in female form, the Victorian novel accomplishes a more important purpose than simply venting hostility toward actively aggressive women. These women served their primary purpose, I argue, by directing the reader's attention away from the contradiction that threatened to puncture the fantasy of the liberal individual as complete unto himself and capable of caring for others. By pathologizing and criminalizing these women, Victorian fiction justified beating, drowning, burning, hanging, or exiling them for possessing qualities that the same novels would persuade us to forgive in such male characters as Heathcliff, Mr. Dombey, Rawdon Crawley, Stephen Guest, Michael Henchard, or Frank Greystock.

Victorian fiction portrayed the despicable qualities of ruling-class masculinity as truly despicable *only* when those qualities appear to animate women. By providing such a cover, these women provide a means of simultaneously establishing and disavowing the competition, aggression, and domination that were well on their way to becoming necessary and natural properties of male individuals alone. In this way, the violence directed toward women in Victorian fiction actually protected the ideology of individualism: the claim that one could compete successfully with other men within the public sphere and serve as caretaker to his dependents in the factory and the remote outreaches of empire as well as in the home. This contradiction not only shaped the scientific and literary discourse of the period but also proved virtually impossible to resolve: Victorian culture was of one mind in maintaining both the continuity and incompatibility of the two aspects of British masculinity. To create continuity between savage and citizen, the human sciences adopted Scott's strategy of historical dislocation and figured the savage as the primitive forebear of modern man. To maintain the essential difference between our primitive forebears and modern man, fiction developed any number of formal means of transferring the most objectionable masculine features to women, where those features could be sensationally objectified and their potential for violence eliminated.

In concert with the human sciences, Victorian fiction produced a modern individual who incorporated within him all the qualities of the savage. What modern man had that savage man lacked was a distinctive capacity to keep his natural aggression in check and channel that energy toward socially acceptable goals: how one succeeded or failed to contain and redirect his desire—not the mere fact that he possessed and dared to act on it—determined that individual's identity. Such a scenario obviously upset the perfect equipoise achieved by Scott and Shelley and reversed the relation between the supplementary subjectivity and social subjection that shaped British fiction up through Austen. Something entirely new, a cultural ideal that existed outside the individual until that individual could incorporate and dwell within its parameters, assumed the position of self and soul maker formerly occupied by the bad subject.

Rethinking the Bad Subject for
the Culture of Capitalism

I draw on the concept of displacement to explain the use of spectacle to distract us from some problem that is too disturbing to express and thus too basic for fiction to resolve by means of incorporation and synthesis. In his early studies on hysteria, Freud uses this term to describe a psychic mechanism that manifests itself in the rhetorical structure of both symptom formation and dreams. I find it more than a little suggestive that this term also characterizes the rhetoric of fiction written during the period between the 1832 and 1867 Reform Bills, the very time when Charles Darwin was trying, as Freud would later do, to establish a connection between language—indeed, all cultural production—and biology.[3] Coming at the end of the period in cultural history that positioned humans, especially the male of the species, within a developmental narrative, it also seems fitting that Freud should adopt the figure that gave Victorian fiction its distinctive form as his way of explaining how the adult dealt with the residue of desires and fears that had once ensured the survival of the species. According to Freud's early model for managing the emotional energy generated by this archaic psychic equipment, the individual displaces this energy along neurological pathways that seek to disperse it and establish temporary stasis or inertia. Displacement allows the individual to transfer the cathexis attached to an idea that individual cannot express without endangering his or her social identity from the domain of ideas to the domain of the body, where it expresses itself as a physical symptom.[4]

Freud did his most interesting work on displacement in conjunction with dream work, where the focus of the dream tends to differ significantly from that of the manifest content. "Displacement" takes on new precision in *The Interpretation of Dreams*, when Freud develops the notion of transference to describe general shifts in emotional energy from one idea to another. He reserves "displacement," in the words of J. LaPlanche and J.-B. Pontalis, "to refer to a descriptively striking phenomenon, more noticeable in dreams than in others, whose upshot is the shift in focus of the whole emphasis of the dream." "Such a transformation occurs along a chain or chains of associations," they continue, which links "an abstract idea and an equivalent lending itself to visualization."[5] In the process, importantly, the emotional energy invested in some pervasively threatening idea is not dispersed but acquires sensory sharpness and intensity that serve to objectify, localize, and thereby manage it. For Freud, such behavior in dreams testifies to a more primary process of human thought, a relic of those desires he considered essential to the organism's survival in a state of nature.

Victorian fiction uses displacement to accomplish a very different purpose. While dreams provide a means for speaking what is unspeakable in a code that protects the individual from self-knowledge, Victorian fiction provides a purely symbolic means of resolving a conflict among cultural categories that might render their social experience incoherent were a mass readership to confront those conflicts head on. In using displacement to explain how Victorian fiction shifts its initial emotional investment from one object to another, I attribute this mechanism neither to the individuated unconscious nor to some mass anxiety. I prefer to look at the novel as a way of thinking in its own right, the culture's way of maintaining, upgrading, and perpetuating its most basic categories in the face of pressures that changing social conditions bring to bear on them.

After demonstrating the rhetorical ingenuity by means of which Victorian fiction defended masculinity against its own violence, I use Darwin's *The Descent of Man, And Selection in Relation to Sex* to suggest that nothing less than the survival of humanity as an autonomous and enduring category was at stake in transferring the competitive energy of the ruling-class male onto a female who could then be purged from the newly domesticated world of the text. Through forms of displacement, the novel worked hand in glove with the emerging human sciences to sustain the ideal of modern Britain as an inclusive community during the period between the Reform Bills of 1832 and 1867, when pressure from disenfranchised groups within Great Britain combined with the expansion of empire to stretch that fantasy to the breaking point. So pervasive was the strain on the fantasy of humanity as a single, cohesive body that it would not be too much of a stretch, I believe, to chalk up what Georg Lukács considers the premature disappearance of the historical novel to the fact that it had become all but impossible to think of savage man as one's progenitor.[6] How could a novelist relegate his ancestors to the past, to memory, and to art, as Scott had, when that ancestor continued to carry on his violent and obscene practices at the periphery of the modern state?

For an example of the textual behavior I have in mind, one need look no further than Emily Brontë's *Wuthering Heights*. This novel is all the more remarkable for its persistent attempts and spectacular failures at shaping the available examples of masculinity into a ruling-class male who can compete with other men and still be good to women. The question of how these two cultural criteria produced irreconcilable differences between Heathcliff and Edgar Linton, both of whom were ultimately terrible husbands, has received more than its share of critical attention. I want to stress two moves by which the novel encourages us to regard its male characters as somewhat appealing and worthy of pity.

First is the conspicuous presence of precocious women, who include not only the two indomitable Catherines but the willful Isabel Linton and the loquacious Nelly Dean as well. That women shall disrupt rather than stabilize domestic relations and ensure their perpetuity is overdetermined in *Wuthering Heights*. Consider, for example, a scene that allows a visitor in Yorkshire to attribute his own viciousness to a local woman from an earlier period in cultural history whom he accuses of entering his bedchamber. As Lockwood recounts the episode, he was roused from his sleep by a branch tapping on his window and reached out to stop it,

> instead of which, my fingers closed on the fingers of a little ice-cold hand! . . .
> "Catherine Linton," it replied, shiveringly . . . "—I'm come home, I'd lost my way on the moor!"
> As it spoke, I discerned, obscurely, a child's face looking through the window—Terror made me cruel; and, finding it useless to attempt shaking the creature off, I pulled its wrist onto the broken pane, and rubbed it to and fro till the blood ran down and soaked the bed-clothes: still it wailed, "Let me in!" and maintained its tenacious gripe [sic], almost maddening me with fear.[7]

Never mind that Lockwood has made himself at home in Catherine's bedroom and begun to thumb through her diary. Never mind that she may have returned as a spectral child to reclaim the private life that he seems intent on consuming throughout the novel. The reader is conducted along a metonymic chain from the auditory stimulation of the branch outside the window, to the child's hand that he evidently grabs by thrusting his own through the pane of glass, and from there to Lockwood himself. The surge of energy reverses course as he locks hands with the child and rubs her wrist against the broken pane until "the blood ran down and soaked the bed-clothes." The metonymic chain accomplishes its purpose as it relocates Lockwood's aggression in an image that transforms his violence into an act of self-defense. As he explains it, "I discerned, obscurely, a child's face looking in through the window—Terror made me cruel." After rubbing the child's wrist against the broken pane, his fear only intensifies, as the phantom "maintained its tenacious gripe, almost maddening me with fear." Indeed so persuasive is the rhetorical sleight of hand—by which I mean the image that relocates the source of violence from the one hand to the other—that most readers excuse Lockwood's aggression by translating the image of a child into the presence of the ghost of Catherine Earnshaw, a woman notably lacking in feminine self-restraint.[8]

A second set of events dispersed over several pages and not nearly so memorable as the first repeats the encounter of a passive male with a supposedly aggressive female in a manner that switches the positions that eighteenth-century fiction had assigned to their respective sexes. Trapped in a room with Linton Heathcliff, Catherine the younger attempts to bribe her frail tormentor into allowing her to leave through the window and go to her father's deathbed. This sets off a chain reaction whereby Linton alerts Heathcliff to her intention. Heathcliff promptly seizes Catherine's most personal possessions, some treasured books and miniature portraits of her mother and father, and then strikes her across the face. "And were you pleased to see her struck?" asks Nelly Dean. Linton's answer merits our attention: "I was glad at first—she deserved punishing for pushing me: but when papa was gone, she made me come to the window and showed me her cheek cut on the inside, against the teeth, and her mouth filling with blood; and then she gathered up the bits of the picture ... and she has never spoken to me since, and I sometimes think she can't speak for pain. I don't like to think so! but she's a naughty thing for crying continually; and she looks so pale and wild, I'm afraid of her!" (214–15). This scene contains the same elements as the previous one: the window, the cut, the blood, the child crying, the mutation of violence into fear. All are facets of a curious interaction between the sexes that repeats itself at these two crucial junctures in the story: a female appears to draw agency away from a male, who in the first instance literally cuts her off at a window to keep her from entering and in the second instance cuts off her attempt to escape through that same window until she promises to return and share his cramped apartment. Men in both cases occupy the woman's position within claustrophobic domestic interiors. In defending themselves, these men are gratuitously cruel, and Victorian readers would have surely hated them were they not in some sense victims.[9] By switching the positions usually occupied by male and female, Brontë goes a long way toward excusing both men for the violence it takes to keep the first Catherine out of the house and the second Catherine in. But this is by no means the whole story.

Another metonymic chain links Catherine Earnshaw's ghost to her daughter, Catherine Linton, where the mother's aggression again reverses its course and heads back toward the male, as the daughter sets the stage to assume the place of the mother and become Catherine Earnshaw through marriage to Hareton, heir to the Earnshaw bloodline and property. Having displaced Earnshaw violence onto a second generation, however, the novel transforms that aggression into the means of redirecting the sexual energy of the male to a culturally acceptable substitute: "He was a young man, respectably dressed, and seated at a table, having a book before him. His handsome features glowed with pleasure, and his eyes kept impatiently wandering from the page to a small white hand over his shoulder, which recalled him by a smart slap on the cheek, whenever its owner detected such signs of inattention" (234). The "little ice-cold hand" toward which the novel first directed Lockwood's cruelty reappears in this final scene as "a small white hand" that serves as an erotically invested instrument of discipline.

But rather than follow the novel's chain of associations through a second generation to this final scene that transforms punishment into discipline, the tradition of reading extends that chain from Catherine Earnshaw beyond the novel to the author, Emily Brontë herself. It is fair to say that sister Charlotte encouraged this way of reading in her preface to the 1850 edition of *Wuthering Heights*, when she painted Emily as a "nursling of the moors" (314), a cultural primitive who embodied the same masculine energy that bound Catherine to Heathcliff in a relationship of like to like that ultimately destroyed them both. Ignoring the fact that the displacement of masculine aggression from mother to daughter transforms that aggression into a distinctively modern form, those who track the first Catherine's open defiance back to the author tend to regard Brontë's negative depiction of the new men who were moving into the country as her personal rejection of modernity itself. Such readers deny Emily her rightful place at the beginning of a tradition that had difficulty representing modern masculinity in positive terms. We are all too familiar with the claim that Brontë curiously identified herself with the figure of Heathcliff.[10] Even after we have come to see that claim as a rather silly way to think about female authorship, something about the prefeminist biographical tradition surrounding this author has kept us from noticing a similarity between the unsavory men who mark her fiction and those whose violence punctuates novels by Charles Dickens. Because he is willing to include the occasional philanthropist, noble artisan, long-suffering worker, and well-meaning but incompetent father, Dickens appears to be more even-handed than Brontë in creating masculine characters. In fact, he is not.

In both cases, violence erupts when the individual achieves individuality, hence masculine identity, by subordinating and controlling femininity. Femininity in turn produces the illusion of masculinity's social independence and economic autonomy. That fantasy necessarily collapses if we understand the relation between masculinity and femininity in terms of rivalry. Were competition between the two genders to pursue a dialectical path, it would eventually transform male-male rivalry into stable male-female relations within a household dominated by women. According to what cultural logic would masculine identity be thus reduced to a state of dependency? The male would have to go after any traces of individuality in the feminine as a threat to the domestic order, but in true dialectical fashion the masculine compulsion for social recognition would turn out to be self-defeating, because that recognition depends on its dependents. Thus the violence that seeks to maintain masculine identity by subordinating femininity inevitably travels back along a chain of displacements to shake the foundations of masculinity and make it vulnerable to new forms of social rivalry.

That such violence permeates the household in which the novel sought to produce a new ruling-class masculinity, one that could both compete successfully with men and take good care of women, is nowhere so clear as in Dickens's *Dombey and Son*. Dickens introduces Dombey to us as a man who regards his family members as extensions of his business and, in this respect, extensions of himself. To indicate the source of Dombey's anger at the first Mrs. Dombey for giving up the ghost before she had ensured the future of that business, Dickens writes: "Mr. Dombey had remained in his own apartment since the death of his wife, absorbed in visions of the growth, education, and destination of his baby son. Something lay at the bottom of his cool heart, colder and heavier than its ordinary load. . . . That Dombey and Son should be tottering for [want of] a nurse, was a sore humiliation."[11] Dombey regards his wife's physical weakness as an assault on his own economic strength. Until the last fifty pages or so of this three-decker novel, Dickens takes enormous pleasure in exposing this peculiar form of misogyny as a cover for Dombey's rivalry with women.[12]

As he questions Dombey's reaction to his daughter's grief upon her little brother's death, Dickens implies that such rivalry indeed defines Dombey's relationship to Florence. The novel asks if in seeing her, "Did [Dombey] see before him the successful rival of his son, in health and life? Did he look upon his own successful rival in that son's affection? Did a mad jealousy and withered pride, poison sweet remembrances that should have endeared and made her precious to him?" (272). By means of these outrageous questions, Dickens indicates that the drive compelling Dombey to compete with other men for success in the world of business has spilled over into the household, where it compels him to compete with his daughter for affection. As if to hammer home the point that, yes, competition does indeed infiltrate the domestic sanctuary, Dickens has Dombey remarry. After the disintegration of his second marriage, the novel returns to the interrogative voice with a vengeance.

The second time around, the mock incredulity characterizing the first set of questions hardens into the conviction that Dombey actually considers his daughter, Florence, a competitor. But where the previous questions came from the narrator and were aimed at Dombey, this second battery of questions is couched so as to put words to thoughts that come from within Dombey himself in the form of accusations aimed squarely at his prepubescent rival: "Who was it who could win his wife as she had won his boy! Who was it who had shown him that new victory, as he sat in a dark corner! Who was it whose least word did what his utmost means could not! Who was it who, unaided by his love, regard, or notice, thrived and grew beautiful when those so aided died!" (593–94). From narrator to Dombey, then from Dombey to Florence, the acquisitive drive travels along a chain of displacements that repeatedly puts the object of that drive into question. The resulting sequence of questions relocates competitive aggression in what the Victorians would consider the most inappropriate object of all, Dombey's devoted daughter. By displacing onto her his own acquisitive desire, Dombey transforms Florence into an object of fear, according to the same pattern we observed in *Wuthering Heights*: "Who could it be, but the same child at whom he [Dombey] had often glanced uneasily in her motherless infancy, *with a kind of dread*" (594, my emphasis). So determined is Dickens to expose the murderous discrepancy between moneymaking and caretaking that he tops off his attack on ruling-class masculinity by having Dombey turn from emotional to physical violence in order to defend himself against the only character in the novel capable of loving him.

Like his first wife and son, Dombey's daughter appears to lack the competitive drive that turns love into the kind of fear that justifies violence. The short, unhappy lives of Florence's mother and brother indicate that individuals who lack this drive will be turned into objects by those who have it. In contrast with her mother and brother, however, Florence not only proves uniquely capable of loving without return, she also proves uniquely capable of resisting objectification. Apparently threatened by the resilient selfhood he has thus far failed to crush, Dombey "lifted up his cruel arm and struck her, crosswise, with that heaviness, that she tottered on the marble floor" (704). With this blow, Dombey hastens the downfall of a household already "tottering" for want of maternal affection. In doing so, he reproduces the crime by which Bill Sikes inspired the public outrage that led to this villain's death in *Oliver Twist*. Here, too, in *Dombey and Son* a blow struck by a man reverses its direction when received by a woman and flows back the other way. The blow aimed at Florence does not harm her physically but rather destroys what might be called her paternal ideal and with it the basis for the authority Dombey exercises over his household. Dickens could not have rerouted violence through the female to the male more economically than this: Florence "saw him murdering that fond idea to which she had held in spite of him. She saw his cruelty, neglect, and hatred, dominant above it, and stamping it down" (704). Here, more overtly than in *Wuthering Heights*, the transfer of the source of violence from male to female causes it to travel back along another chain of associations to its source in the male, exposing such savagery as his alone. Under what conditions can Dombey eventually be reincorporated in the household? To rescue modern masculinity, Dickens abruptly shifts the reader's attention to the spectacularly scandalous behavior of Dombey's second wife.

I stress the term "spectacular," because Edith has plotted to avenge herself on Dombey by casting him as the betrayed husband of a sensation novel. She locates the melodrama appropriately in France and chooses as her partner in adultery the unscrupulous go-between whom Dombey has used to convey his wishes rather than have to deal with her himself. In so doing, she reveals Dombey's extension and surrogate as his rival, in that Carker is motivated by the same need for recognition. His obsequiousness aims exclusively at acquiring domination over those things that constitute his master's mastery: Dombey's business and wife. Andrew Elfenbein puts it succinctly when he says that "in Carker, Dickens invents a Victorian nightmare, the subversive manager as the second-in-command who is more in charge than the boss."[13] In a remarkable reversal of melodramatic convention, Edith informs her husband's rival that their romance is mere spectacle; he will only play the part of the rival and never succeed in possessing what Dombey too was unable to enjoy. Laying bare the cultural logic of the plot in which she has ensnared her husband's competitor, Edith takes full advantage of the fact the Dombey has placed her at the intersection of two metonymic chains. In one, she is the object for whose affection Dombey competed against Florence, and, in the second, she is the object for which Carker competed with Dombey, the object to which Dombey himself, by inserting Carker in his domestic relations, gave his rival access. Fully aware of her position the terminus of two chains, Edith receives the competitive energy traveling along both and redirects that energy so as to make each man the victim of the other's need for recognition: " 'In every vaunt you make,' she said, 'I have my triumph. I single out in you the meanest man I know, the parasite and tool of the proud tyrant, that his wound may go the deeper, and may rankle more. Boast, and revenge me on him! You know how you stand cowering there; you see yourself in colours quite as despicable, if not as odious, as those in which I see you. Boast then, and revenge me on yourself' " (806–7). Here again we encounter the wonderful economy of spectacle. Not only does this scene shift the locus of aggression from male to female, exposing femininity as the true rival to masculinity. It also drains the competitive energy out of homo economicus in the figure of the go-between, who substitutes for Dombey as the object of Edith's wrath and then wanders, terrified, into the path of a locomotive.

During the period of decline that brings Dombey to the brink of physical death, Dickens never says what causes his near-fatal malady, whether it is the humiliation Dombey suffers from this public scandal, the conditions under which bankruptcy forces him to live, or the fact that he has cut himself off from the only source of genuine love in the novel. The point is that it takes a great deal to knock the aggression out of Victorian masculinity before it can be incorporated in the household on which Dombey now openly depends for his existence, master and dependent having changed places. After more than seven hundred pages in which he gives us absolutely no reason to admire Dombey, Dickens asks us to pity the man precisely because he has lost his power to compete with other men and so dominate women. Dickens asks us, in other words, to see Dombey as the victim of his own masculinity. Once reduced to a child, he can be treated as one and subjected to the maternal ministrations of his daughter, becoming one of those benignly incompetent old men who can populate ideal households in Dickens precisely because they are no longer qualified breadwinners.[14]

The Impersonal Subject

The conversion of male into female aggression was not strictly an early Victorian phenomenon. As it was transferred to and transformed by female embodiment, this essential feature of masculinity changed character and began to serve as the means of individual discipline. In her 1860 novel *The Mill on the Floss*, George Eliot offers a significant variation on this displacement and transformation of antifamilial aggression. Eliot endows her heroine with the rationality and will to move out of a provincial town and into the mainstream of modern life. But Eliot puts that rationality and will in a sexually attractive body that compels men to compete for it. Try as she might to be loyal to her father and brother, Maggie Tulliver is inexorably drawn into a sexual relationship with their competitors, historically later versions of ruling-class man. She succumbs first to the intellectual companionship of Philip Wakem, whose father destroyed hers in protracted litigation, then to the blandishments of Stephen Guest, son of the firm that oversaw the economic ruin of the Tulliver mill, a firm that clearly comes to represent the emergence of a professional class and the ascendancy of intellectual capital over the kind of local management represented by the old mill. Maggie is just as devoted a daughter as Florence Dombey and sacrifices every emotional need of her own to her father's competitive rage. Paradoxically, however, this novel refuses to let its heroine renounce desires hostile to the fabric of provincial society. Nor, on the other hand, will it let her carry out some scandalous display of self-expression that would defy the archaic kinship rules by which such communities regulated marriage. Both too bad to be Florence and too good to be Edith, Maggie incorporates a contradiction that other novels finessed by doubling the heroine.

Like her predecessors, Eliot sets in motion two metonymic chains, one objectifying and localizing bad desire in the woman who is its object, the other redirecting that desire back toward its masculine source in a form that maintains rather than destroys the modern family. Where Brontë and Dickens relied on double heroines to accomplish this displacement, Eliot has both chains converge in Maggie. Eliot does invoke the convention with the appearance, near the end of the novel, of little cousin Lucy as Maggie Tulliver's foil. Rather than a full-fledged double, however, Lucy is a placeholder, a Victorian stereotype that indicates what Maggie would be like if she were either less susceptible to the impersonal desire that grabs hold of her or less capable of the renunciation that battles such desire for control of her body. Lucy is not a solution to the contradiction embodied in Maggie but an indication that such a contradiction, even when contained within a single body, cannot be resolved except in patently conventional terms.

F. R. Leavis considers Eliot's fiction a milestone in "the great tradition" of British fiction that culminated in the internally conflicted subjects of Henry James and Joseph Conrad.[15] Although *The Mill on the Floss* is not a novel he uses to make this case, it certainly does the work of translating the conflict played out by means of double heroines into an internal struggle between self-expression and self-discipline within a consequently complex and layered individual. In assuming that this struggle is internal, however, the reader is likely to miss the point that very little about Maggie Tulliver comes from and belongs to Maggie Tulliver. Victorian readers would have known that her forms of self-renunciation come straight from that culture's most limited notion of femininity, a limitation Eliot herself conspicuously refused to observe. But what of the desire to which she strives in vain to apply these conventions? Given its tendency to exceed the limits set by provincial English society, surely such desire must come from within Maggie herself, chafe at those limits, and compel her to violate them. Not necessarily.[16] If we read *The Mill on the Floss* as a rethinking of the displacement that relocates masculine aggression in a female body where the threat it poses can be localized and contained, then it is masculine energy that works its way along a chain of associations from Philip Waken and Stephen Guest to Maggie's body, where it finds a local habitation and a name. Inherently masculine but belonging to no individual, this form of desire gathers momentum during the course of the novel as it accumulates participants and intensifies with every effort at renunciation.

Where other Victorian novelists relied on melodramatic words and ultimately violent actions, Eliot offers a sequence of hydraulic metaphors to create the metonymic chain that transfers such desire from men to the body of her heroine. Well before this desire materializes as a turbulent pair of boat rides down the river Floss, the novel starts thinking about masculine desire as a substance capable of flowing from one individual to another. In doing so, it has already realigned the traditional relationships between genders and generations that ensures the community's internal coherence and continuity over time. Caught in the hydraulic model that not only directs sexual energy in the novel but determines the flow of money, information, and modernization as well, Maggie and her brother, Tom, find themselves finally powerless to resist that flow. Indeed, each refusal of desire—Tom's rejection of Maggie's feelings for Philip Wakem, Maggie's rejection of Stephen's feelings for her—constitutes a chain of associations that eventually opens the floodgates of larger-than-individual emotions, destroying the possibility of self-containment so essential to individualism. Once Maggie persuades Stephen to honor his engagement to Lucy Dean, their passion grows: "She refused it less and less, till at last the evening for them both was sometimes made of a moment's mutual gaze: they thought of it till it came and when it had come they thought of nothing else."[17] Here the novel brings into direct conflict two quite different metonymic chains. One proceeds in terms of the individualism of old, which manifests itself in personal choices in turn predicated on the power to say no, while the other set of connections is forged by a transindividual force that reverses all choices that dare run counter to its flow. The confrontation of the two not only wipes out an earlier generation along with its basis for interpersonal relations but also dissolves the link between sexual precocity and individuality, locating desire outside the individual in a nature heedless of both personal wishes and social conventions.

Driven into silence by this force, Stephen becomes the instrument of a curiously impersonal lyric voice: "One other thing Stephen seemed now and then to care for, and that was, to sing; it was a way of speaking to Maggie. Perhaps he was not distinctly conscious that he was impelled by a secret longing—running counter to all his self-confessed resolves" (372). This "secret longing" radiates outward to transform one individual plot after another into components of an unwitting conspiracy to possess the single object that can put an end to such longing. The exchange of glances between Maggie and Stephen makes Philip—a former suitor renounced out of loyalty to brother Tom—so ill that he can't bring himself to show up as planned and join the group for a boat ride. Sensing in part correctly that her rift with Philip is responsible for Maggie's low spirits, Lucy decides to bow out of the excursion and give Philip and Maggie an opportunity for reconciliation. These small derailments of a plot designed to sublimate the lovers' passion actually conspire to bring Maggie and Stephen together alone and set them adrift on a current of emotion that seems all the stronger for their attempts to block it. The novel makes it clear that neither Maggie nor Stephen choreographs the boat ride that expresses the emotional truth of their relationship: "Maggie felt that she was being led down the garden ... all by this stronger presence that seemed to bear her along without any act of her own will, like the added self which comes with the sudden exalting influence of a strong tonic.... They glided rapidly along" (376). Yes, Stephen is leading her into a scandalous situation from which she and not he will emerge as the one to objectify this disruptive flow of energy and make it legible in the form of gossip.

But the kind of desire I have in mind is not one that can originate in Stephen, Philip, Tom, his father, or any other individual. The kind of desire I have in mind drives a plot in which all are merely characters. In this respect, we might compare Maggie's place in the shifting constellation of characters in *The Mill on the Floss* to the purloined letter in Lacan's reading of Poe's story.[18] Like the errant letter, she is out of place. Beginning with her father and ending with her brother, a number of men compulsively try to master her. But rather than fix her in a subordinate relation, each is in turn mastered—rendered quite passive—by whatever it is about her that compels them to seek such mastery. Maggie's presence within their respective domains automatically redefines all other subjects—or what we might consider the collective subject of the novel—as a differential system that shifts as she travels from one man to another. By this process, members of the group trade in one kind of individuality, based on desires shaped by rivalry, for another, in which each performs in a minor key the act of renunciation enacted on a spectacular scale by Maggie and her brother Tom. Their inability to submit to a less than gratifying position in a world that would no longer accommodate earlier forms of gratification leaves them both without any position in the modernized social order that emerges from their destruction.

At the same time, Maggie is the only one of the lot to experience "the added self which comes with the sudden exalting influence of a strong tonic" (376). In that this libidinal supplement violates the limits that Victorian culture placed on expressive individualism in a woman, it seems to recall the bad subject that propelled eighteenth-century heroines into positions of imagined fulfillment within the social order. Maggie believes herself to be inhabited by just this form of selfishness when she renounces her desire for Stephen out of a counterdesire to avoid causing pain to family and community, but in fact the desire to which she finally succumbs absorbs her last drop of individual agency, including the will to say no: "this stronger presence... seemed to bear her along without any act of her own will" (376). In relinquishing all claims to a position within the social order represented by the novel, Maggie becomes not only less of an individual but also more of a human being than Lucy, who lacks the capacity to be caught up in something larger than herself and be carried away on the a current of an impersonal desire that appears to have something more like the interests of the species in mind. The libidinal supplement is, in this case, not one that can adjust society to serve individual needs. On the contrary, it sets the individual whom it possesses forever outside society, as society's symptom, embodying those elements of humanity that must be excluded in order for the social body to maintain internal coherence and durability over time.

No major Victorian novel could allow Maggie and Stephen to elope together, as to do so would be to reward those who capitulate to the reproductive drive, which must, above all else, be regulated if it is to serve the community. But does this mean that Eliot is capitulating to the most puritanical convention of her day when she is so hard on Maggie? What else can be made of the fact that this heroine is scorned, sent from the Tulliver house, rejected by the people of St. Ogg's, and even forbidden counsel with her clergyman, before being swept away in the flood, mowed down by a flotilla of machinery, and finally drowned together with Tom? What is Eliot saying if not that such a woman is better off dead, leaving her former lovers to linger mournfully over her grave?—"There was a tomb erected, very soon after the flood, for two bodies that were found in close embrace; and it was visited at different moments by two men who both felt that their keenest joy and keenest sorrow were for ever buried there" (422). Such overkill is not about punishing Maggie, I must insist, so much as defending the liberal individual against a most devastating attack.

Let us assume that the metonymic chain taking Eliot's protagonist from St. Ogg's down the river Floss a second time finds its terminal point in this graveside scene. Propelled by desire that transcends the individual, the first chain of associations locates masculine sexual energy in the female body. The novel defines this body as a bad object, one that simultaneously threatens the perpetuation of the community and guarantees its autonomy by identifying what must by definition be kept outside. Motivated by an equally compelling urge that arises out of sympathy, or her ability to understand the pain of others, Maggie's second boat ride also produces a memorable female body that clasps her brother in mortal embrace. Where the first body objectified a transindividual desire and contained it within a woman, the second body is composed of brother and sister, void of sexual energy, and therefore lacking any gender. This curious form was what it took to reintegrate that first body, which we might quite accurately call the bad object, into the community. It is as a lost object, the missing piece of every Victorian subject, that Maggie's body contains the sexual energy that seemed so threatening to the community and redirects that energy back toward the men of the new ruling class in a radically altered form.

The previous chapter explained how the mourning process might end abortively were the mourner to refuse to forgive the beloved, preferring to blame her for abandoning him and taking with her a piece of himself. This leaves him with a keen sense of a lack within himself and compulsion to objectify it in a form he can possess. This is very much like the condition of melancholy. Something like this same refusal to produce the kind of synthesis of self and lost other shaped fiction that resisted the turn against individualism. According to most authoritative accounts, the mourning process arrives at a successful conclusion when the melancholic abandons the search for the lost object, accepts the fact of permanent separation, and incorporates within himself certain idealized features of the beloved. With this act of partial incorporation, the bad object loses its hold on the individual. Mourning concludes as he reclassifies what remains of that object as ordinary humanness. If by virtue of its repeated phantasmatic construction of the Scottish past, Scott's fiction remains resolutely melancholic, then surely Eliot's can be characterized as the conclusion of a long process of mourning. The process I have in mind in fact kills off the robust individualism of an earlier epoch in favor of homogeneous normativity and realism.

This, I am suggesting, is what the lyrical conclusion of *The Mill on the Floss* finally yields: two men, once rivals and polar opposites, now more alike than different. By means of Maggie's death, each man loses the object that set him in rivalry against the other, and each consequently acquires something of a woman's capacity for self-renunciation. In so doing, these examples of ruling-class man could be said to have arrived at the point, in Freud's theory of narcissism, where the child gives up the satisfactions of childhood and aspires to be something else, something more—in this instance, a member of the professional class. Growing up in these terms requires them to incorporate certain elements of an earlier masculinity (as culture) and abject others (as nature), all of which elements originated in them but circulated through Maggie. Masculinity not only seems to gain independence as it incorporates features of the loved one but also acquires individuality by means of the aggressive tendencies the novel has routed through a woman designed by nature for this purpose and returned to their sources transformed.[19] Thus each also seems somehow domesticated, as if he had incorporated something of the domesticity that his culture assigned strictly to women but that consistently eluded Maggie's grasp.

The conclusion of the novel offers an especially striking example of how Victorian fiction revised the bad subject of earlier fiction so as to redirect the energy created when individual excess produces a corresponding lack in the forms of fulfillment made available to nonelite but literate people by the early modern state. Without going into great detail, let me just assert that something like the logic of displacement I have described in *Mill* also operates in most if not all the late novels we consider "mainstream" or "realistic." *Tess of the D'Urbervilles* offers perhaps the clearest comparison to *Mill on the Floss*, but Thomas Hardy's other major works of fiction should not be counted out of the larger thought process I am describing simply because they seem to shift our focus away from women and onto men. It is entirely possible to read *Jude the Obscure* as an ingenious variation on the model that situates the male body as the terminus of metonymic chains responsible for transforming the quality of transindividual desire into something locatable within and manageable by the individual. *The Mayor of Casterbridge* thinks through the same problem from the perspective of male-male rivalry that, though marginalized, was nevertheless moving events forward in *Mill*. Michael Henchard's rival is successful precisely because he assumes the role of caretaker to the family that Henchard abandoned in entering into economic rivalry (gambling) with other men. As suggested by the striking image of two siblings locked in a lethal embrace, Tom Tulliver's consuming rivalry with his sister's suitors cuts his generation off from every available form of domestic authority and gratification.

WHAT'S LOVE GOT TO DO WITH IT?

The novels on which I have focused to this point consider individual competition an essential component of modern masculinity and hold it at least partly responsible for the rise of the modern ruling class. Given that novelists routinely acknowledged this principle, the question remains, why should they then go to such lengths to attribute competition to sexual desire, relocate that desire in a woman, and enjoy repudiating it? To address this question, let me first recall the overarching argument of Charles Darwin's *On the Origin of Species by Means of Natural Selection; or, The Preservation of Favoured Races in the Struggle for Life* (1859), which I shall regard as another example of this rhetorical behavior rather than an explanation for it. Against the backdrop of the fiction that preceded and followed its publication and rapid notoriety in 1859, Darwin's theory of evolution can be understood as a response to the self-contradictory cultural imperative to acknowledge and repudiate those forms of desire considered natural and primitive. Like Scott, Darwin uses history to relocate the very competitive qualities that eighteenth-century novelists and political theoreticians had installed in modern man. In contrast to Scott, Darwin situates the so-called primitive qualities not "sixty years back" in cultural history but at a remote distance in natural history.[20] Thus he displaced the definitive characteristics ascribed to the capitalist onto forebears who had to survive in a thoroughly predacious animal kingdom, making violence a fact of human nature.

This not so subtle change in the relocation of acquisitive individualism from a cultural to a natural body challenged the tenuous link that Adam Smith had forged between competitive vigor and sympathy, the ability of one man to feel for others as if they were oneself.[21] In setting man against man in territorial competition, Darwin's theory set the competitive drive on a collision course with the very notion of sympathy that had performed the cultural work of transforming individuals into a collective body. In equating masculinity with man's competitive relation to other men, Darwin also set sex in opposition to love, as men competed among one another for territorial supremacy in order to determine whose features might be reproduced in future generations. In this way, the male of the species might be said to achieve something like the self-objectification that Hegel's "master" sought through the slave's labor. In Darwin's account, however, the master's need for recognition is not construed as a need on the part of the individual ego but as one that only inadvertently may bring individual recognition by ensuring the biological perpetuation of the species.

In implicit contradiction to the principle of the survival of the fittest, Darwin argued that natural selection could account for man's evolution from a predacious competitor to the modern culture bearer. Just as children grow up and became respectable adults, so primitive people learn to control their natural aggression and strive for culturally sanctioned goals. Where this account of natural history sought to unite the species in a single epic narrative that culminated in the contemporary European, it actually set intellectuals to wondering exactly when in the past and under what pressures our anthropoid forebears made the quantum leap from nature to culture. Whether paleontologists found evidence for the fundamental difference between savage and modern in the shape of a cranium or in relics of early symbolic behavior, their enterprise succeeded in breaking the continuum of prehistoricial development into two components: the species before and the species after Western civilization. This made it more rather than less difficult to think of man as a single species. To keep his natural history from dividing in two on this basis, Darwin went back to the drawing board and wrote *The Descent of Man, And Selection in Relation to Sex*. Published in 1871, this effort to make sex do double duty—as the object of male-male rivalry and as a civilizing force—adopts the same strategy of displacement that seemed to work so well for novelists.

In his later work, Darwin preserves the vital link between modern masculinity and an inherently competitive nature. Here, however, he relies on gender to make the leap from nature to culture. The sexual struggle is of two kinds, he declares: "In the one it is between the individuals of the same sex, generally the males, in order to drive away or kill their rivals, the females remaining passive; whilst in the other, the struggle is likewise between the individuals of the same sex, in order to excite or charm those of the opposite sex, generally the females, which no longer remain passive but select the more agreeable partners" (398). Like so many novels of its time, Darwin's model of natural selection in relation to sex assumes that females are naturally passive and stand on the sidelines while men compete among themselves for the resources to support a family. After this phase has concluded, women take over. Although men actively strive to "excite or charm" them, nature leaves it to women to decide which attributes of appearance and behavior, among those who survive the preliminary competition, will be perpetuated generations to come. Sex and love part company in this second kind of sexual struggle, as women select as their mates those men capable of converting competitive energy into the elaborate courtship rituals that usher in domestic life.

Darwin goes to some lengths to make it appear that a man's success in this second phase of natural selection depends on the energy and ingenuity with which he strives to make himself attractive to the gentler sex. But there is nothing in his theory to indicate that a man's ability to prevail over other male competitors will make him the least bit attractive to women. It is entirely up to women to find, say, intelligence more exciting and sociability more charming than raw virility. It is up to women, in other words, to discipline the species itself, much as the Brontës' heroines disciplined the men whom they eventually married. And if men happen to be deficient in the cultural accoutrement necessary for a gratifying domestic life, then the blame can be placed squarely on women's failure to select men who can be satisfactorily domesticated.

Although it was relatively easy to hold natural selection responsible for man's triumph over other species, it was rather difficult to see how that same competitive drive promoted sociability. A novelist of sorts, Darwin had to tack on a second phase of natural selection that would favor the bloodlines of those examples of humanity who transformed their primitive impulses into fellow feeling and companionate love. In this way, Darwin sought to correct the troubling contradiction built into his earlier account of this process. But the notably shrill conclusion to *The Descent of Man* reveals that he did not, after all, succeed in localizing and managing the source of anxiety by gendering the process of selection: "He who has seen a savage in his native land will not feel much shame, if forced to acknowledge that the blood of some more humble creature flows in his veins. For my own part I would as soon be descended from that heroic little monkey, who braved his dreaded enemy in order to save the life of his keeper... as from a savage who delights to torture his enemies, offers up bloody sacrifices, practises infanticide without remorse, treats his wives like slaves, knows no decency, and is haunted by the grossest superstitions" (404). The first statement pays lip service to the Victorian reader who would be persuaded by his theory and sufficiently humanitarian to recognize the humanity he or she shares with savage man. But the final sentence shifts into the confessional mode by throwing the full weight of authorial approval behind the "heroic little monkey" portrayed as far more capable than Darwin's human ancestors of subordinating his own interests to the collective good. If he wrote *The Descent* in order to shift our focus from the struggle for survival to the spectacle of courtship, then here he finds it necessary to compound that first displacement with a second, as he relocates the source of human violence from the monkey's rather incredible homosociality to the depravity of primitive marriage.

My next chapter argues that late-nineteenth-century intellectuals and authors felt somewhat less compelled than their predecessors to place the natural predator on the same continuum with the culture bearer. Indeed, they seem rather eager to equate masculine aggression with recidivism and a form of degeneracy that made them essentially different and ontologically hostile to modern man. These later works see no reason to sustain the fantasy of a single natural history for man in which some groups had simply progressed further than others. Such novels as Bram Stoker's *Dracula*, Oscar Wilde's *Picture of Dorian Gray*, and H. Ryder Haggard's *She* reshape the developmental narrative of monogenesis to accommodate the fantasy of polygenesis, which holds there is more than one natural origin and thus more than one species of man. Polygenesis emerges from its residual position within Darwin's monogenetic account of human difference to displace the linear plot of communal destiny with multiple affiliations springing from different origins holding forth different possibilities for and limits on the success of humanity in a struggle among species to survive. These novels pay lip service to the kind of cover-up I have been describing when they cast the female as the bad object of sexual desire and a major threat to the cohesion of the community. Lucy Westenra's latent promiscuity may well have made her susceptible to Dracula's bite, and Sybil Vane's desire for Dorian Gray initiated his corruption. These women nevertheless do more to expose the absolute contradiction within modern masculinity than to cover it up.

To conclude, let me rephrase my initial question in terms of ideology writ large: why do modern cultures feel compelled both to maintain and to displace the contradiction posed by man's inherent capacity for violence, on the one hand, and his capacity for self-restraint, on the other? Modern cultures must claim to be inclusionary. A lot rests on maintaining the belief that virtually anyone with sufficient will and a modicum of education can belong to the respectable classes and enjoy full citizenship. The conviction with which the West exported the ethnographic practices of such a limited group of people as one and the same as Westernness itself rested in turn on a belief in universal man. The fantasy of a common origin and single trajectory of development defined the working classes and colonized populations as less advanced or underdeveloped versions of those economically and politically above them: one species struggling against its own natural instincts to reach a common good, as opposed to the kind of class warfare that Marx imagined when he rewrote Hegel's dialectic. To keep this ideal of the modern state alive and well, fiction had to represent differences as cultural equivalences, much as Kant did, for example, when he laid out the conditions for universal hospitality in his essay on perpetual peace. There, as I have already explained, he imagined a future in which all men, "by virtue of their common possession of the surface of the earth... cannot infinitely disperse and hence must finally tolerate the presence of each other."[22] Kant represents the arrival at tolerance in terms that strongly suggest the group ego's transformation from a state of rivalry, where all others are either self or other in the sense of a threat to self, to a dialectized ego, an ego capable of internal and external difference, able to recognize the other without requiring the kind of mirroring that leads to aggressivity.

The Victorians did not pursue this way of dealing with the problem of difference. My reading of Victorian fiction shows some of the most important novelists coming up with highly individuated ways to sustain a contradiction within masculinity. By doing so, paradoxically, they almost always turn the cultural equivalences that would be tolerated in Kant's cosmopolitan community into essential differences that require some definitive gesture of exclusion. This change is evident even in an early novel like *Wuthering Heights*. Brontë initially argues that what distinguishes Heathcliff from Earnshaw and Linton is his behavior, education, and treatment at the hands of others, but by novel's end she has turned those differences into nature and represents them as emanating from Heathcliff himself, whose lack of self restraint is so profound as to prevent him from breeding successfully with those who have it. If such polygenetic thinking became increasingly difficult for both novelists and even Darwin to resist, then we really ought to consider whether, by the end of the century, the contradiction within masculinity could have offered a solution to a problem rather than a problem to be solved.[23]

I want to suggest that the imagined community produced by Victorian fiction is one that could only be defined in terms of its limits, or which elements of humanity it had to exclude in order to remain what it was. None of the novels from this period that we still care about produces a synthesis of the forms of masculinity it sets in contradiction each to the other. I do not consider this a failure in either aesthetic or ideological terms. To formulate such an ideal image of middle-class man would, I suspect, have somehow damaged his claim to universality. Instead, Victorian fiction characteristically used gender—the illusion of sexual difference—to maintain the illusion of inclusiveness. Once a novel recast the inassimilable features of masculinity as a woman, it could then proceed to cast out those features without sacrificing either the fantasy of universal man or the belief that certain human qualities were by definition outside the limits of Western culture and therefore less than human. Even at this level of abstraction, two kinds of violence are set in play: the violence of inclusion became our natural heritage when modern man incorporated savage man within the category of the human, and the violence of exclusion became our cultural heritage when modern man cast out certain manifestations of that natural heritage in order to maintain the difference between modern Europe and its others.

4

THE POLYGENETIC IMAGINATION

Let me turn from what I have been calling mainstream Victorian fiction and consider two popular Victorian novels that don't seem especially concerned about the plight of the individual forced to choose among unaccommodating social options. In the fiction I have in mind, what often begins as a traditional question of how to achieve individual fulfillment quickly evaporates. An imaginary social body composed of individuals positioned each according to his or her worth turns out to be a flimsy conceptual obstacle in the path of an alien form of energy that ripples through the human aggregate. In such novels as H. Rider Haggard's *She* (1887) and Bram Stoker's *Dracula* (1897), we are asked to imagine what happens when the boundaries distinguishing individuals no longer exist. Whether it was because of their anatomy, their emotional volatility, their isolation from the public sphere, or their penchant for reading romance, women were always considered particularly porous in this respect, thus susceptible to desires that enter the mind from outside the body. In late-nineteenth-century romance, men became equally susceptible. Where mainstream Victorian fiction concerned itself with the problem of how to harness the individual's energy for social purposes, I argue, this other kind of fiction explored the alternative possibility that we are nothing but points of intensification through which these desires circulate to form one all-encompassing and mindless mass of humanity.

The nineteenth-century argument between monogenesis and polygenesis becomes especially important here. The assumption that all human beings descended from a single pair and so constitute one unified species distinct and apart from the rest of nature provided the conceptual bedrock of British ethnology with the publication of James Pritchard's *Researches into the Physical History of Mankind* in 1848. This theory was as old as the Old Testament and required an act of divine creation rather than a process of gradual development to get us from ape to man, but it nevertheless provided such men as John Lubbock, Edward Burnett Tylor, and John Ferguson McLennan with the rationale for extending Darwin's natural history into modern cultural history. To do so, the exponents of cultural evolutionism reasoned backward from the demonstrable differences between civilized and savage peoples and then forward from antiquity along a tree structure of which the varying states of civilization in recorded history formed the outermost branches. As George Stocking explains, "contemporaneity in space was therefore converted into succession in time by rearranging the cultural forms coexisting in the Victorian present along an axis of assumed structural or ideational archaism—from the simple to the complex, or from that which human reason showed was manifestly primitive to that which habitual association established as obviously civilized."[1] To bridge the gaps in archaeological research, gaps in which divine intervention could arguably operate, cultural evolutionists used the metaphor of growth, especially the cumulative growth of ideas, based on the process by which a child develops into an adult. Drawing on a model of individual maturation (still largely indebted to Lockean epistemology), cultural evolutionism revised the figure of the child to recapitulate the sociocultural process by which savage thinking developed into the ideas worthy of modern civilization.[2] Western researchers needed look no further than their own children to grasp exactly how the savage thought, spoke, and interacted socially. Stocking articulates this tautology most succinctly. Given that "these ideas were the product of basically uniform mental processes ..., the processes of savage thought were recapitulated in the minds of children and could be recreated in the minds of evolutionists. Psychic unity made it possible to think oneself out of the Miocene, both for the primitives who had been there originally, and the evolutionists who attempted to reconstruct the process" (174). Darwin himself embraced this theory, despite the fact that it still required a moment of ontological transformation when apes suddenly stopped being animals and became human beings.[3]

By way of contrast to monogenesis, polygenesis early on renounced this theological residue and relied on physical anthropology instead of a reconstructed cultural history. In *The Races of Men* (1850), Robert Knox made an important statement of this position by offering what he promoted as a new definition of race. Dismissing such external causes as education, religion, or climate, Knox argued that different races had different points of origin in nature, different patterns of growth, and thus different limits in their development. In the 1862 edition of this work, Knox concluded that certain of the races were "entitled to the name of species" (Stocking, *Victorian Anthropology*, 65). Although definitely marginal to the mainstream of Victorian thought, the poly-genetic viewpoint troubled theories of monogenesis. The survival into contemporary history of savage people could support the idea that mankind was a single species with a common origin and history only if one agreed that such peoples were "earlier" in developmental terms rather than "different" in kind. Is it any wonder the Victorians were so fascinated with the so-called primitive peoples of Africa and the South Pacific islands? Members of tribal cultures could be either ear-lier, childlike versions of European humanity or a rival species lacking the salient qualities of rationality and sexual restraint characterizing modern individuals. To complicate the situation further, even from a polygenetic viewpoint the same savages could belong either to a species incapable of developing into some recognizably more civilized form or to a species that had reached the limit of its development in antiquity and from there degenerated to a primitive state.

In support of the single-origin hypothesis, archaeologists and an-thropologists pointed out similar patterns across different cultures. On the other hand, as the advocates of polygenesis argued, such similarity could simply indicate that each variation of man passed through a stage where it resembled all others before it underwent its own particular development and emerged as another species. This, in their estima-tion, would account for the remarkable differences between cultures better than a theory that insisted on the participation of all humanity in one continuous process of growth. The cultural evolutionists used a Darwinian tree structure to conceptualize the development of a single human culture from savage to civilized man. But, as Stocking points out, "because its lower branches had been obscured in the mist of human time, [the evolutionists] used the ladder of cultural evolution to get from the presumed ground level of human antiquity to a point higher up the trunk that led to European civilization" (183). This ladder resembled, uncannily, the static classification system produced by polygenetic thought. Thus attempts to draw a clear line between monogenesis and polygenesis only made it murkier and the idea of exactly what constituted a species equally so.

Without slighting the obvious significance of the argument between monogenesis and polygenesis in the context of British imperialism, I want to consider briefly what these two positions share politically: what assumption do they hold in common in order that they might so sharply disagree? If monogenesis defined Western man as culturally improved in relation to members of degraded cultures, then polygenesis understood this difference as natural. In so doing, it eliminated any basis for sympathetic identification with members of subordinated groups. As for the purity of the modern middle-classes, the advocates of polygenesis counted on civilized man's natural aversion to other races and the failure of most hybrids to reproduce themselves. In much the same way, the novels I am going to discuss ultimately colluded with mainstream Victorian fiction to create a difference within humanity between savage and civilized man that imaginatively subordinated most of the world to Western civilization.

This chapter addresses the question of how some novels used polygenetic thinking to expose the implicit conflict between a subject compelled to pursue his or her desires and a social order that demanded conformity to moral and sexual norms. I also show how the gulf in formal terms between those novels we still consider aesthetically important and what tends to be dismissed as popular fiction actually allowed for a powerful complicity between them at the level of ideology. For examples, I have chosen two novels that were part of the romance revival of the 1880s and 1890s, both of which suggest that individualism puts Western cultures at a distinct disadvantage in relation to less civilized or "degraded" peoples. At the same time, these novels understand individualism as the one thing that keeps Europeans from going over to the dark side and losing their humanity. Refusing the kind of compromise formation that resolves novels belonging to the great tradition, She and Dracula create so clear a contradiction between a civil society composed of individuals and versions of mass man that the two cannot possibly mingle or even share the same planet but must engage in a battle to the death.

To understand what, if not rampant racism, created this contradiction and gave it so much appeal, I find it instructive to translate the argument between monogenesis and polygenesis into the figures of reproduction and repetition, each of which places limits on individualism in its own distinctive way.[4] The figure of reproduction obviously lends itself to a linear developmental narrative, where an individual starts off as less than a full and independent individual and progresses, as Moll, Jane Eyre, Pip, and other protagonists do, to a social level where his or her individuality can be socially recognized and sanctioned. To signal this achievement, the story cannot stop there but must reproduce itself. Moll writes her story; Jane has a child and writes her story; Pip vicariously reproduces himself through Biddy and Joe and tells his story. Even Maggie Tulliver is reproduced postmortem as a lost love object in the memories of her lovers. To indicate such individual growth and development, the novel eliminates certain traits of a historically earlier subject, hangs on to other traits, and adds new ones. But it cannot perform these acts of abjection and displacement arbitrarily, not if it wants to maintain the illusion of a single individual, whole if not yet entire. Observing a single master narrative, these stories tell the same story. By thinking in terms of the individual and how he or she might fit into the given social order, the same figure of reproduction lends itself to such collective narratives as the ascent of man and the march of civilization, both of which understand the vicissitudes of the collective as the progression of a semiautonomous entity—analogous to "the individual"—toward what Tennyson described as "one far-off divine event."[5] To think with the logic of reproduction on a collective scale, in other words, fiction has to repeat the past—whether self or social body—and change that past in some significant way; ontogeny recapitulates and exceeds past ontogenies.

In his revisionary reading of Darwin's theory of natural selection, Daniel C. Dennett contends that, despite the tree structure organizing Darwin's account of the ascent of man, today's reader can hardly overlook "the underlying process [that] always consists of nothing but a set of individually mindless steps succeeding each other without the help of any intelligent supervision; they are 'automatic' by definition: the workings of an automaton. They feed on each other, or on blind chance—coin flips, if you like—and on nothing else."[6] I argue that Dennett's reading of the "underlying process" in Darwin's theory of evolution describes precisely how Haggard and Stoker exhume the process "underlying" the linear narrative organizing mainstream Victorian fiction. Only by keeping these novels at the margins of the canon or else appropriating them for the mainstream can literary criticism continue to read the collective subjects of narrative fiction as semiautonomous units that move forward in time enacting much the same conflicts—between master and slave, masculinity and femininity, self and other—that we believe individuals actually pursue in achieving an identity. In this respect, we repeat the marginalizing gestures of modernism itself. At the very moment when psychoanalysis was establishing itself as the way to read psychosocial phenomena, authors and intellectuals associated with modernism insisted that novels should not only tell the story of the group as that of the individual (take, for example, the literary historiography of Virginia Woolf's *Room of One's Own* and *Orlando*); novels should also tell the story of the group from the perspective of that individual (hence stream of consciousness and the other techniques associated with modernism). Novels that did not observe what can only be called an aesthetic imperative were considered outside the tradition, where they could be regarded as idiosyncratic, disruptive, degraded, or deviant. In marked divergence from the grand narratives that define human groups—indeed, humanity itself—by way of analogy to the individual subject, such novels as *She* and *Dracula* imagined collectivity as a radically different mode of being fundamentally opposed to individualism.[7]

Freud's essay "The Uncanny" remains the most influential attempt to come to terms with fiction that challenges individual autonomy and continuity in time. In discussing E. T. A. Hoffman's "The Sandman," his example par excellence of the uncanny tale, Freud attributes the curious repetitions that challenge the autonomy of individuated consciousness and therefore the reality principle itself to the persistence of infantile thought modes oblivious to the difference between what originates within the individual and what comes from outside in his or her cultural environment. With this move, Freud relocates a challenge to individuated consciousness within the individual unconscious, reestablishing the difference between inside and outside. But when he turns from fiction to explain how and why the uncanny disrupts real life, his essay begins to erode the very difference between inside and outside on which his model of modern consciousness depends. His essay takes on some of the features of its uncanny subject matter, as his recollection of a particular experience destabilizes the generalizations it was called on to support. Freud remembers strolling through a foreign city, when he inadvertently entered "a quarter of whose character I could not long remain in doubt. Nothing but painted women were to be seen at the windows of the small houses, and I hastened to leave the narrow street at the next turning. But after having wandered about for a while *without enquiring my way*, I suddenly found myself back in the same street, where my presence was now beginning to excite attention. I hurried away once more, but only to arrive yet a third time by another *détour* at the same place yet a third time."[8] Convinced that the street was not just another street in a foreign city but one that directed him back to the very place he wished to leave, he repeated his initial journey. Rather than move from point A to point B as planned, his stroll observes the logic of repetition, or AB, AB, AB. The loss of agency that accompanies this structural transformation of his account is preserved in the curiously intransitive phrasing of his description of the street, where "women were to be seen," to which he had "wandered without enquiring his way," and where he "suddenly found [him]self" against his will. The city street operated as a *"détour"* capable of returning him to the forbidden zone against his intention. As he reasons some years later, however, the force that turned him from his intended path was not something foreign and therefore outside his body after all. It was something internal that he had repressed. Indeed, he reasons, something at once so foreign and yet familiar can only be one thing. Several pages later, he concludes that "whenever a man says to himself [in a dream], 'this place is familiar to me, I have been here before,' we may interpret the place as being his mother's genitals or her body. In this case too, the *unheimlich* is what was once *heimisch*, familiar" (2:245).

Those who smile knowingly as Freud recounts the process that returned him for a third time to what he understood to be the red light district of a foreign city have been successfully enlisted as his partners in a joke. The Freud who temporarily regresses to an infantile thought mode plays the butt of the joke. The Freud who objectifies and debases magical thinking is the one who tells the joke and so regains interpretive authority over what is obviously troubling material. It is possible, however, to give this particular joke one more turn of the screw. Let us suppose that, instead of the fantasies that are supposed to form the unconscious core of modern consciousness, what we encounter in those moments Freud characterizes as uncanny is the periphery and limit of individual consciousness, something inherently foreign to the self-enclosed subject and endowed with the power to change human nature. Let us suppose, moreover, that whatever it is, this phenomenon is neither concealed nor working undercover but has been made to seem so by a culture that reads human phenomena as much the same contest between desire and will that organizes mainstream fiction. Reading otherwise, we could take Freud's circular itinerary at face value and assume there is indeed something about the city that draws visitors toward its red light district. Perhaps it is not, after all, a degraded version of Freud's own sexuality in the form of an infantile wish that he enacts in this place but another libidinal economy that does not understand itself in relation to the bourgeois family and refuses to privilege that unit. From this other perspective, Freud is clearly at a loss to explain what has happened. He is the butt of the joke not because he has wandered into foreign territory but because he fails to consider that once in the city he is something other than he was before entering. He can neither imagine himself without a "self" that he can carry with him into foreign settings nor entertain the possibility of a social body that is not composed of individuals.

He admits that uncanny experiences can be the result of another thought mode, one that modern individuals believe themselves to have surmounted but that can temporarily put individual consciousness on hold. In taking what he considers a detour to the scene of "painted women," we could argue that Freud is no more returning to his beginning in the genitals and body of reproductive woman than to his proper end in the family that reproduces that origin. In a letter to his fiancée, Martha Bernays, in 1883, he admits to being something of a snob. "'The people,'" he contends, "judge, think, hope and work in a manner utterly different from ourselves."[9] In a letter to his fiancée's sister, written after wandering the streets of Paris, he describes the people as "a different species: 'uncanny.'"[10] Given the implicitly polygenetic turn of phrase that Freud used in 1883 to describe humanity en masse, we might see the account of a later stroll through Rome as a denial of the possibility that he may not have been directed by his own unconscious to return to the scene of "painted women" but by an alien populace, who think in "a manner utterly different from ourselves." Caught in the force field of those city streets, Freud performs according to the logic of repetition that strips desire, will, and action of their individuality. The repetition that brings him face to face with "painted women" signals the culture's hostility to Freud's assumption that every human story begins and ends in private life with the birth and death of an individuated consciousness.

Locke first imagined a modern civil society as proceeding from the ground up, individual by individual, household by household, to form a citizenry of heads of household responsible for women, children, and servants, who do not qualify as self-governing subjects. The fantasy he fostered is that to be governed by such a citizenry is to be governed by oneself. But what happens when that model of collective man gives way to notions of "the people," "the masses," or "the crowd," all terms that indicate the human aggregate is not the sum total of individuals, as the logic of the social contract would have it. In his study of the nineteenth-century crowd, John Plotz argues convincingly that nineteenth-century British culture began to define both individual and civil society not so much in opposition to each other as against the background of variable, fluid, heterogeneous, and mesmerizing images of the crowd.[11] Long regarded as more or less self-evident, the figure of mass man remains conspicuously undertheorized, despite the fact that it lends human collectivity a form not only radically different from the Lockean ideal of civil society but radically different from itself from one moment of history to the next as well. The logic governing this figure during the modern period is none other than that which Freud will call "the uncanny" and attribute to "primitive" thought modes "that exist within us ready to seize upon any confirmation" (2:247).

As Gilles Deleuze explains, this logic should not be confused with that of reproduction. Reproduction compels us to think in terms of a sequence of resemblances that are measured according to an implicit norm. Thus we read *Jane Eyre* as a sequence of Janes that approach the normative Jane who serves as narrator; we read this novel, in other words, as a narrative of growth and development. But repetition tells another story, one without beginning or end, because it has occurred before and will occur again. No individual can possibly matter in a process whose sole purpose is to repeat itself.[12] To understand such a formation, Deleuze asks us to think of crabgrass as it sends out shoots in all directions, any one of which may operate as center, or of a line of ants, which may appear to have direction but can be broken at any point and rerouted, or of nomads, a collective that neither arrives at nor departs from a destination but exists perpetually "in the middle, between things, interbeing, *intermezzo*."[13] Rather than a linear narrative of development, then, repetition yields a disrupted, redirected, decentered, multidirectional spread. As opposed to the kind of civil society that forms as individuals acquire positions within it, the mass body takes shape as "a pullulation of individuals absolutely identical in respect of their concept, and participating in the same singularity in existence (the paradox of doubles or twins)."[14]

Repetition generates a form at once spatial and fluid. This is not a form one encounters from outside, as one does an object, but something one experiences as a loss of individual boundaries, an infusion of curious sensations that do not appear to be one's own, and a compulsion to dance, so to speak, to someone else's tune. Deleuze famously uses the figure of the rhizome to account for the formal consequences of repetition: "Unlike the tree, the rhizome is not the object of reproduction: neither external reproduction as image-tree nor internal reproduction as tree-structure. The rhizome is an antigenealogy. It is a short-term memory, or antimemory. The rhizome operates by variation, expansion, conquest, capture, offshoots. Unlike the graphic arts, drawing, or photography, unlike tracings, the rhizome pertains to a map that must be produced, constructed, a map that is always detachable, connectable, reversible, modifiable, and has multiple entryways and exits and its own lines of flight" (21). Deleuze insists that a rhizome can only be defined as the undoing of the tree structure dominating Western thought and is in this sense conceptually parasitic upon that structure, much, as I show, the novels of Haggard and Stoker are. Themselves products of the individualistic culture of the novel, *She* and *Dracula* cannot help portraying the alien thinking of the rhizome in highly artificial and negative terms.

WHEN REPRODUCTION BECOMES REPETITION

In 1798 Thomas Malthus claimed that it was dangerously short-sighted to understand human reproduction individualistically. His *Essay on the Principle of Population* argued for a quantitative understanding of humanity that submerged the individual in great tides of human desire checked only by such natural catastrophes as war, plague, and famine. Thus he linked the fate of the nation to that of something on the order of a species, a social body that could not be broken down into distinct individuals. What many thought to be individual gratification was, in Malthus's view, nothing more than a limited view of an impersonal reproductive drive curbed only by the limited resources nature provided. To launch his assault on the novelistic assumption that individual gratification on a mass scale would lead to collective well-being, Malthus situates himself in the aftermath of the French Revolution and surveys the period stretching before him as one "*big* with the most important changes, changes that would in some measure be decisive of the future fate of mankind" (my emphasis).[15] He offers this promising image of his historical moment as a pregnant woman, only to roll this metaphor over and expose its sinister underside.

With this turn, reproduction ceases to rely on a linear progressive narrative and begins to observe the logic of repetition. Food increases according to a simple linear progression, he reasons famously, while hungry mouths increase geometrically, the population doubling itself twice over in the time it takes to double food production. According to this line of reasoning, times of relative plenty are especially dangerous. When resources seem abundant, more people are likely to marry and have children, thereby ensuring an even greater disparity between the growing population and a diminishing food supply. Where one would expect the figure of a woman "big with the most important changes" to inaugurate a narrative of progressive development, this one behaves as the figure of repetition, a body that spreads wherever there are resources to consume; it expands from the middle, we might say, beyond recognition, without any direction or constraints except those checks that nature throws in its way. The collective body that results from Malthus's calculus is fundamentally hostile to the concept of civil society. Some individuals will certainly fare better than others as the population amasses, but even their stories are ultimately subject to the ebb and flow of population.

In redefining the terms in which fiction henceforth imagines individual fulfillment, Malthus also implies a solution to the problem of a geometric increase in mouths to feed, a solution that Victorian fiction would also embrace. Simply by resorting to the figure of the female body, Malthus translates a problem that unfolds according to the logic of repetition into one that can be solved according to the logic of reproduction—cultural reproduction, that is, rather than sexual reproduction. Assuming that sexual desire is not only natural but also the cause of overpopulation—which in turn gives rise to war and misery—he proposes to solve the problem, in theory at least, by bringing human nature under cultural control. If the female body is the object of sexual desire, then we can control that desire by controlling her body. In order to show how culture might intervene in nature and resolve the problem that emerges when one understands the social body as a population, Malthus uses the narrative of individual development to present the case of a man with an education but without the income sufficient to support a family: "The woman that a man of education would naturally make the object of his choice would be one brought up in the same tastes and sentiments with himself and used to the familiar intercourse of a society totally different from that to which she [would] be reduced by marriage. Can a man consent to place the object of his affection in a situation so discordant, probably, to her tastes and inclinations? Two or three steps of descent in society, particularly at this round of the ladder, where education ends and ignorance begins, will ... be considered by the generality of people ... a real and essential evil" (33). Having set his quantitative model of human growth against the twin narratives of individual development and social progress, Malthus returns to those narratives as the means by which an individual can avoid the fate of the mass body. Education directs desire toward a woman whose sexual appeal resides in her cultural rather than her biological attributes. The "man of education" will fear pulling "the object of his affection" off the lower rungs of the social ladder and plunging with her into an undifferentiated humanity. He can remain the individual that one becomes through education, in other words, only by relinquishing the immortality he would achieve through sexual reproduction.[16]

Such late Victorian novels as *She* and *Dracula* reject this solution in favor of the principle that the fate of one is the fate of all. To insist that what works for the individual no longer applies by analogy to the whole, these novels abandon the problem of how the individual fits into a rigidly exclusive social order and pick up the line of thought abandoned when Frankenstein tore up his female monster midway through production.[17] Initially, Shelley's novel appears to argue against a mode of production that divides the world into economic and domestic spheres only to subordinate feminine to masculine, destroy the organic community, overvalue scientific rationalism, instrumentalize the human body, and unleash individualism at the expense of every sentimental bond. If, as feminist readings demonstrate, the novel calls attention to dismembered families, aborted births, and a bride destroyed on the marriage bed by the intellectual ambitions of her husband, then it also supports Marxist readings that focus on the destruction of an older agrarian economy by the new order of manufacturing that spawns an alien subspecies of human beings to work in factories.[18] To understand this story in either psychosexual or socio-political terms is, I believe, a way of avoiding the intractable fact that the monster is not quite human.[19] From a purely formal perspective, this makes all the difference.

Adopting a monogenetic argument, the monster claims that like a human being he can improve, in which case his creator should finish what he started and civilize his progeny: "I intended to reason. This passion is detrimental to me; for you do not reflect that you are the cause of its excess. If any being felt emotions of benevolence towards me, I should return them an hundred and an hundred fold; for that one creature's sake, I would make peace with the whole kind!"[20] Rather than inspire sympathy, the monster's excesses give him away. In making the case that he resembles a human being and can therefore grow progressively human, his penchant for hyperbole reveals his radical difference from what he calls "the whole kind"; his rhetoric positions the monster outside humanity and in a mimetic relationship to the community he would join. Thus what starts out as an argument based on reproduction (I am an extension of your being and will grow progressively human as you socialize me) observes the logic of repetition (I am like you but not the same as you and will therefore repeat your course of development as a competitor). Initially persuaded that he owes this creature, "all the portion of happiness that it was in my power to bestow," Frankenstein begins to assemble a body of the choicest female parts (99). To muster the courage required for this task, he adopts the same logic that Malthus used to think his way out of the dilemma posed by mass man: what the monster needs is a good woman to domesticate his otherwise destructive energy. Soon enough, as I noted in chapter 2, Frankenstein imagines the female monster turning with disgust from her mate "to the superior beauty of man" (114).

To the degree that the monster is an extension and reproduction of his maker, we can think of him in analogous relation to the marginalized groups that lag historically behind modern man on a developmental time line. In such a relation of resemblance, the monster would necessarily fall far short in comparison "to the superior beauty of man." But on the off chance that the female monster might find her male counterpart agreeable even so, the outcome would be far worse. As Frankenstein continues to pursue this line of thinking, the sinister figure of repetition rears its hungry head, and the logic of monogenesis momentarily falls prey to the polygenetic imagination: "if they were to leave Europe, and inhabit the deserts of the new world, yet one of the first results of those sympathies for which the dæmon thirsted would be children, and a race of devils would be propagated upon the earth, who might make the very existence of the species of man a condition precarious and full of terror" (114). At this point in the novel, the problem initially created by Frankenstein's misconceived and botched production recedes into the background. In view of the fact that reproduction on a mass scale might become repetition and amass a population, the manufacture of a female companion for this monster suddenly promises not only to destroy Frankenstein's immediate community but also to set all humanity on a path to extinction.

With this possibility in view, Frankenstein must reject any idea of the monster as an objectification of his own arch individualism. Once doubled, the monster will continue to double, transforming a one-of-a-kind demon into a "race of devils" with its own pattern of development. By recasting the monster as this radically different being, Frankenstein nullifies all sense of responsibility for his creation. Indeed, the very possibility that the monster might be something other than his dependent allows the scientist to dismember the half-completed female monster and reclaim his status as an ethical protagonist: "Had I a right, for my own benefit, to inflict this curse upon everlasting generations? . . . I shuddered to think that future ages might curse me as their pest, whose selfishness had not hesitated to buy its own peace at the price perhaps of the existence of the whole human race" (114–15). This is for me the most interesting moment in the novel, where Shelley allows Frankenstein to arouse and then quell the anxiety that Malthus sought to generate in his *Essay on the Principle of Population*. To produce a nightmare scenario that anticipates Frankenstein's "race of devils," Malthus had to imagine the nation as a bounded agricultural territory beset by a monstrous body exponentially sprouting mouths to feed and subject to cycles of scarcity and plenty that put it on a collision course with progressive accounts of human advancement.[21] Shelley explicitly rejects this fantasy.

In this momentary inversion of the image of a world of dwindling desire into one of unquenchable demand, Shelley's novel foresaw the same interchangeability of deficiency and excess that Malthus himself would exploit within just a year or two in another assault on liberal economic thinking. His 1798 *Essay on the Principle of Population* began with the premise that all human beings are driven by a natural desire to reproduce, which would in aggregation exponentially increase demand until it exhausted all available natural resources. By 1819, however, he had drafted *Principles of Political Economy*, which challenged the idea that either supply or demand was a natural phenomenon. In the motion of the new commodity culture, he evidently saw the prospect of too little demand as a more serious threat to a robust national economy than the problem of a diminishing food supply.[22] This change in his understanding of supply required him to reconceptualize the principle of population: "We hear of great splendour among princes and nobles in every period of history. The difficulty was not so much to inspire the rich with a love of finery, as to break down their immense properties and to create a greater number of demanders in the middle ranks of life who were able and willing to purchase the results of productive labor.... Thirty or forty proprietors, with incomes answering to between one thousand and five thousand a year, would create a much more effectual demand for the necessaries, conveniences, and luxuries of life, than a single proprietor possessing a hundred thousand a year" (374). In this passage, Malthus's concern with a geometric increase in demand has given way to what evidently seemed to be the larger problem of a geometric decline in demand. As the rich grow richer, the number of rich decreases, and there are fewer consumers to purchase goods, which continue to increase in number. To solve this problem, Malthus reasons, it will be necessary to reverse the inevitable decline in demand by whipping up consumer desire to keep pace with an exponentially increasing supply of goods. For starters, he suggests abolishing the principle of primogeniture, as the distribution of property from father to eldest son necessarily produces a linear rather than a geometric increase in big consumers.

In thus shifting focus from humanity in general to England in particular, Malthus hangs on to "taste" as the means of controlling the discrepancy between supply and demand. Rather than curb desire, as it did in the case of the "man of education," taste here affords the stimulus essential to increasing consumption. An ever-expanding economy depends on a new kind of middle class who "derive their power of purchasing [not from land] but from the various professions, from commerce, from manufactures, from wholesale and retail trade, from salaries of different kinds, and from the interest of public and private debts" (379). I won't speculate as to why Malthus considered this particular group of "demanders... more likely to acquire tastes more favourable to the encouragement of wealth than the owners of small properties on the land" (379). He does not spell out exactly how their acquired tastes would increase geometrically and so keep pace with commodity production. But the principle that people of wealth who have not inherited property would feel compelled to distinguish themselves by means of conspicuous consumption was certainly borne out well before the end of Victoria's reign. The new commodity culture operated on the principle that the more people exchange goods for money, the greater the national wealth. This fantasy of an ever-increasing number of consumers completely reversed the calculus of the principle of population. No longer driven by a mindless nature to consume as much as possible, the consumer now required cultural inducement like that at work in Marx's "The Commodity Fetish and the Secret Thereof."[23] The very fact that reproductive desire was no longer considered natural implicitly transformed humanity into a body over which desire might spread contagiously and around which goods could circulate until the flow reversed its course and receded. By offering dwindling desire as the counterphobia of ever-increasing desire, then, Malthus did not abandon the figure of repetition so much as transform that figure into one that could spread and shrink erratically according to its own libidinal economy.

DEFENSIVE INDIVIDUALISM

It is commonplace to read Stoker's *Dracula* (1897) as an expression of the anxiety experienced by middle-class Englishmen and women who found themselves in an economy flooded with goods and people from every corner of the globe. In recent years, Stoker's novel has generated a body of criticism that links it to other characteristically fin-de-siècle aberrations: fetishism (where objects take control of subjects), consumerism (where supply determines demand), hysteria (where infantile phobias overcome adult desire), degeneration (where inferior traits dominate superior ones), and decadence (where foreign fashion supplants the practical robustness associated with English food, dress, and fiction). These cultural readings of the novel are bolstered by historical readings that suggest such anxieties accompanied the increasing number of foreigners pouring into England and indications that the empire was no longer expanding but contracting.[24] Suggestive as they are, however, each of these readings of Stoker's best-known novel steers clear of the very questions that it begs. If English readers were as anxiety ridden as scholars say, then why did they embrace a novel so bent on intensifying that anxiety? If the Victorian readership favored domestic realism and colonial adventure stories, then why did romances that effectively killed off both genres flourish during the 1880s and 1890s? This much is clear: late Victorian romance marks one of those instances in the history of the novel where a residual form of thinking emerged and temporarily overwhelmed the conventions of the genre.

So long as we regard *Dracula* as a fantastic demonstration of what happens when individual desire gets out of hand, it makes sense to say that the novel portrays a consumer-driven culture as a threat to humanity. According to this reading, the novel teaches us not to let artificially implanted desires run away with us, especially if we happen to be women. And there is reason to think that this is indeed the moral one should draw from the story. The attractive Lucy Westenra resembles a traditional heroine, except for indications of her wanton consumerism, first in her ability to attract a variety of suitors and then in the aggressive eating habits she acquires from the vampire. Pursued by a number of men, she correctly selects the one born of English gentry, but she confesses to her friend Mina Harker that she felt like accepting all of them. Does this apparent lack of discrimination point to latent promiscuity in Lucy herself that sets one suitor against another and makes her susceptible to Dracula? I would say no, on the grounds that Lucy is caught in a transformation that robs her of individuality, both of the capacity for sympathetic identification with her rejected suitors and of her own desire. Once infected with Dracula's blood, she no longer can be said to have the decision-making power that a woman supposedly exercises in selecting a mate but responds only to the needs of the vampire body as a whole. That these needs not only fulfill themselves through her but also cancel out anything resembling erotic desire becomes ironically apparent when Lucy nearly persuades her fiancé to "leave these others and come to me. My arms are hungry for you." As he reaches to embrace her, she proceeds to bare "the pointed teeth, the bloodstained, voluptuous mouth—which it made one shudder to see."[25] Haggard's Ayesha resembles the heroine of romance until she reveals that she too is murderously compelled to possess her lover's body and soul at the cost of his humanity: "Like the old sphinx of Egypt," She tells him, "shalt thou sit aloft from age to age, and ever shall they cry to thee to solve the riddle of thy greatness that doth not pass away, and ever shalt thou mock them with thy silence!"[26] Much as the vampire's bite strips Lucy of any choice in the matter, Ayesha's gaze turns Leo Vincey into her ancient lover, Kallikrates, not simply into his descendant and spitting image but into somebody else, a second Kallikrates (the first lies after centuries perfectly embalmed in her dual-purpose tomb and bedroom).

Neither the vampire's bite nor Ayesha's gaze exaggerates some desire already residing at the core of the victim's individuality. Both implant an alien desire within the victim that destroys his or her human core.[27] The problem with Lucy Westenra, from this perspective, is not her tendency to desire men too liberally but the total annihilation of her sexual appetite and sex appeal by something else. As one witness to her transformation, a former suitor, testifies: "I call the thing that was before us Lucy because it bore her shape" (271). Nor are men immune to the seductive effects of this desire. Early on in the novel, the male protagonist, Jonathan Harker, describes his helplessness before the blandishments of Dracula's minions: "The skin of my throat began to tingle as one's flesh does when the hand that is to tickle it approaches nearer—nearer. I could feel the soft, shivering touch of the lips on the supersensitive skin of my throat, and the hard dents of two sharp teeth, just touching and pausing there. I closed my eyes in languorous ecstacy and waited—waited with beating heart" (54). The same logic plays itself out in Haggard's novel, as the narrator finds his will completely taken over by Ayesha's on first meeting her gaze: "Drawn by some magnetic force which I could not resist, I let my eyes rest upon her shining orbs, and felt a current pass from them to me that bewildered and half-blinded me" (159). Knowing full well the cost of desiring Ayesha, the narrator finds himself in the position of an addict with no choice but to desire all the more: "Mortality is weak, and easily broke down by a sense of the companionship that waits upon its end. Take me hence, O Ayesha!" (190). Having slain the native woman to whom Leo Vincey once considered himself married, Ayesha offers him the chance to "be avenged. Strike, and strike home!—so shalt thou be satisfied, Kallikrates, and go through life a happy man." Tragically aware that he has no powers of choice and action, he responds to her invitation, "well thou knowest that I cannot strike thee, no, not even for the sake of her whom thou slewest but last night. I am in thy power, and a very slave to thee" (253).

So that his reader may understand the logic by which the individual is stripped of individuality, Stoker spells it out in the case history of the mental patient Renfield that runs parallel to his account of Lucy's gradual transformation from heroine to vampire. Dr. Seward, keeper of the "lunatic-asylum" observes "a method in [the] madness" (94) of the patient Renfield, as he feeds many flies to fewer spiders, feeds those spiders to "a whole colony of sparrows," and then, in a fit of impatience, eats the tamed birds raw. "What he desires," the doctor concludes, "is to absorb as many lives as he can, and he has laid himself out to achieve it in a cumulative way.... What," Seward considers, "would have been his later steps?" (209). What else but to continue moving further up the food chain to human beings! By the time Seward realizes that his patient's manic-depressive behavior and strange eating habits are manifestations of his inner vampire, it is too late to save either Renfield or Lucy, for both have already been incorporated in the vampire body and automatically repeat its behavior.

Known among the Amahagger as "she-who-must-be-obeyed," Ayesha deploys her telepathic powers to much the same effect as Dracula. Having her inhabit his mind and body renders Haggard's narrator, Ludwig Holly, "so bewildered..., and racked and torn with such a succession of various emotions, that I began to think that I must be going mad" (209). Like the vampire, she uses her powers of mind to rule subjects who are themselves the very antithesis of individuals. As the tribal elder explains, while they can certainly distinguish between an Arab and a white man, the Amahagger lack any respect for individual difference. In carrying this principle to its logical extreme, they perform the same inversion performed by Kant's cannibals: "here there is a custom that if a stranger comes into this country, he may be slain by 'the pot,' and eaten," a custom that turns "hospitality... upside down." As the narrator observes, "In our country we entertain a stranger, and give him food to eat. Here ye eat him, and are entertained" (111).

In both novels, the practice of cannibalism transforms the language of seduction into the logic of polygenesis. For these authors, loss of individuality is tantamount to joining a species not only different but fundamentally hostile to humankind as well. Instead of reproducing himself in a linear manner from one generation to the next, the vampire spreads according to a pattern that repeats itself ad infinitum. He does "not die like the bee when he sting[s] once" (304), explains Van Helsing, a scientist of occult phenomena, "but must go on age after age adding new victims and... so the circle of the world goes on ever widening, like as the ripples from a stone thrown in the water" (275). The vampire body spreads "everywhere that men have been," from ancient Greece and Rome, to Eastern Europe and the Far East, across the Arctic wastes, and finally to modern England. Always in motion, this body is highly mutable. The vampire can "command all the meaner things: the rat, and the owl, and the bat—the moth, and the fox, and the wolf; he can grow and become small; and he can at times vanish and [be]come unknown" (305).

Haggard's Ayesha also starts out as a human being. Disappointed in love during the fifth century B.C., she acquires a curious form of cosmetic immortality that allows her to wait through the centuries in the ruins of an ancient civilization of North Africa for her lover to return, as if in emulation of those domestic heroines who will not settle for less than the perfect ending to their stories. However deserving of admiration this testament to her devotion may initially strike us, Ayesha shares Dracula's lack of humanity, a lack that makes the two more alike than different in the end. The body serves neither Dracula nor Ayesha as the metaphysical enclosure of a singular identity; indeed, they can change their bodies like clothes almost though not entirely at will. Both are, in the words of Haggard's narrator, a "fluid or essence" that so fortifies "these fleshy walls that they [can] from age to age resist the mines and batterings of decay" (123). That Ayesha murdered the first Kallikrates for preferring another woman should suggest that, from the first, her desire would tolerate none of the obstacles that time or human history might throw in her way. Nor could she be any more content to live happily ever after with Kallikrates in North Africa than Dracula was to pass his countless days terrorizing the Carpathians. "Evidently," explains the narrator, "She had made up her mind to go to England, and it made me absolutely shudder to think what would be the result of her arrival there" (255).

The Inhumanity of Repetition

The nineteenth-century novel frequently marks the limit of the human community with a specimen so savage and otherwise ignoble that it neither wills nor wishes to develop into modern man. Heathcliff and Bertha Mason are among the most memorable of these inassimilable beings. Housed within the same body as Dr. Jekyll, Stevenson's Mr. Hyde can be considered the end of the line, the last instance where the recalcitrant savage can cohabit the same conceptual category with the self-governing citizen. In recalling his wish to separate his moral side from the primitive components of his personality, Dr.

Jekyll admits that it is no longer even desirable to contain these human extremes within a single consciousness: "I saw that, of the two natures that contended in the field of my consciousness, even if I could rightly be said to be either, it was only because I was radically both; and from an early date . . . I had learned to dwell with pleasure, as a beloved daydream, on the thought of the separation of these elements. If each, I told myself, could but be housed in separate identities, life would be relieved of all that was unbearable."[28] Stoker obviously begins where Stevenson ends, with fully embodied antagonists, one modern and human, one ancient and not. But there the similarity ends. In shifting from the logic of monogenesis to give full reign to polygenetic thought, Stoker lets the savage out of the bag. That is to say, he recasts the deviant elements that cannot be ascribed to the ambition or sexual desire of a modern individual in the fantastic form of another species, whose features are specifically designed to cancel out what the Victorian readership considered most true of human nature.

The rhizome embodies a mode of thought that neither originates within the individual nor spreads by way of words from one individual to others who are equally self-contained. The fact that the vampire combines in one body the strength of "twenty men," not to mention wolves, bats, and other nocturnal predators, is the least of the problems posed by his lack of individuation. The vampire mind displays all the human passions, only magnified well beyond the reach of human ethics, so that mania and depression sweep across the mass body in alternating waves, as its physical expansion is thwarted or finds a direction in which to spread. Those individuals who embody vampire consciousness are just that: expendable members of a consciousness that does not depend on any one of the bodies it inhabits. Dracula began as a kind of Frankenstein, "a mighty brain, a learning beyond compare" (389). At some point, that intelligence "survived the physical death" and, like Frankenstein's monstrous experiment, took on a life of its own, "though it would seem that memory was not all complete" (389). From this uncontained intelligence, the novel imagines another, nonlinear mode of development that gives the savage—if such it can be called in a polygenetic worldview—an advantage over modern man: "In some faculties of mind he has been, and is, only a child; but he is growing, and some things that were childish at the first are now of man's stature. He is experimenting, and doing it well; and if it had not been that we have crossed his path he would be yet—he may be yet if we fail—the father or furtherer of a new order of beings" (389).

Ayesha is as beautiful to look upon as Dracula is repulsive, but there is, from the first, a link between her body and the embalming skills of the ancient kingdom Kör, and her gauzy drapery keeps us mindful that she should, by all the laws of nature, be long dead. As suits her gender, Ayesha's development is the obverse of Dracula's: her body has survived and maintained its original freshness over the millennia, giving it ample time to absorb—in the manner of Walter Pater's Gioconda—the wisdom of the ages. Though different from the vampire's dark cunning, she has acquired the same linguistic versatility, occult knowledge, and confidence that the curvature into a repetitive cycle of what appears to humans to be linear time will eventually bring Kallikrates back to her. Her only difference from Dracula is that her intelligence requires a man—and thus a domestic plot—where his depends largely on women—and hence a seduction plot—to disrupt human history. As the vampire exchanges blood with his victims, he establishes a communications network that allows him to participate in their thinking with increasing frequency, so that eventually their thinking will be his. Because it is the ultimate transgression of individualism, this intercourse does absolutely nothing to humanize the vampire, no matter how much human blood he drinks or how expert he becomes in the ways of English culture.

In wandering through North Africa over millennia, Ayesha, similarly, comes across a vessel of water that reflects what is in the mind of any individual on whom she happens to focus her attention. Capable of incorporating all knowledge, her consciousness is nothing in and of itself, as she explains, "I am a woman of many moods, and like the water in that vessel, I reflect many things; but they... pass, and are forgotten. Only the water is the water still, and I still am I, and that which maketh the water maketh it, and that which maketh me maketh me, nor can my quality be altered" (193–94). This, reasons the narrator, is an intelligence that—not so unlike that of Lockean man—incorporates whatever it reflects, so that it already exceeds human limits many times over. Only the fact that it has been contained within a domestic narrative has kept this intelligence from rethinking human history. With the rebirth of Leo as the lover Kallikrates, however, "this wonderful creature, whose passion had kept her for so many centuries chained as it were, and comparatively harmless, was now about to be used by Providence as a means to change the order of the world, and possibly, by the building up of a power that could no more be rebelled against or questioned than the decrees of Fate, to change it materially for the better" (256). The operative word here is "materially." Ayesha's knowledge can bring about the scientific advances of the ancient civilization of Kör and free human intelligence from the limits of a perishable body. But we must nevertheless attribute the narrator's belief in the possibility of a rosy future to the fact that Ayesha's hypnotic beauty has colored his thinking. Equally disrespectful of individual autonomy, any future over which Ayesha rules will put an end to human life as surely as Dracula's victory.

Given the overwhelming power of this alien mode of thought and the curious inability of the conventions of domestic fiction to deal with it, how do these novels arrive at anything like a resolution that makes us recognize them as novels? How, more importantly, does Stoker manage to do so in a way that pulls his novel back into proximity with a tradition that suppresses polygenetic thinking? Dracula explains to Mina that he has outfoxed her male protectors in terms that would seem to obviate the possibility of a domestic resolution: "They should have kept their energies for use closer to home. . . . And you, their best beloved one, are now to me, flesh of my flesh; blood of my blood; kin of my kin; my bountiful wine-press for a while; and shall be later on my companion and my helper" (370). Ayesha's account of how she engineered her wedding to Leo similarly overturns the conventions of bourgeois love. Having murdered the faithless Kallikrates, she sent his Egyptian lover "away through the swamps, and it seems that she lived to bear a son and to write the tale that should lead thee, her husband, back to me, her rival and thy murderess" (281). Before the reader's eyes, this sentence turns her impending marriage to Leo into a repetition of the past as Ayesha conflates the husband-to-be with Kallikrates, his murdered ancestor, and identifies herself as his "murderess." No qualitative change, no dialectical synthesis, can emerge from this rivalry, only repetition of the same.

There is no question that we are supposed to read this statement as a forecast that repetition will ultimately put an end to repetition. The principle that repetition kills rather than perpetuates even so fluid and enduring a figure as Ayesha governs the outrageously fantastic climax of the romance plot and sets the novel on the path to realism. Stepping into the immortalizing flame of life a second time, Ayesha subjects herself to a reversal of the process that made her "the loveliest, noblest, most splendid woman the world has ever seen." This time, recalls the narrator, "she lay still before us, near the masses of her own dark hair, no larger than a big monkey, and hideous—ah, too hideous for words. And yet... it was the *same* woman!" (293). Leo returns with the narrator to Cambridge, where they write up the account of their respective roles in a recurring story of love and revenge that kept the world safe for a form of reproduction in which their experience prevents them from ever participating directly. The story of Ayesha is not a novel in that it is not their story, or even Ayesha's story, but a script in which each has been assigned a role that cancels out his individuality. For this reason alone, Haggard's curious foray into an entirely different way of thinking about human history ends up, as any number of such tales did, by marginalizing itself.

Stoker pursues a different tactic when he tempers the polygenetic imagination and so sets his novel in a mutually authorizing relationship to mainstream fiction.[29] First of all, he draws on the convention of doubled heroines to solve the problem posed by repetition. Lucy, the more conventional of the two, begins as a purely feminine being directed exclusively by the cultural imperative to select a husband. Her body is emptied of human blood as it is infused with Dracula's and begins to repeat the act of her own dehumanization. To contain within her body the compulsion to repeat is simply impossible, given that compulsion intensifies as death releases her from the constraints of human affiliation. The vampire hunters find it necessary to kill Lucy herself by means of violence as overwrought as Dracula's own. Once they behead her, drive a stake through her heart, and ritualistically mark her off from human kind with garlic, they can turn their full attention to Mina Harker, who assumes the role of vampire bait and heroine as soon as Lucy is finally put to rest. Resembling Ayesha's second marriage ritual in this respect, the elaborate purification of Mina Harker turns repetition against itself and frees the reproductive body from the compulsion to repeat.

In contrast to Lucy, Mina begins as a mixture of categorical possibilities. Neither masculine nor entirely feminine, not so pure as Lucy but then also not racially marked, of neither high status nor low, Mina, we might say, is nothing in herself but has the potential to become many different things. She receives transfusions from the group of men who encircle and try to prevent her from repeating Lucy's metamorphosis. She is also a typist who repeats and synthesizes information that comes from numerous sources, including the mind of Dracula. She comes to occupy the position of heroine vacated by Lucy as she abjects, or casts out of herself, many of the features of race, class, gender, and nationality that late-nineteenth-century British culture would have found objectionable in a woman. Oscillating between a superior ability to repeat information necessary to the men around her, on the one hand, and utter dependence on their specialized knowledge, on the other, Mina survives a ridiculously protracted purification ritual in order to produce a child that signals the success and futurity of the group. Thus where Lucy began as a sexually attractive woman and subsequently incorporated certain features from other men that disfigure her beauty, Mina begins as something of a hybrid and comes to represent English womanhood, as she casts out everything she copied from and for the group of men. This shift in their positions reverses the spiral whereby repetition took over reproduction, making Mina fit for motherhood. Despite the fact she still incorporates the vampire's blood, the elimination of its source seems to put an end to the threat of polygenesis. The mixture that Mina contains is no longer one of radical difference, two species that do battle for her body and soul, but one of monogenetic resemblances, or variants within the human species.

SOME HELP FROM THE VAMPIRE

By placing modern man on the same historical continuum with his primitive counterpart, Darwin came up with a way to refute once and for all the persistent belief that there might have been several species of man, developing from diverse points of natural origin. Were polygenetic thinking to prevail, the British public would have to understand the colonial enterprise as nothing more than ruthless competition for goods and territory in which Europeans were proving to be the superior predator. By coming up with a theory that opens a temporal gulf between primitive and modern man and yet includes all variations of man within a single species, Darwin's theory provided not only a scientific explanation for British superiority. It also offered a way for the British to consider themselves more humane than the people they dominated while profiting by their competitive superiority over colonial populations. When Stoker exposed the kernel of polygenetic thought lodged within the monogenetic narrative where human variations mark different phases of development within a single species, he dismissed the belief that, with sufficient time and exposure to European culture, a primitive people might develop into modern individuals. As it dawns on Stoker's protagonists that Dracula is making himself at home in England and taking up with English women, the reader discovers that what might at first appear a variation of humanity actually constitutes an altogether different species whose development threatens Western supremacy. What does Dracula achieve by giving formal expression to the residual racism of monogenesis?

Let us suppose that the qualities that polygenesis attributes to a different species are—in some way we can't acknowledge—absolutely essential to the modern individual. At Stoker's moment in history, that individual needed something only its primitive counterpart could provide; call it the thought of another species or, better yet, another species of thought. Dracula has the edge on his European antagonists because his thinking is not his own but a fundamentally synthetic process. Having transcended the limits of individual embodiment, the vampire's mind can travel across categories of gender, class, nation, and species. It automatically assimilates information gathered in different forms from disparate sources and puts that information to work spreading his domain. As in Freud's description of the primitive thought mode that modern man has by definition "surmounted," the vampire mind preoccupies itself with "the omnipotence of thoughts, with the prompt fulfillment of wishes, with secret injurious powers and with the return of the dead" ("Uncanny," 247). Thus it matters not a whit if fiction, legend, rumor, or the ravings of a madman is at odds with scientific knowledge and historical fact. All become equivalent in the vampire's mind, which therefore seems more comprehensive in this novel than conventional realism or the empirical knowledge to which it plays lip service.

To conquer the vampire, the vampire hunters have to think like their prey. Each has to shed his autonomy, for individualism only hampers a campaign where each exists only to defeat a common foe. Forget privacy, reason, and morality of the conventional kind. Vampire hunters have license even to intrude in each other's most intimate moments; if the vampire can enter the Harkers' bedroom, then the vampire hunters must do so as well. What matters is the survival of human reproduction. Or so the novel suggests when it gives the Harkers' son "a bundle of names," names that, as Mina puts it, "link our little band of men together" (485). Given that the child incorporates the blood of all the male characters in the novel, thanks to his mother's need for transfusions and the community's willingness to provide them, his birth signals the novel's achievement of the purpose of sending humanity to war against the vampire. Baby Harker indeed changes the composition of the individual and future citizen, while maintaining the illusion that he is nevertheless the universal human being capable of synthesizing all differences within a single body. It is crucial, however, that Mina no longer houses the consciousness acquired with Dracula's blood.

She always had a talent for reading other people's minds and was among the first to sense that the members of her community were being taken over by something that entered the mind through the body. Her transcriptions made it possible for the group of scientists and businessmen to think like the vampire. But it ultimately requires the vampire's bite to magnify Mina's sensibility, so that this group of otherwise unremarkable men can hunt him down in his lair. Indeed, as Van Helsing says of Mina, "She has a man's brain—a brain that a man should have were he much gifted—and a woman's heart" (302). As her infection progresses, however, it dawns on her male companions that if she directly shares the vampire's thoughts, then he is likely to be directly sharing hers and gaining access to their plans through the conduit of sensibility. They conclude that she can no longer "be of our council, but [must instead] be simply guarded by us" (416). The kind of thinking that she shares with Dracula and transmits to his competitors completely vanishes with her infection.

The cure that rids Mina of the traces of vampirism is so much more elaborate, arcane, and protracted than killing off the vampire itself that we can, I think, regard it as Stoker's way of both acknowledging and suppressing the fact that his heroine thought like a vampire before her male companions did. By repeating information, she makes it possible for her male counterparts to receive information from sources they would otherwise overlook. By synthesizing that information, she provides them with knowledge of its ebb and flow. But she must cease to serve as their medium for these men not only to think like the vampire but also to claim that thinking as their own, a testament to masculine mastery of a competitor. Never mind that it takes repetition to end the tyranny of repetition or that the purification ritual that prepares Mina for motherhood suppresses without diminishing the hybridity of her child. Before reproduction can be restored, her ability to think as a group must be severed and her manuscript stripped of its authority. What marks the success of this heroine is her capacity for biological reproduction alone. Because the words she typed were not hers but came from a variety of other sources, written, spoken, and enacted in a range of documents by various people, even Dracula himself, the manuscript that results is nobody's story. It abandons the arboreal logic of a progressive narrative in order to recount the rhizomatic amassing and contraction of the vampire body. As her husband recalls some years later, "I took the papers from the safe where they had been ever since our return [from Carpathia] so long ago. We were struck with the fact, that in all the mass of material of which the record is composed, there is hardly one authentic document; nothing but a mass of type-writing" (486). Thus the novel identifies its own body as a patchwork affair, the product of repetition that lacks an identifiable human source. That the novel nevertheless ends with Jonathan Harker's disavowal of repetition (in the form of Mina's manuscript) and celebration of reproduction (in the form of her baby) redefines *Dracula* itself as an attempt to defend the tradition—as well as the individual—from the polygenetic thinking required to adapt individualism for a new historical moment.

Reproduction with a Difference

During the last decade of the nineteenth century, a shift in public concern away from the problem of overpopulation to the problem of degeneration marked the emergence of a new class of experts.[30] Unlike older avatars of the so-called middle class, this new class was not made of self-employed artisans, shopkeepers, investors, or farmers. It was formed of those employed by capital to consolidate its cultural hegemony over the traditional proletariat and migrant workers within Great Britain proper as well as the ruling elite of dependent populations throughout the empire. The position of the modern middle classes was not secure until it had established its specific ethnic practices as those of British culture itself. If the authority of the new cast of experts and professionals depended on its ability to standardize and carry out those practices, then its authority would naturally increase along with capital. That authority would also increase in proportion to the anxiety of the expanding number of prosperous people whom it served.

Dracula registers the emergence of a culture of experts as it has a motley "bundle" of otherwise quite ordinary men assume responsibility for most, if not all, the cultural functions that the novel identifies as feminine and the domain of middle-class women.[31] These include the medical knowledge ensuring successful childbirth, education, regulation of the emotions, family management, and all aspects of communication—in other words, knowledge necessary to the reproduction of the modern middle class. In this way, the novel makes it clear that the superior femininity of middle-class women no longer provides an adequate example and curb on the sexual behavior of those around them. An apparent epidemic of hysterical symptoms in what seemed the most eligible of young women indicated not only to Freud but to popular fiction writers as well that the taste and refinement Malthus once represented as a promising deterrent to sexual reproduction had gone too far. Terrified by signs of desire within themselves, women of taste and sentiment were reacting phobically to signs of desire in men as well. Men of education, in their turn, often seemed more interested in one another than in the company of young women of taste and sentiment. Popular fiction expressed concern that the middle-class body was losing its traditional robustness with the waning of desire, while lower-class populations continued to increase in number. Literature written during the period is of one mind in this respect.

The late Victorian imagination completely abandoned the anxiety that Malthus sought to reproduce in his *Essay on the Principle of Population*. Authors and intellectuals who contributed to the twin myths of imperial decline and human degeneration that cast a shadow over the end of the nineteenth century worked within the problematic of his *Principles of Political Economy*, where Malthus argued that surplus production would turn against itself and brings about a progressive dwindling of desire. In view of their consolidation as a class of experts and professionals, however, we need to ask whether these authors and intellectuals simply responded to the catalog of aberrant appearances and behaviors for which the fin-de-siècle is known. Or did they produce the anxieties that flowered into the symptom of a middle class whose reproductive capacities were declining, its men being too crude and its women too refined of sensibility to mate?

It is important, I believe, to acknowledge yet another feature appropriated for modern masculinity from the gender whose ethos and function in modern cultures it was usurping. This new group represented their power as producers of cultural capital as entirely dependent on an earlier generation of rugged individuals who came into power on the basis of capital alone. In Stoker's novel, significantly, this role is represented only by the stalwart American capitalist Quincey Morris, whom Stoker kills off in hand-to-hand combat with the vampire. The

Harkers give their child Quincey's name not to celebrate the aggression of the capitalist so much as to bury and memorialize it; this group acquires its identity not as a dependant of the capitalist businessman but as a body whose knowledge keeps England safe for motherhood. To do so, as I have explained, its members must appropriate Mina's role as the gatherer, classifier, synthesizer, and disseminator of information. In thus revising middle-class masculinity, Dracula suggests as surely as does She that individuals don't in fact unfold from within themselves and pursue their own innate desires for objects that society deems appropriate. On the contrary, they perform a score or enact a melodrama that does not have the reproduction of the modern individual in mind.

From the beginning, novels were accused of implanting ideas in the minds of women who lacked knowledge of the world, ideas capable of rendering them unfit companions to men and mothers to children. While I doubt that most educated people thought that novels, like vampires, would actually change the individual who consumed them, at least not if that individual were educated, our culture does in fact still think that even highly fictional accounts of the world can distort the way that the public at large understands its relation to the real. Thus the question of censorship, or what we should not be hearing, seeing, or reading, arises along with displays of violence, sexual promiscuity, or disregard for family and government. Seduction or poison—a bad lover, bad food, a drug, or a disease—these figures continue to describe the danger of exposure to impermissible cultural production. Mainstream Victorian fiction considers the difficulties that arise when individual ambitions and desires take antisocial forms and choose the wrong objects as a problem that originates within the individual and requires education, sublimation, and self-restraint. Romance in contrast sees that problem as one that originates outside the individual in a world that allows no alternatives but to belong to the human community as defined by the West or to turn monstrous and perish.

At the same time, novels so different as She, Dracula, The Picture of Dorian Gray, The Heart of Darkness, and The Turn of the Screw, to mention a few obvious cases in point, acknowledge the degree to which fiction had to imagine what was unnatural and aberrant in order to maintain the normative subject and make readers want to embody it. Fiction, I am suggesting, had to think beyond the envelope of individualism in order to pronounce certain of its excesses unthinkable. Late-nineteenth-century romance did exactly that. It offered up the unthinkable, allowing its reader to pursue possibilities that did not originate within them, because those possibilities were only and explicitly literary. We still take pleasure in destructive creativity that temporarily overthrows the norms of realism in order to expose its limitations as the limitations of individualism itself. Nevertheless, as my concluding chapter will suggest, the fact that this fiction equates the pleasure of escaping the limits of individualism with the loss of humanity itself ultimately compels us to defend individualism at any cost. In this respect, we are of one mind with the genre that gave form to the modern individual and continues to defend and update it.

5

THE NECESSARY GOTHIC

To think utopically is to imagine how that insatiable being known as the modern individual might acquire the means to perfect and gratify him- or herself. A conceptual countermove always accompanies such utopian imaginings, as we must immediately devise measures to check the selfish excesses of that individual, lest they encroach on the rights of others. Isn't this the dilemma we confront, for example, in advocating free speech? No sooner do we imagine the possibility of free self-expression than we also feel compelled to curb speech at the point where it turns into hate speech, permits telemarketers to violate the sanctity of our dinner hour, or puts salacious material in the tremulous hands of children. Economic theory observes the same paradox when it insists that capitalism be left to work according to its own laws but then hastens to define those laws as either self-regulating or in need of external controls to bring supply in line with demand. Arguments for free sexual expression similarly limit the scope of their application with such qualifiers as "in the privacy of the home" and "between consenting adults." Throughout this book, I have been interested in the question of when and by what cultural means people came to be softwired with this compulsion to imagine the future in terms of expanding possibilities for individual fulfillment, only, it would seem, so that those same people would fear such possibilities and slap limits on them.

I have identified this pervasive cultural paradox with a change in the novel form that occurred during the Victorian period and fostered great expectations. This body of fiction invites us to imagine better worlds and then turns those wishes so sour that we come to prefer the present reality, fraught as it is with social inequities. Indeed, my favorite novels turn fantasies of unlimited inclusion and human perfectibility into scenes of dashed hopes and monstrous forms of self-gratification with a regularity that tells me that this is precisely the point. Victorian fiction is out to convince us that partial gratification is preferable to a social alternative that indulges what is presumed to be man's unlimited appetite for more. But like most definitions of realism, the model I have just offered is both too loose in logic and too close in terminology to the very paradox it seeks to describe.

In order to provide some sense of the curious turn of cultural thought this paradox actually performed for Victorian readers and the rhetorical power that it still exercises on us as a result, I will pursue two critical tactics. First, I want to approach this paradox by way of the form it took and what it did and did not accomplish as recent feminist theory appropriated certain narrative strategies from Victorian fiction and used them to argue for new reading procedures and a more inclusionary literary canon. Presumably, readings informed by feminist theory sought to make it easier for educated people to imagine both a more diverse faculty and a more democratic social world. Naomi Schor reminds us that feminism's interrogation of power in the academy expressed a "perhaps utopian longing for a different university, a university of differences."[1] Victorian fiction provides the occasion and material for mounting this argument, I believe, because recent feminist criticism sought much the same objective as Victorian novelists once did. Given that feminism's success in the literary disciplines has not made it any easier than Victorian fiction did to imagine expanding the means for self-expression without simultaneously limiting those possibilities, it should be instructive to find out why both fiction and feminism failed to get beyond this paradox. Should this line of questioning succeed, we stand to learn how this feature of Victorian culture continues to inflect our political thinking. After pointing out what feminism shares in this respect with the Victorian novel, I want to try reversing the critical undertow that accompanies modern utopian thought and consider where a reading of Dracula might lead us politically were we to identify with the vampire in rejecting the limits of a realism designed to maintain the autonomy of nation, family, and individual.

What Women Lack

Until the 1980s, when feminism emerged as a major force in novel studies, scholars and critics by and large read novels novelistically. By reading novelistically, I mean that one identifies a lack in the protagonist that he must overcome. Once the protagonist does acquire the missing element—as Robinson Crusoe does land, Tom Jones does a patrimony, or Edward Waverley does British identity—that individual can overcome the obstacle that kept him from improving his position in life and achieve recognition within the community whose order and vigor he consequently renews. The protagonist's lack defines the magical ingredient that both enables self-fulfillment along with social empowerment and creates a reader who feels that lack of social recognition and wants to see it remedied. Self-fulfillment so defined calls for nothing less than a seismic shift in the prevailing social order. The small shock of incorporating a Pamela Andrews, Tom Jones, Fanny Price, or Jane Eyre throws open imaginary doors to individuals with the energy, wit, and desire to occupy positions formerly closed to them. The novel, I have argued, was born as authors gave narrative form to this wish for a social order sufficiently elastic to accommodate individualism.

Feminist literary theory made a swift and telling intervention in this way of reading British fiction when it created a reader willing to consider what a female protagonist lacked and how that lack could be corrected. Feminists identified the feminine lack in terms of agency, by which they usually meant such things as property and patrimony enabling men to effect some kind of social change, however local and temporary. But, taking their cue from fiction, these same critics rarely sought a masculine remedy for this lack in terms of property or position. Instead, feminists established a specific verbal performance as the precondition for achieving authority. Novels from Defoe's to those of Virginia Woolf indicate that an author-heroine has to represent herself as rational, consistent, durable, and personally resourceful before she can argue against some form of bias, do what that bias would not let her achieve, and gain recognition within a community that appears progressive for thus extending the limits of acceptable feminine behavior. This move convinced a generation of readers that acquiring a voice—access to print, or what might be called cultural agency—could compensate for the forms of property that traditionally authorized the rights-bearing citizen.[2]

Thus, for example, in their groundbreaking study *The Madwoman in the Attic*, Sandra Gilbert and Susan Gubar ask us to read novels authored by women as the author's way of gaining compensation through the speech of a fictional surrogate for what she lacked in economic and political terms. They claim that "by projecting their rebellious impulses ... into mad or monstrous women ... female authors dramatize their own ... desire both to accept the strictures of patriarchal society and to reject them. What this means ... is that the madwoman in literature written by women is ... in some sense the *author's* double, an image of her own anxiety and rage."[3] Guided by this model, the reader feels the author/protagonist's lack but refuses to accept it as something she is missing simply because she's a woman. Like Jane Eyre, the reader projects her lack of political agency onto a madwoman who enacts the outrage of every woman's dependency and confinement within a masculine culture. But as the novel detaches action from the heroine and displaces it onto a debased surrogate, one cannot help noticing that the speech act itself acquires a form of power superior to action, one that consequently authorizes not only Brontë's narrator and Brontë herself but also those critics who identify her lack with their own as members of a masculinist discipline. By shifting responsibility for this lack from the natural condition of being female to the cultural institutions that reserve power and privilege for men, feminism clearly made a move in the right direction.

During the 1980s, this way of reading changed which novels were read and taught in British and American classrooms as well as the imagined relationship between individual and nation that compels one to identify with a protagonist. Feminist critics began to read Daniel Defoe's *Moll Flanders* in place of his *Robinson Crusoe*, Samuel Richardson's *Pamela* for Henry Fielding's *Tom Jones*, and Jane Austen's *Emma* rather than Walter Scott's *Waverley*. Because *cultural* authority, as feminism had defined it, depended on a lack of *political* authority, however, this argument left a new generation of feminists with the difficult task of overcoming their lack of political authority without losing the rhetorical power that same lack had given them. Wendy Brown explains this dilemma as a version of what Nietzsche termed *ressentiment*, the claim that because power corrupts truth and compromises moral authority, those without power are especially qualified to speak. To move from a position of lack to one of power, according to this logic, feminism would have to let go of the lack of power, or injury, on which it has based its claims to occupy the moral high ground and explore alternative ethical possibilities.[4] The solution rested on reattaching voice, or cultural power, to politics. Instead of saying that men have what women lack and use that power to prevent women from having it, feminist scholars of the late eighties and nineties, myself included, identified the feminine difference itself as a positive source of authority, though not the same authority reserved for men.[5] Others argued that their exclusion from the public sphere made it possible for women writers to develop new and interesting ways of displaying psychological breadth and subtlety.[6] Before long, still others noticed that eighteenth-century novels used women as the source of feelings that united in a community of sensibility those individuals whom acquisitive individualism would otherwise put asunder.[7] During the 1990s, literary criticism consequently looked to sentimental novels as the imaginary seedbed of a more inclusive nation, increased class mobility, and aesthetic innovation.

The publication of Judith Butler's *Gender Trouble* simultaneously validated and demolished the premise that voice could compensate women for the lack of the forms of political power that men came by naturally.[8] Where Foucauldian historicism had seriously undermined the naturalness of gender and placed women on the same cultural playing field with men, Butler's notion that identity was no more or less than a performance effectively turned the tables on the primacy of the unmarked term, or universal masculinity. Butler made the marked or excluded term—woman, queer, and ultimately drag queen—into the model for all identities, including "straight men." As she famously put it, "the 'presence' of so-called heterosexual conventions within homosexual contexts as well as the proliferation of specifically gay discourses of sexual difference... cannot be explained as chimerical representations of originally heterosexual identities.... The replication of heterosexual constructs in non-heterosexual frames brings into relief the utterly constructed status of the so-called heterosexual original. Thus, gay is to straight not as copy is to original, but, rather, as copy is to copy."[9] According to Butler's model, the individual begins as a mix of possibilities and acquires a gender as he or she drops either feminine qualities or masculine qualities from his or her performative repertoire to become masculine or feminine, respectively. The lack of masculinity is both something women acquire from their culture and the very basis of their identity. Acquiring such an identity is no giddy one-night stand but a lifetime commitment to repeat performances. With this model, one can read novels as culture's way not only of naturalizing, stigmatizing, and updating categories of identity but also of setting the standard for an individual performance: Which performances must a protagonist repeat and which discard? What categorical violations can a heroine get away with and which must she eschew as foreign to her very being? Fiction should have shown us not only that interiority comes from an external source (i.e., writing) but also that repeated performances have over time wrought significant changes on our culture's standard for gender difference. Informed by the understanding that performance—or, for my purposes, fiction—produces identity, feminism might have hijacked certain narrative strategies and reworked them to imagine an order whose authority depended on its responsiveness to the needs and desires of disenfranchised and dependent groups rather than to the claims of property. Let us consider what kept us from doing so.

MOTHER OF FALSE UTOPIAS

In recuperating the softer side of femininity, it seems to me, critics and scholars repeated that event in the history of the European novel known as the inward turn. Georg Lukács identifies 1848 or thereabouts as the moment when the novel abandoned its attempts to imagine a more flexible and inclusive social order.[10] After the midcentury mark, even such consummate novelists as Dickens and Flaubert fill what they define as lacking in the social world not through some small shift in social relations but through a change of heart, the excesses of sentimentalism, escapes into exoticism, and the pleasures of domestic life. Herbert Marcuse's analysis of this moment puts Lukács's disappointment into useful historical perspective. In "The Affirmative Character of Culture," Marcuse describes the moment of the novel's inward turn as a rupture in modern culture that caused an ideal domain of the mental and spiritual to break off from the rest of culture. The decisive characteristic of this new domain is, he claims, "a universally obligatory, eternally better and more valuable world that must be unconditionally affirmed: a world essentially different from the factual world of the daily struggle for existence, yet realizable by every individual for himself 'from within,' without any transformation of the state of fact."[11] Marcuse identifies this displacement of material gratification onto a purely cultural plane as the liberal solution to the problem of economic inequity. The idea is that each individual is responsible for finding within him- or herself emotional, spiritual, or aesthetic compensation for whatever forms of gratification he or she may lack in material terms. Marcuse's account of the inward turn also goes a long way toward explaining how the utopian imagination came to be stalked by a disingenuous counterpart in the form of nostalgic rein-carnations of precapitalist communities that were notably powerless to transform the world defined by realism. As he explains, "the truth of a higher world, of a higher good than material existence," became the means of concealing "the truth that a better material existence" might actually be achieved.[12]

The novel performed its own version of the inward turn as it used a class-specific model of the household to displace the ideal of civil society as the collective body on which one depended for care and protection. In so doing, the novel made that household the model for imagining social relations. Over two decades ago, Nancy Chodorow explained how this peculiar apparatus—peculiar, that is, to capitalist economies—produces gendered individuals, each differentiated from the other in terms of traits specific to a social stratum more or less de-termined by the mother.[13] The household so conceived not only serves as the primary means of interpellation in relation to which we con-tinue to individuate ourselves through repeated acts of compliance to or deviance from familial norms; the modern household also provides the reward one receives for meeting those norms. This household is formed and perpetuates itself on a principle of exogamy that compels us to find a partner outside the maternal household with whom we can reproduce something very much like that household, with the result that it appears both natural and available to everyone.[14]

The formation of a community at the end of *Jane Eyre* encapsu-lates the cultural-historical process that I have in mind: "My Edward and I, then, are happy: and the more so, because those we most love are happy likewise. Diana and Mary Rivers are both married: alter-nately, once every year, they come to see us, and we go to see them. Diana's husband is a captain in the navy: a gallant officer, and a good man. Mary's is a clergyman: a college friend of her brother's; and, from his attainments and principles, worthy of the connexion."[15]

Why Charlotte Brontë must strain to create difference between households that are almost indistinguishable from the heroine's should be obvious. She has her protagonist describe the formation of a new society as the reproduction of the private sphere through a set of marriages that mimic and normalize Jane's marriage to Rochester. Brontë does not even try to assemble this social ideal out of the heterogeneous population that her protagonist encounters during the course of the novel. On the contrary, she begins with Jane's blood relatives—cousins Mary and Diana—and so implies that civil society is made of men whom such women deem "worthy of the connexion." The novel consequently leaves us with a social order that has been renovated one household at a time, until all other forms of kinship have been banished either to the colonies or to Catholic Europe. As it slowly but surely exiles or kills off those characters who dare to exist in alternative living arrangements, *Jane Eyre* universalizes a radically restricted notion of kinship based on the married couple and their biological offspring.[16] In this respect, the novel offers a prolepsis of the formal development of nineteenth-century British fiction itself. After Austen, the exemplary protagonist rarely grows up to become a member of civil society. The Dickensian hero, for example, enters a household that displaces any semblance of the complex and fraught social world he has successfully negotiated. At this point, the limits that the novel has set on his happiness miraculously vanish, along with the fact that such happiness is an exception to the social rule. It is by means of this move, when repeated countless times over, that one class established its own ethnic practices as the national norm and ensured their reproduction in future generations.

If the family in this precise cultural-historical sense served as the mechanism by which the novel canceled its own democratic mission and naturalized the gendered division of labor and political authority, then why did feminist theory and criticism fail to perform a sustained critique of such literary behavior? Unless we can challenge what happens at the level of literature, what chance do we have in political terms? Yes, feminism has produced important examples of antifamilialism over the course of the movement's history. But when examined in a harshly critical light, most such political critiques end up replacing a household composed of the heterosexually monogamous couple and their biological offspring with another version of that household that can in fact do little to change the way a nation distributes goods and services to its population.[17] Judith Butler confronts this problem in an essay on gay marriage when she refuses to say whether extending the legitimacy of the family to lesbian and gay couples would threaten or authorize traditional marriage.[18] This is the way with hegemonic formations, I would suggest: deviations at once threaten and maintain what culture has defined as nature.

The Return of the Repressed

Once novelists displaced the expanded and renewed society imagined by their Enlightenment predecessors with a constricted and idealized household, anyone who tried to imagine a different model of social relations had to grapple with the family first. This, I believe, is how Victorian fiction painted modern utopian thinking into a corner, where it either had to come up with a genuine alternative to the modern family or else offer readers a reformed version of the status quo. At the same time, however, that same fiction banished nonfamilies to a domain resembling the one that Freud identified with the uncanny: a domain that asserts itself in literature and life by suspending realism and common sense, thus undermining our taken-for-granted relation to the real. I would go so far as to say that uncanny experiences are fundamentally collective, involving not only a loss of the difference between inside and outside but a loss of the difference between individual and aggregate as well. Freud's essay on the uncanny labors to separate the thinking of primitive people—always implicitly collective—from the queasiness a modern individual feels when suppressed fantasies well up and overpower the categories on which he or she relies for understanding people, things, and their behavior. But, as Freud himself admits, it is virtually impossible to maintain this difference even in theory.[19] And if that difference cannot be so maintained, I would argue, then the fantasies peculiar to the uncanny provide one way of understanding what our relationships to one another might be like were we not to undergo the separations, identifications, and abjections that turn us into modern individuals. If, as Freud's difficulty in maintaining the boundary between individual and group at the level of the uncanny suggests, modern individuals are first collective and only secondarily individual human beings, then when and how were such individuals made to feel that their very existence would be threatened were they not to form a nuclear family? The problem, as I see it, begins as Victorian fiction offers its readership a glimpse of alternative kinship practices only to demonstrate spectacularly that such alternatives dissolve gender differences and so produce monsters.

Hence Emily Brontë's incestuously similar Catherine and Heathcliff, Mary Shelley's parthenogenetic monster, and Robert Louis Stevenson's Jekyll internally split into Jekyll and Hyde. This is indeed the job of the nineteenth-century gothic: to turn any formation that challenges the nuclear family into a form of degeneracy so hostile to modern selfhood as to negate emphatically its very being. Where the great tradition of Victorian fiction saw modern consciousness as the means to resolve the widening gap between self-fulfillment and what was socially permissible,[20] novels associated with the romance revival took an outward turn. Rather than struggle to keep the Victorian gentleman on the same developmental timeline as his savage forebears, the better to justify the dominion of the West over the rest, Stevenson converts these contraries into a contradiction. In his famous story of 1886, he has Mr. Hyde periodically take over Dr. Jekyll's body and occupy his place in time. Although springing from a single origin, this story proves, the pair can no more live as one than it can live as two independent beings. With the publication of *Dracula* in 1897, as the previous chapter demonstrated, Bram Stoker pushed the logic of monogenesis past the breaking point. Rather than the same ontology with the entirely different temporalities that we encounter in Stevenson, self and other confront each other in Stoker's novel as competing varieties of human being between whom the production of some compromise formation is no longer possible. This is the full-blown logic of polygenesis at work, rendering phobic the idea of humanity as a single family, autonomous, relatively self-sufficient, and dedicated to caring for all its members.

Clearly marked as imaginary, vampire practices represent precisely that notion of kinship as one that reproduces itself at the expense of humanity. Natural reproduction is hardly the issue, however. In one of the more peculiar bedroom scenes in modern literature, Stoker identifies the threat posed by the vampire as primarily cultural, as Dracula systematically undoes the naturalized relations of the modern family:

> On the bed beside the window lay Jonathan Harker, his face flushed and breathing as though in a stupor. Kneeling on the edge of the bed facing outward was the white-clad figure of his wife. By her side stood a tall, thin man, clad in black. His face was turned from us, but the instant we saw, all recognized the

Count.... With his left hand he held both Mrs. Harker's hands, keeping them away with her arms at full tension; his right hand gripped her by the back of the neck, forcing her face down on his bosom. Her white nightdress was smeared with blood, and a thin stream trickled down the man's breast which was shown by his torn-open dress.[21]

Were we to stop reading here, we could anticipate the unfolding of a classic pornographic scenario. But Stoker adds one more sentence designed to quell all conventional eroticism: "The attitude of the two resembled a child forcing a kitten's nose into a saucer of milk" (363). This statement transforms the metonymic chain linking man to woman and woman to man into a set of metaphoric substitutions that reverses the dynamic of normative desire.

The facts that Dracula must keep her hands "away with her arms at full tension" and force "her face down on his bosom" tell us that something like a rape is in progress. Her husband's flushed face and heavy breathing indicate that he is in something like a postcoital "stupor." Kneeling before Dracula, Mrs. Harker's position may suggest fellatio, but she is actually subject to an act of maternal aggression performed by a male who has already enjoyed her husband. By thus usurping the positions of wife, mother, and lover, Dracula strips these figures of their meaning in nineteenth-century porn and subjects them to another libidinal economy. This is a radically overwrought scene: a menstruating male with bodice ripped, a polluted female with nightgown stained, a castrated father, and a phallic mother. For a flickering instant of iconographic confusion before the final sentence reasserts the difference between what this strange man is doing to a woman and how an impatient child might feed a kitten, the rapist behaves as a mother, the lover is truly bisexual, and oral gratification prevails. Against the tide of recent critical opinion, I want to argue that this passage is not using sex to render intolerable the foreigner, the Jew, the Oriental, or the immigrant, the features of which Dracula bears. This novel uses the foreigner, the Jew, the Oriental, and the immigrant to render intolerable all social groupings hostile to the family.[22] What then are these antifamilial rules of kinship, and just why are they so dreadful?

The novel begins by proposing an ideal family and concludes with a family that has incorporated certain qualities of the vampire. This family is detached from geography. Jonathan Harker is the real estate agent responsible for the transaction that allowed Dracula to invade England in the first place. The hybrid child whom he fathers contains some of Dracula's blood, along with the blood of the other men who supplied transfusions to combat the vampire blood within Mina's body. This group forms a polyandrous community to care for one quite ordinary woman and their collective child. Thus here, at the end of the nineteenth century, the family still shapes the community. Finding no safe haven in the English countryside, however, this family requires an international community of experts to secure its reproductive capability.[23] The cast of experts in turn lacks something that it must have before it can perform this service and revitalize a society in decline. As I have pointed out, this cast overcomes that lack only as it incorporates certain features of the vampire. By absorbing these residual cultural elements, the modern middle class adapts to and endures through changing historical conditions.

Still more important to my argument than the forms of aggregation that can be incorporated into a new and less individualistic ruling-class ethos are the gothic elements that cannot be so subsumed in Stoker's holy family. Topping my list of such elements is the curious formation of the heroine that inverts the formation of earlier domestic heroines. Initially, Mina Harker is one of those secondary characters born to serve as man's helpmate. But once bitten she takes over center stage and becomes the focal point and purpose of the labor carried out by her entourage of masculine types: a doctor, a scientist, an American capitalist, and a member of the English gentry, as well as her husband, a real estate agent. In contrast with conventional heroines, Mina is full of information that she has copied from and synthesized for members of the community. Her synthesis blurs the distinction between fact and fiction along with the difference between masculine and feminine labor. Thus Mina, as I have argued, provides the means of transferring certain qualities of vampire culture to the masculine half of her community. By incorporating and then being purified of the very qualities that modern men lack—a common object of desire, collective thinking, and so forth—she comes to embody that lack. In order to become the traditional reproductive woman, she must stop managing information and leave the work of cultural reproduction to men.

In ridding the world and her body of Dracula, the novel eliminates the possibility that individual identity can be formed according to the principle of addiction, which was understood by Victorian medical science as the invasion of an individual's mind and sensibility by a foreign substance capable of overriding that individual's natural desire.[24] While under Dracula's spell, Mina's desire comes from elsewhere and belongs to someone else. Contrary to the domestic novel—which pits a desire that wells up from within the self against the limits imposed on that individual by her social position—the culture of the vampire acknowledges that all identity is cultural at base, therefore external in origin, especially sexual appetite. In Mina's case, however, to say that the individual's desire is not her own but that of someone external to herself does not mean that she is enacting someone else's desire, not if the entire group is made of individuals no different from herself.

The end of individuated desire spells the undoing of any need for fiction to defend the community against excessive individualism, which was, according to Enlightenment versions of the social contract, the main purpose of civil society. With the assumption that individual desire was not only natural but also excessively present in human beings, the idea of property was born: the need to have it as well as the need to protect it. If, however, each individual were to enact the desire of all, then there would be no reason to protect each from all others, thus no need for civil society to defend the autonomy of the home.[25] The same inverse logic holds true for intellectual property. It is one thing for members of a culture of experts to pass around diaries, notes, books, newspapers, and documents. Doing so only reinforces the idea that this printed material arises from thoughts originating in the mind of a specific individual. But it is quite another thing to know what someone is thinking as she thinks it, for this eradicates the boundaries that make her an individual. Having no individuality, Dracula can mimic virtually anyone, male or female. In mimicking, he enters them and knows what they know. In containing him, they in turn know him; indeed, they share the knowledge of all those so incorporated. If any member of the group can carry all that group's knowledge, then what is the point of experts or, for that matter, authors. In this respect, we can say, vampire thinking reverses the gendered division of intellectual labor that Mina Harker was predisposed to violate anyway.[26] Rather than hoarding information for herself, she recasts it in a form that offers the big picture necessary for the group's strategic control of battlefield and institution. Like the desire she feels, the ideas that Mina produces come from and rightfully belong to the group.

But the novel makes Dracula's penetration of her mind less shocking than his melodramatic usurpation of the rights of the Harkers' marriage bed, a violation that overtly eradicates sexual difference. The figure of the breast-feeding male cancels out the categorical distinctions between man, woman, and child maintained by the family, a cancellation represented in and produced by the vampire's needy, all-consuming, and yet inseminating mouth. This organ affords Stoker the means of challenging the natural difference between family and civil society, the one expressing woman's nature and the other man's. Wendy Brown's analysis of the symbolic weight that modern cultures place on the gendered difference between public and private spheres provides a sense of how much, besides sex, is at stake in the difference between man and woman. As she explains, "the autonomous liberal subject is a fantastic creature, born into and existing wholly in the realm of civil society, who disavows the relations, activities, and subjects that sustain him in civil society from their sequestered place in the family. This creature is not only fantastic, however, but ultimately dependent: the 'autonomous' subject depends on the subjection of [his dependents] for emotional and physical sustenance."[27] Dracula's bite may cancel out the principle of difference that inevitably subordinates a marked term to an apparently universal term, as in the difference between woman and man, but the figure of the breast-feeding male makes Stoker's vampire disturbing in another respect as well. Contradicting his traditional role, which is to drain an individual of the humanity that restrains his most basic, presumably bestial impulses, here Dracula performs as the bad breast incarnate to infuse the world with the infectious otherness of foreign blood, along with desires hostile to the reproduction of the human species, as modern culture defines it.[28] Where such a novel as *Jane Eyre* allowed the family to eclipse civil society as the symbolic means of resolving social contradictions, *Dracula* turns the tables and allows a radically inclusive society to render the family obsolete, ending the regime of the liberal individual.

Negating the Negative

Although Stoker's novel makes it all but impossible for us to see the demise of the nuclear family in positive terms, European culture did offer readers the means of doing so. To negate the negative implications of vampire, we might turn to the fantasy of a cosmopolitan world order that lost out and was finally demonized in its struggle with modern nationalism to dominate the modern political imagination. In his 1795 essay "Perpetual Peace," Immanuel Kant argues that a representative republic is the only state capable of rule by law rather than violence. To eliminate the conflict associated with despotism, Kant contends, the rule of law must extend beyond national boundaries and embrace, in theory, all humanity. Thus, as I explained in an earlier chapter, he asks his reader to imagine an all-inclusive world republic that guarantees to all people, no matter their origin, "the conditions of universal hospitality." Hospitality, as he explains it, depends on "the right of a stranger not to be treated as an enemy.... It is not a question of being received as a guest," he continues, "it is rather a right of visit, a right of demanding of others that they admit one to their society."[29] The desires of one group will offset another's, Kant contends, so as to neutralize conflicts that inevitably arise within and among such populations, "if only they are intelligent."[30] By the time Stoker set pen to paper a century later, the situation must have looked entirely different. The migration of people from metropolitan core to colonial periphery and back again, as well as the cultural circulation among metropolitan centers, evidently made it seem as if cosmopolitanism was challenging the nation's autonomy, thus the principle of nationalism itself. By running roughshod over national differences, Stoker's vampire transforms the utopian fantasy of universal hospitality into the xenophobic fantasy of a nation that welcomes strangers only to become something other than itself, a colonizer colonized from within.

Writing at the beginning of the nineteenth century, as I have explained, Kant places the American savage at the limit of those peoples who could be included in the human community, on the grounds that the practice of cannibalism completely inverted the respect for difference required for hospitality. Where the cannibal engulfs the individual in a composite body and so destroys his individuality from without, the vampire enters the individual from without and so destroys his individuality by introducing foreign pollutants. Both produce much the same composite body. Hence the appearance of cannibalism in these novels alongside forms of mesmerism and addiction. For most readers, the categorical violation linking vampirism to cannibalism would be enough to put the final nail in the conceptual coffin I am exploring. Indeed, one might well ask, what new possibilities can be teased from a model where the dead feed on the living?

But this question, I must insist, invites yet others: What if there is no such thing as a new idea? What if new ideas come into being only as we mine history for residual materials and recombine them so as to alter the way we understand our relations to one another? It is fair to say that Locke and Rousseau did precisely this when each came up with a model of the state that reworked sovereignty so as to imagine each individual as the sovereign of his own private domain. Two centuries later, Freud argued that the unconscious mind expressed an individual's deepest and most personal needs by similarly reworking the debris of culture, or "day residue" material.[31] Fast-forward another fifty years to the last half of the twentieth century, and one finds Claude Lévi-Strauss explaining cultural change as just such a recycling process in which categories congeal out of earlier material, rise into dominance, and then disperse once the cultural conflict for which they afford symbolic resolution becomes obsolete.[32] Close on the heels of structural anthropology, Foucault's *Discipline and Punish* turns this process of narrative transformation into a theory of history, as dressage passes from a mere display of horsemanship, or tactic, into a strategy, or method of social engineering essential to the growth and maintenance of the kind of population required for industrial capitalism.[33]

Stoker invites us to listen to the residual, the repressed, the past, the ostensibly dead, much as Freud, Lévi-Strauss, and Foucault do. But in contrast to theories that try to explain how what is outside, past, and dead gets inside our minds and determines what we desire, thus how we imagine the future, Stoker emphasizes the bone-chilling truth that to invite the past in the form of alternative kinship relations into our present may well mean our extinction as liberal individuals. By associating Stoker with twentieth-century theories that lack his apocalyptic edge, I am certainly not implying that he went overboard in making this prediction. I believe he was simply being more forthright on this point than most modern theoreticians. What I am suggesting is that there is something important to be gained from a positive reading of what the Victorian novel deliberately abjects as antagonistic to the very terms in which it negotiates the fraught relationship of self to society. To assume a positive form, a genuinely new way of conceptualizing this relationship will necessarily invalidate all the categories that support and lend their features to differences among classes, races, sexualities, and ethnicities.

That feminism has brought us to a crossroads in cultural history is clear. The line of argument that rests on the politics of difference leads us indirectly back to the liberal individual and wins us the power accruing to negative rights: the right not to be violated in one's body, the right not to be unrepresented, implicitly, then, the right to speak for oneself, the right to be different within specified limits. It goes against all common sense to undervalue these rights, especially in today's political climate. Another line of argument is poised within literary theory, however, and ready to challenge the prevailing notion of identity based on the differences we maintain within the category of the human. This counterargument inverts the concept of difference so as to emphasize what we all share by virtue of our individual deviations from the cultural norms naturalized by the modern family.[34] During the 1990s, feminist theory and criticism together began to mount an argument for the superior reality of identities designated as marked, specific, or dependent in contrast with that normative masculine individual who *depends* on his family of dependents for a semblance of realism. Dominant and subordinate, universal and marked, are, according to the logic of this model, two faces of the same cultural coin. Feminist theory intuited this fundamental truth when it staked out the undervalued, or marked, term as its own, only to back away from this conviction as a variety of groups challenged the right of women to speak as and for those in such a position.

Feminist literary theory had by this point come to understand "women" as nothing more or less than a placeholder for just about everyone who did not feel completely at ease within the category of straight white masculinity, including straight white men. A generation of readers informed by Lacan and Foucault understood full well that modern individuals achieve specificity on the basis of how they either fall short or defy the human standard set by the fantasy of the liberal individual. We knew, in other words, that feminism was not about us so much as an argument for the primacy of the marked term itself, an argument potentially capable of destroying that fantasy. As I have tried to show by pointing out the utopian potential in *Dracula*, the trick of formulating a more adequate notion of the human is to find a way of articulating what we lack in positive rather than negative terms: as the sameness we acquire by virtue of always and necessarily falling short of the cultural norms incorporated in the modern individual and reproduced by the nuclear family.

Notes

Introduction. How Novels Think

1. In *The Making of the Modern Self: Identity and Culture in Eighteenth-Century England* (New Haven: Yale University Press, 2004), Dror Wahrman identifies Reynolds as "the leader of the artistic pack" in producing "a sharp rise in artistic interest in young children" that shifted focus "on their individuality and character." Wahrman notes that Lady Grantham, Reynolds's contemporary, commended him for showing viewers that "children had characters to be 'discovered'" (284). For an analysis of how Reynolds not only built a reputation for himself equivalent to what we now call celebrity but also endowed his subjects with certain of the same qualities, see Martin Postle, "'The Modern Appelles': Joshua Reynolds and the Creation of Celebrity," in *Joshua Reynolds: The Creation of Celebrity*, ed. Martin Postle (London: Tate, 2005), 17–34.

2. Quoted in Richard Dorment, *British Painting in the Philadelphia Museum of Art: From the Seventeenth through the Nineteenth Century* (Philadelphia: University of Pennsylvania Press, 1986), 294.

3. See Fredric Jameson, *The Political Unconscious: Narrative as Socially Symbolic Act* (Ithaca: Cornell University Press, 1981). My description of what it is that novels must compulsively reproduce in order to be novels or what, throughout this study, I call "the individual" is clearly indebted to Fredric Jameson's concept of the "master narrative."

4. For a fuller explanation of the implications of Locke's groundbreaking move, see Nancy Armstrong and Leonard Tennenhouse, "A Mind for Passion: Locke and Hutcheson on Desire," in *Politics and the Passions, 1500–1850*,

ed. Daniela Coli, Victoria Kahn, and Neil Saccamano (Princeton: Princeton University Press, 2005). That work shows, moreover, how Hutcheson reformulated Locke's model of mind to include the internal senses of beauty and virtue.

5. In *Sir Joshua Reynolds: The Subject Pictures* (Cambridge: Cambridge University Press, 1995), Martin Postle explains the relationship between what Reynolds called "fancy pictures," which "allowed Reynolds freedom to try out new ideas," and his portraits of name-brand people (60). The two genres tend to merge in his portraits of children. Of one such portrait, Girl Reading, Postle claims, "the painting becomes not merely a representation of Reynolds's niece with a book, but a representation of the way in which sensibility enters the consciousness, through the self-educative discipline of reading" (77). I find Master Bunbury more interesting for leaving open the question as to whether stories discipline a self that was already evident in the boy or are to be held responsible for endowing his image with individuality. For a fascinating study of Reynolds as a figure who lived out the novelistic logic of individualism I am elaborating, see Richard Wendorf, *Sir Joshua Reynolds: The Painter in Society* (Cambridge: Harvard University Press, 1996).

6. To understand the success of this rhetorical strategy, one need only think of the early modern malcontents—who were at best ridiculous (Malvolio) and at worst lethal (Iago)—and consider how differently we regard the equally ungrateful protagonists of novels from *Robinson Crusoe* to *Jane Eyre* and *Great Expectations*, whom we expect the modern world to accept and reward even so.

7. John Locke, *As Essay Concerning Human Understanding*, ed. Peter H. Nidditch (London: Oxford University Press, 1979), II.xx.6. All citations are of this edition and will henceforward be provided in the text.

8. "*Emma*: A Novel," in *Sir Walter Scott: On Novelists and Fiction*, ed. Ioan Williams (New York: Barnes and Noble, 1968), 230. All citations of Scott's essays on fiction are of this edition and will henceforward be provided in the text.

9. Scott explains that the novel arrived at maturity only with Austen's fiction in these terms: "In its first appearance, the novel was the legitimate child of the romance; and though the manners and general turn of the composition were altered so as to suit modern times, the author remained fettered by many peculiarities of derived from the original style of romantic fiction. These may be chiefly traced in the conduct of the narrative, and the tone of sentiment attributed to the fictitious persons" ("*Emma*: A Novel," 227). In *Institutions of the Novel* (Philadelphia: University of Pennsylvania Press, 1997), Homer O. Brown points out that in using this distinction to equate his moment in time with the maturity of the genre, Scott is producing a history of the novel that itself resembles a novel (187). All citations of Brown are of this edition and will henceforward be provided in the text.

10. Robert Miles, "The 1790s: The Effulgence of Gothic," in *The Cambridge Companion to Gothic Fiction*, ed. Jerrold E. Hogel (Cambridge: Cambridge University Press, 2002), 42.

11. F. R. Leavis, *The Great Tradition: George Eliot, Henry James, Joseph Conrad* (New York: New York University Press, 1964).

12. For this insight, I want to thank Rey Chow, Naoki Sakai, and my other interlocutors at the International Institute for Visual Theory and Cultural Studies at National Chiao Tung University, Taiwan, in June 2002.

13. As J. Paul Hunter has argued extensively and well, "no single word or phrase distinguishes the novel from romance or from anything else, and to settle for 'realism' or 'individualism' or 'character' as the defining characteristic trivializes the conception of a literary species" (*Before Novels: The Cultural Contexts of Eighteenth-Century Fiction* [New York: Norton, 1990], 22–30). I am holding the form of individual that came to dominate British thinking by the end of that century responsible for marginalizing most of the contrary forms that actually gave shape both to the category of the individual and the genre of the novel.

14. In *The Second Treatise of Government*, in *Two Treatises of Government*, ed. Peter Laslett (Cambridge: Cambridge University Press, 1991), John Locke famously defines property in individualistic terms: "Though the Earth, and all inferior Creatures be common to all Men, yet every Man has a *Property* in his own *Person*. This no Body has any Right to but himself. The *Labour* of his Body, and the *Work* of his Hands, we may say, are properly his. Whatsoever then he removes out of the State that Nature hath provided, and left it in, he hath mixed his *Labour* with, and joyned to it something that is his own, and thereby makes it his *Property*" (V.xxvii.287–88).

15. David Hume, *An Enquiry Concerning Human Understanding* (Oxford: Clarendon, 1975), 18. All citations are of this edition and will henceforward be provided in the text.

16. Rousseau's version of this scene has outlived Mandeville's arguably because Mandeville's presupposes a reader who is not quite a modern subject, thus not ready to make the leap of sympathetic identification. Rather than sympathy, Mandeville is interested in exemplifying "pity," of which he says, "all Mankind are more or less affected with it; but the weakest minds generally the most." To prove his point, Mandeville asks us "to look on the defenceless posture of tender limbs first trampled on, then tore asunder; to see the filthy snout digging in the yet living Entrails, suck up the smoking Blood, and now and then to hear the Crackling of the Bones, and the cruel Animal with Savage Pleasure grunt o'er the horrid Banquet" (*The Fable of the Bees* [Hammondsworth: Penguin, 1970], 264–65). I want to note that, rather than emotional events, this version of the scene puts the actions of the "cruel Animal" front and center by converting "the child" into a grisly assemblage of part objects that engage all the senses, making it a scene more

on the order of Foucault's spectacle on the scaffold than a scene of sympathetic identification.

17. Jean-Jacques Rousseau, "Discourse on the Origins and Foundation of Inequality Among Men," in *The Discourses and Other Early Political Writings*, trans. and ed. Victor Gourevitch (Cambridge: Cambridge University Press, 1997), 152.

18. Adam Smith, *The Theory of Moral Sentiments* (Amherst, N.Y.: Prometheus, 2000), 4. All citations are of this edition and will henceforward be provided in the text.

19. In *Imagining Inclusive Society in Nineteenth-Century Novels: The Code of Sincerity in the Public Sphere* (Baltimore: John Hopkins University Press, 2004), Pam Morris makes the point that "when understood as the medium of an urbane harmony of sentiment, as described by Smith, ... natural sympathies were believed to be the natural underpinning of the social fabric" (19).

20. Horace Walpole, *The Castle of Otranto: A Gothic Story*, ed. W. S. Lewis, with introduction and notes by E. J. Clery (New York: Oxford University Press, 1996), 17. All citations are of this edition and will henceforward be provided in the text.

21. Henry Mackenzie, *The Man of Feeling* (New York: Norton, 1958), 23.

22. Jane Austen, *Emma*, ed. James Kinsley (New York: Oxford University Press, 1995), 192. All citations are of this edition and will henceforward be provided in the text.

23. Jane Austen, *Northanger Abbey*, ed. James Kinsley and John Davie (London: Oxford University Press, 2003), 147. All citations are of this edition and will henceforward be provided in the text.

24. In *An Essay Concerning Human Understanding*, Locke was also very careful to invalidate any information that presumed to tell us about the world and yet could not be traced to an origin in the external world. So, for example, he explains, if "[I] frame an *Idea* of the Legs, Arms, and Body of a Man, and join to this a Horse's Head and Neck, I do not make a *false Idea* of anything.... But when I call it a *man* or *Tartar*, and imagine it either to represent some real Being," then "I may err" (II.xxxii.25).

25. In the first chapter of *Scenes of Subjection: Terror, Slavery, and Self-Making in Nineteenth-Century America* (New York: Oxford University Press, 1997), Saidiya V. Hartman offers an example that comments importantly on Rousseau's, in which John Rankin describes in an epistle to his brother the scenes of slavery to which he bore witness. As Hartman points out, although Rankin projects himself onto the victims of whipping, rape, mutilation, and suicide in order "to better understand the other," he confounds his own attempt to identify with the enslaved. "Yet if this violence can become palpable and indignation can be fully aroused only through the masochistic fantasy [of identification with the slave], then it becomes clear that empathy is double

edged, for in making the other's suffering one's own, this suffering is occluded by the other's obliteration" (19).

26. In *Bodies, Masses, Power: Spinoza and His Contemporaries* (London: Verso, 1999), Warren Montag points out that Locke, the architect of British individualism, was haunted by the figure of "the multitude," as "the destructive or destroyed double" of "the people." The multitude, he contends, "is that force partly inside and partly outside the political nation [of property owners] that either, as in Locke's early writings, causes the destruction of government or, as in the *Second Treatise*, is the result of a dissolution of society, the sum of dissociated individuals 'without order or connection,' deprived of any juridical status except a purely negative one" (113).

27. In "Gothic Fiction and the French Revolution," *ELH* 48 (1981), Ronald Paulson says of the prevailing assumption that the term "riot" must refer to some popular rebellion, "in the context of *Northanger Abbey*, the irony is that the exaggeration of the sign falls short of the given reality. But precisely *what* reality?" (533).

28. Ian Watt, *The Rise of the Novel: Studies in Defoe, Richardson, and Fielding* (Berkeley: University of California Press, 1957).

29. In *The Crowd: British Literature and Public Politics* (Berkeley: University of California Press, 2000), John Plotz takes an important stand against the highly influential tradition of thinking that began with Gustave Le Bon's 1895 *Les Foules*, which he holds responsible for a tradition of social scientific thinking about crowds that seizes on Le Bon's method and terminology "to make the passing appear permanent, and the contingent configuration of working-class protest seem a deep-seated fact of the human psyche" (4). It seems to me that in his tendency to hypostasize crowds as the negative image of collective humanity, Le Bon is as much a product of his moment as Stoker is. The problem is that Le Bon's empirical method turns phobia into fact, where Stoker made sure his negative representation of the human aggregate as inhuman would be understood as fantasy down through the generations.

30. H. Rider Haggard, *She: A History of Adventure* (London: Penguin, 2001), 184.

31. In *Imagining Inclusive Society*, Morris associates the appearance of figurations of mass man during the 1860s with a second transformation of the public sphere that resulted from linking direct expression of feelings to "uncontrolled bodily excess" (27). Especially relevant to my project is her observation that "the domination of corporeality in the imagining of mass culture was a decisive factor in the further transformation of the public sphere.... Bodies, within this process of imagining, constituted a complex system of signification to various degrees of abstraction and figuration: signifying bodies, engulfing bodies, brutish bodies, class-ified bodies" (25). Haggard's image of mass humanity includes all the above.

32. In *Cannibals and Philosophers: Bodies of Enlightenment* (Baltimore: Johns Hopkins University Press, 2001), Daniel Cottom offers what I consider the best explanation for the centrality of this figure in modern thought. Having pointed out how cannibalism intrudes on Robinson Crusoe's island kingdom along with the mysterious footprint, Cottom goes on to show how it exerts a subtle pressure across the field of Enlightenment letters and leaves its mark on the nineteenth century: "Through the historical issue of cannibalism we can see that the boundaries of the Hegelian philosophical concept, like those of culture and identity, can be articulated only through a dramatic struggle over signs, territories, and bodies. Cannibalism is imaginable only in and through the self-dividing articulation of cultural, psychological, and conceptual borderlines: through a positing of sameness that must subvert itself in the excessiveness of its every assertion" (178).

33. For a sense of how, by the mid-nineteenth century, the individual was understood in relation to a threat posed by the masses, we might recall that despite his best intentions Friedrich Engels described the Irish living in the slums of Manchester in 1848 much as one would another species:

> The lack of cleanliness, which is not so injurious in the country, where population is scattered, and which is the Irishman's second nature, becomes terrifying and gravely dangerous through its concentration here in the great cities. The Milesian deposits all garbage and filth before his house door here, as he was accustomed to do at home, and so accumulates the pools and dirt-heaps which disfigure the working-quarters and poison the air. He builds a pigsty against the house wall as he did at home, and if he is prevented from doing this, he lets the pig sleep in the room with himself. This new and unnatural method of cattle-raising in cities is wholly of Irish origin.
> (*The Condition of the Working Class in England*, ed. David McLellan [New York: Oxford University Press, 1999], 103)

In *London Labour and the London Poor: The Condition and Earnings of Those that Will Work, Cannot Work, and Will Not Work* (London: C. Griffin and Company, ca. 1861), Henry Mayhew uses the same figure to contrast members of the respectable poor to "the slop-workers of the different trades—the cheap men or non-society hands—who constitute the great mass of paupers in this country. And here lies the main social distinction between the workmen who belong to societies and those who do not—the one maintain their own poor, the others are left to the mercy of the parish" (3:232). In "On Liberty" (1859), John Stuart Mill sees individualism as all but helpless in the face of a new mass culture: "At present individuals are lost in the crowd. In politics it is almost a triviality to say that public opinion now rules the world. The only power deserving the name is that of the masses, and of the governments while they make themselves the organ of the tendencies and instincts of masses" (*On Liberty and Other Essays*, ed. John Gray [Oxford: Oxford University Press, 1991], 73).

1. How the Misfit Became a Moral Protagonist

1. I accept Max Weber's claim that the many of the elements of what he calls "the spirit of modern capitalism," commonly known as the Protestant work ethic, "are the same as the content of the Puritan worldly asceticism, only without the religious basis." But this similarity does not mean the secular ethic of industrial capitalist cultures "was born ... from the spirit of Christian aestheticism" (*The Protestant Ethic and the Spirit of Capitalism* [London: Routledge, 2002], 120–21). On the contrary, I argue, fiction rhetorically appropriated certain elements of Christian asceticism—specifically, the "sanctification of work as a calling," which entails delayed gratification—for an entirely new purpose: the harnessing of desire to serve the material ends of an emergent middle class (121). The secularization of morality, from this perspective, is not the mechanism or wish on the part of that class to exploit the labor of others so much as the symptom of a cultural hegemony inducing members of that class themselves to embrace that rhetoric as truth and live out its master narrative.

2. Nancy Armstrong and Leonard Tennenhouse, "A Mind for Passion: Locke and Hutcheson on Desire," in *Politics and the Passions, 1500–1850*, ed. Daniela Coli, Victoria Kahn, and Neil Saccamano (Princeton: Princeton University Press, 2005) argues that by cutting the operations of the mind free, John Locke's epistemology effectively renders obsolete the early modern passions, as described, for example, in Thomas Burton's *Anatomy of Melancholy* (1621). Claiming that reason alone could not explain the individual's affective responses to stimuli, Thomas Hutcheson was among those who proceeded to argue for internal senses of beauty and morality that worked analogously to the external senses to produce an aesthetic sensibility and capacity for moral judgment. While not all individuals developed their responses to beauty and virtue, each possessed as part of his or her natural equipment the capacity to do so, just as each possessed the capacity to develop rational judgment.

3. Jacques Derrida, *Of Grammatology*, trans. Gayatri Chakrovorty Spivak (Baltimore: Johns Hopkins University Press, 1976), 144–45.

4. In *Family Fortunes: Men and Women of the English Middle Class, 1780–1850* (Chicago: Chicago University Press, 1987), Leonore Davidoff and Catherine Hall show that a new class of businessmen did not actually come into power in England until the 1830s. And when they did, it was not on the basis of capital. The hegemony of the modern middle class was made possible, they contend, in the decades following the French Revolution, while England was off the gold standard and the basis for credit shifted suddenly and decisively

to a man's character as displayed in the external signs of morality: a charming wife, a handsome house with servants, and a robust family.

5. Government by what Althusser calls the ideological state apparatus and I have called simply fiction, or the ability to shape how a literate population imagines its relation to the real, not only establishes itself by means of violence but also needs to back up the threat of force with the very real possibility of force. Most of the time and in the vast majority of cases, as Althusser claims, "subjects 'work,' they 'work by themselves,'" insofar as they understand themselves to be self-governing subjects. This is not true, however, of "the 'bad subjects' who on occasion provoke the intervention of one of the detachments of the (repressive) state apparatus" ("Ideology and Ideological State Apparatuses [Notes Towards an Investigation]," in *Lenin and Philosophy, and Other Essays*, trans. Ben Brewster [New York: Monthly Review Press, 1971], 181). These subjects serve, as do Crusoe's five hostages, as examples that support the representation of violence and so turn it into an effective means of state control.

6. See Raymond Williams, *The Long Revolution* (New York: Columbia University Press, 1961); and Nancy Armstrong and Leonard Tennenhouse, *The Imaginary Puritan: Literature, Intellectual Labor, and the Origins of Personal Life* (Berkeley: University of California Press, 1992).

7. Louis Althusser, "Rousseau: The Social Contract," in *Politics and History: Montesquieu, Rousseau, Hegel, and Marx*, trans. Ben Brewster (London: NLB, 1972), 113–61.

8. Only under the terms of the exchange Rousseau called the social contract does the individual submit solely to his own authority in the form of the social body, because that body, "being formed of the individuals that compose it, neither has nor can have any interest contrary to theirs" (*The Social Contract*, ed. Lester G. Crocker, trans., Lester G. Crocker and Henry J. Tozer [New York: Washington Square, 1967], 21).

9. "For the mechanism [of the contract] to carry out its function properly," Althusser argues, Rousseau must add the condition that "'the people must have adequate information,' i.e. there must be enlightenment" ("Rousseau: The Social Contract," 150). Thus, Rousseau explains, a body politic that includes all citizens depends on their being "made to see objects as they are, sometimes as they ought to appear." Individual desire must be directed toward these objects in just the right way. Not only must the public be "shown the good path it is seeking," but it must also "be guarded from the seductions of private interests" (*The Social Contract*, 41).

10. In *Wayward Contracts: The Crisis of Political Obligation in England, 1640–1674* (Princeton: Princeton University Press, 2004), Victoria Kahn argues that early modern contract theory was distinguished from its predecessors by its emphasis on the power of the political contract to bring new obligations into existence.

This emphasis on the constitutive power of contract ... makes the new politics part of the history of poetics.... What this meant in practical terms was that, from thinking of politics as a prudential activity, an activity often linked to a normative conception of virtue, many seventeenth-century men and women came to think of politics as a realism of poetics, even fabrication. The fiction of the political contract was the single most important way of thinking about politics in the early modern period. (15–16)

Where early modern culture converted contractual thinking into poetics, I would argue, the culture of the novel returned the favor and turned the two parties implied by the contract into the conceptual categories organizing social experience.

11. David Hume, "Of the Original Contract" (1748), in *Political Essays*, ed. Knud Haakonssen (Cambridge: Cambridge University Press, 1994), 201. All citations are of this edition and will henceforward be provided in the text.

12. It is worth noting that in his essay "Of the Origins of Government," Hume universalizes the tension between the subject who freely expresses himself and the subject of government, thus granting the individual much the same supplementary energy that novels granted to their misfit protagonists: "In all governments, there is a perpetual intestine struggle, open or secret, between Authority and Liberty; and neither of them can ever absolutely prevail in the contest" (*Political Essays*, 22).

13. Daniel Defoe, *Robinson Crusoe*, ed. Michael Shinagel (New York: Norton, 1994), 65. All citations are of this edition and will henceforward be provided in the text.

14. In his chapter "Of Paternal Power," Locke imagines the child much as he imagines unowned territory, that is to say, as a lack of reason that translates directly into a lack of political rights; at that point, the child is under paternal government. But once the son's "Understanding be fit to take the Government of his Will," then father and son "are equally Subjects of the same Law together, without any Dominion left in the Father over the Life, Liberty, or Estate of his Son" (*Two Treatises on Government*, ed. Peter Laslett [Cambridge: Cambridge University Press, 1988], II.59.26–30).

15. In *The Imaginary Puritan* (184–95), Leonard Tennenhouse and I make the argument that as the sign of individualism Crusoe's property is a result of intellectual rather than manual labor from the beginning. Confronted with threats to his individualism, Crusoe quickly delegates to Friday the violence required to maintain himself, thereby effectively denying the degree to which government by ideology depends on the very forms of force that it displaces.

16. Daniel Defoe, *Moll Flanders*, ed. Edward H. Kelly (New York: Norton, 1973), 146. All citations are of this edition and will henceforward be provided in the text.

17. See Carole Pateman, *The Sexual Contract* (Stanford: Stanford University Press, 1988), 50–60, 154–89. Following Pateman, a tradition of feminist literary criticism called attention to the vast body of literature demonstrating that, in being represented in civil society in and through fathers, brothers, husbands, and even sons, women were not represented so much as oppressed, even in some cases enslaved. Most recently, Wendy Brown has argued that the entire fantasy of the liberal individual depends to a great extent on the fact that men exceed the domestic limits embodied in the women and children on whom they depend for both emotional and physical support; see *States of Injury: Power and Freedom in Late Modernity* (Princeton: Princeton University Press, 1995).

18. As Moll explains, "My true name is so well known in the Records, or Registers at *Newgate*, and in the *Old-Baily*, and there are some things of such Consequence still depending there, relating to my particular Conduct, that it is not to be expected I should set me name or the Account of my Family to this Work" (7). Roxana similarly fears exposure: "The Scene is laid so near the Place where the Main Part of it was transacted, that it was necessary to conceal the Names and the Persons; lest what cannot be yet entirely forgot in that Part of the Town, shou'd be remember'd, and the Facts traced back too plainly; by the many People yet living, who woul'd know the Persons by the Particulars" (Daniel Defoe, *Roxana; or, The Fortunate Mistress*, ed. John Mullan [Oxford: Oxford University Press, 1996], 1; all citations are of this edition and will henceforward be provided in the text).

19. John Mullan, "Appendix: The Textual History of *Roxana*," in *Roxana*, 338.

20. Samuel Richardson, *Pamela; or, Virtue Rewarded*, ed. Peter Sabor (London: Penguin, 1985), 265.

21. See Jay Fliegelman, *Prodigals and Pilgrims: The American Revolution Against Patriarchal Authority, 1750–1800* (Cambridge: Cambridge University Press, 1982), 83–89; and Dorothea E. von Mücke, *Virtue and the Veil of Illusion: Generic Innovation and the Pedagogic Project in Eighteenth-Century Literature* (Stanford: Stanford University Press, 1991).

22. On the success of Richardson's heroine, Henry Fielding famously expressed these sentiments in the preface to *Shamela*:

> The Instruction it conveys to Servant-Maids is, I think, very plainly this, To look out for their Masters as sharp as they can. The Consequences of which will be, besides Neglect of their Business, and the using of all manner of Means to come at Ornaments of their Persons, that if the Master is not a Fool, they will be debauched by him; and if he is a Fool, they will marry him. . . . my Friend, the whole narrative is such a Misrepresentation of Facts, such a Perversion of Truth, as you will, I am perswaded, agree, as soon as you have perused the Papers I

now inclose to you, that I hope you or some other well-disposed Person, will communicate these Papers to the Publick, that this little Jade may not impose on the World, as she hath on her Master.

> ("Prefatory Letter from Parson Oliver to Parson Tickletext,"
> in *Shamela*, ed. Judith Hawley
> [London: Penguin, 1999], 12)

23. See Homer O. Brown, "The Institution of the English Novel: Defoe's Contribution," *Novel* 29 (1996): 299–318.

24. Jane Austen, *Persuasion*, ed. Patricia Meyer Spacks (New York: Norton, 1995), 165–66.

25. Jane Austen, *Pride and Prejudice*, ed. Donald J. Gray (New York: Norton, 1966), 75. All citations are of this edition and will henceforward be included in the text.

26. Benedict Anderson, *Imagined Communities: Reflections on the Origin and Spread of Nationalism* (London: Verso, 1983).

27. Jeremy Bentham, *Bentham's Theory of Fictions*, ed. C. K. Ogden (New York: Harcourt, Brace, 1932), 123.

2. WHEN NOVELS MADE NATIONS

1. See my "The Nineteenth-Century Austen: A Turn in the History of Fear," *Genre* 23 (1990): 227–46.

2. During this period, members of and aspirants to the modern middle class went to great lengths to distinguish themselves as English in comparison to the more primitive folk populating the so-called Celtic periphery; see, for example, Michael Hechter, *Internal Colonialism: The Celtic Fringe in British National Development, 1536–1966* (Berkeley: University of California Press, 1975). The point I want to make here is a version of the one Foucault makes in *Discipline and Punish: The Birth of the Prison*, trans. Alan Sheridan (New York: Vintage, 1979), namely, that the modern middle classes never required members of the cultures they colonized to practice forms of self-constraint that they had not first tried out on themselves.

3. Étienne Balibar, "Subject and Subjectivation," in *Supposing the Subject*, ed. Joan Copjec (London: Verso, 1994), 9.

4. Ibid.

5. Gilles Deleuze, "Repetition for Itself," *Difference and Repetition*, trans. Paul Patton (New York: Columbia University Press, 1994), 100–101.

6. Étienne Balibar, "Citizen Subject," trans. James B. Swenson Jr., in *Who Comes After the Subject*, ed. Eduardo Cadava, Peter Connor, and Jean-Luc Nancy (New York: Routledge, 1991), 51.

7. Georg Lukács, *The Historical Novel*, trans. Hannah Mitchell and Stanley Mitchell (London: Merline, 1962), 54, 63.

8. See Homer O. Brown, *Institutions of the English Novel* (Philadelphia: University of Pennsylvania Press, 1997), 138–70.

9. In her introduction to *Frankenstein*, ed. J. Paul Hunter (New York: Norton, 1996), Mary Shelley explains, "I busied myself to *think of a story*... one which would speak to the mysterious fears of our nature, and awaken thrilling horror—one to make the reader dread to look around, to curdle the blood, and quicken the beatings of the heart. If I did not accomplish these things, my ghost story would be unworthy of its name" (171). All citations of *Frankenstein* are of this edition and will henceforward be included in the text.

10. In *Circles of Fear and Desire: A Study of Gothic Fantasy* (Chicago: University of Chicago Press, 1985), William Patrick Day spells out what is still the prevailing opinion, namely, that "no discussion of the Gothic can avoid discussing Freud," because, he maintains, "Gothic fantasy is the expression of fears and desires created, but unacknowledged by conventional culture. Like a dream, it reveals the inner life of the individual" (177). More recently, in *Gothic Writing, 1750–1820: A Genealogy* (Manchester: Manchester University Press, 2002), Robert Miles seeks to modify the assumption that "Gothic represents the subject in a state of deracination, of the self finding itself dispossessed of its own house, in a condition of rupture, disjunction, fragmentation" on grounds that gothic writing "should be understood as literary 'speech' in its own right, and not the symptom, the signification, of something else 'out there,' or 'in here.' ... Gothic formulae are not simply recycled, as if in the service of a neurotic, dimly understood drive; rather, Gothic texts revise one another, here opening up ideologically charged issues, there enforcing a closure" (3).

11. Sir Walter Scott, *Waverley: or, 'Tis Sixty Years Since*, ed. Claire Lamont (Oxford: Oxford University Press, 1981), 5. All citations are of this edition and will henceforward be included in the text.

12. Ian Duncan offers an especially compelling version of this formula in *Modern Romance and Transformations of the Novel: The Gothic, Scott, Dickens* (Cambridge: Cambridge University Press, 1992): "In short, the utopian 'marriage of Scotland and England' with which *Waverley* closes turns out to be a delicate and complex exchange, in which the young Southron is the donor of revived historical possibility in the form of capital and political connections. Fresh English wealth is the romance currency that restores the real historical place, lean and battle-scarred and wily, of old Scotland" (98). In *Bardic Nationalism: The Romantic Novel and the British Empire* (Princeton: Princeton University Press, 1997), Katie Trumpener argues against critical readings of the marriage plot in early-nineteenth-century fiction as deceptively transparent: "these novels are also engaged, from the outset, in a complicated political reconciliation process. What they attempt is not only the cultural rapprochement of a colonizing nation and colonized one, but also, more paradoxically the reconciliation between the imperialist project of a United Kingdom and

Wolf Tone's vision of an internally united Ireland, in which shared purpose transcends differences of creed and culture" (137).

13. In "The 1790s: The Effulgence of Gothic," in *The Cambridge Companion to Gothic Fiction*, ed. Jerrald E. Hogel (Cambridge: Cambridge University Press, 2002), Robert Miles identifies the 1790s with an "upsurge in Gothic works.... From 1788 until 1807 the Gothic maintains a market share of around 30%.... If there was a peak," he concludes, "it is in 1800, the year in which the largest number of Gothic novels were published" (42). Miles also identifies such "marketing cues" as "geographical features," "architectural features," "ghost and its cognates," "exotic names," and "generic or historical figures" that can characterize this fiction (41–42).

14. Contrasting the situation in early-nineteenth-century England with that of France, Lukács attributes the epic scope of Scott's novel to the fact that his "world-view ties him very closely to those sections of society which had been precipitated into ruin by the industrial revolution and the rapid growth of capitalism. Scott belongs neither with the ardent enthusiasts of this development, nor with its pathetic, passionate indicters. He attempts by fathoming historically the whole of English development to find a 'middle way' for himself between warring extremes. He finds in English history the *consolation* that the most violent vicissitudes of class struggle have always finally calmed down into a glorious 'middle way'" (*The Historical Novel*, 32, my emphasis). I agree with Lukács's use of the language of mourning to describe Scott's political position but disagree with the assumption that the novel managed to resolve the ambivalence generated by the author's peculiar affiliation with both sides of a struggle in which one was destined to lose. What I describe as a failure to mourn successfully is not one that can be located in Scott or any individual author so much as in a consistent failure to make the novel perform political work hostile to the ideology of the novel form itself.

15. In *The Psychic Life of Power: Theories in Subjection* (Stanford: Stanford University Press, 1997), Judith Butler explains how "melancholia rifts the subject, marking a limit to what it can accommodate. Because the subject does not, cannot, *reflect* on that loss, that loss marks the limits of reflexivity, that which exceeds (and conditions) its circuitry. Understood as a foreclosure, that loss inaugurates the subject and threatens it with dissolution" (23). Although melancholia, in contrast to mourning, may be understood as a process that keeps the fact of loss outside the self and in abeyance, melancholia may also have internal manifestations: "If in melancholia a loss is refused, it is not for that reason abolished. Internalization preserves loss in the psyche; more precisely, the internalization of loss is part of the mechanism of its refusal. If the object can no longer exist in the external world, it will then exist internally, and that internalization will be a way to disavow the loss, to keep it at bay, to stay or postpone the recognition and suffering of loss" (134). By preserving the difference between self and other, melancholic incorporation

structurally contradicts the synthesis and acceptance of the internalization of loss that marks successful mourning.

16. In *Culture and Truth: The Remaking of Social Analysis* (Boston: Beacon, 1989), it makes sense to view what Renato Rosaldo calls "imperialist nostalgia" in precisely these terms, where the missionaries to oceanic cultures first saw the cultures they hoped to "improve" as debased versions of Western modernity and, later, represented the result of improvement as the destruction of a pure and unsullied exoticism (69). The same can be said of Eric Hobsbawm and Terence Ranger's account of the archaic Scottish and Welsh folk traditions that were created out of the local ways of life decimated in the making modern Britain; see *Invention of Tradition*, ed. Eric Hobsbawm and Terence Ranger (Cambridge: Cambridge University Press, 1983), 1–4.

17. Duncan sees the renovation of Tully-Veolan in terms of "the figure of an essential, original, authentic British place or ground, concealed or 'underneath' history.... The essence of the myth is that, at the end, social relations are not transformed ... they resume their place, idealized within the imagination of the property-owner as the function of his privilege.... [A] world torn apart by historical force of economic and political difference is brought together in an extended patriarchal family" (*Modern Romance and Transformations of the Novel*, 104–5).

18. Percy Bysshe Shelley, introduction to Shelley, *Frankenstein*, 5.

19. My point in introducing the term *terra nullius* here is to suggest that by situating us in the Artic, Shelley indicates that nothing less is at stake in her novel than a revision of Locke's liberal individual and his basis in property. Since the Middle Ages, international law—following Roman law—could recognize a nation's legal occupation of a foreign territory by declaring it *terra nullius*, a blank land over which no one yet had dominion (see Andrew F. Burghardt, "The Bases of Territorial Claims," *Geographical Review* 63 [1973]: 225–45). At the advent of the modern period in British letters, John Locke seized on this figure to assert that human intelligence began as "white paper void of all characters," which was subsequently inscribed by the sensations received through encounters with the world. For a fully developed account of this cultural event and its consequences, see Nancy Armstrong and Leonard Tennenhouse, "A Mind for Passion: Locke and Hutcheson on Desire," in *Politics and the Passions, 1500–1850*, ed. Daniela Coli, Victoria Kahn, and Neil Saccamano (Princeton: Princeton University Press, 2005).

20. Victor Frankenstein's brief encounter with the Irish says it all: "I was exceedingly surprised on receiving so rude an answer from a stranger; and I was also disconcerted on perceiving the frowning and angry countenances of his companions. 'Why do you answer me so roughly?' I replied: 'surely it is not the custom of Englishmen to receive strangers so inhospitably.' 'I do not

know,' said the man, 'what the custom of the English may be; but it is the custom of the Irish to hate villains'" (120).

21. For the best examples of this way of reading the novel, see Margaret Homans, *Bearing the Word: Language and Female Experience in Nineteenth-Century Women's Writing* (Chicago: University of Chicago Press, 1986), 100; and Sandra Gilbert, "Horror's Twin: Shelley's Monstrous Eve," in *Critical Essays on Mary Wollstonecraft Shelley*, ed. Mary Lowe-Evans (New York: Hall, 1998), 55.

22. Immanuel Kant, "Perpetual Peace: A Philosophical Sketch," in *Kant: Selections*, ed. Lewis White Beck (Englewood Cliffs, N.J.: Prentice Hall, 1988), 439. All citations are of this edition and will henceforward be provided in the text.

23. In "Remarks on Frankenstein," *Blackwood's Edinburgh Magazine* 2 (1818), Sir Walter Scott classified *Frankenstein* as one of those tales of horror that, "though wild in incident, is written in plain and forcible English without exhibiting that mixture of hyperbolical Germanisms with which tales of wonder are usual told. . . . The ideas of the author are always clearly as well as forcibly expressed." Amid this praise for the novel's fidelity to the vicissitudes of human nature, Scott notes that "the author has however two apologies—the first, the necessity that his monster should acquire those endowments [of a sophisticated education], and the other, that his neighbours were engaged in teaching the language of the country to a young foreigner" (619).

24. In *Romanticism and the Human Species: Poetry, Population, and the Discourse of the Species* (Cambridge: Cambridge University Press, 2000), Maureen McLane argues, "The novel demonstrates, perhaps against itself, that acquisition of 'literary refinement' fails to humanize the problematic body—the ever-unnamed monster. The monster thus introduces and embodies an anthropological problem which literature fails to resolve (within the novel) and yet which literature displays (in the fact of the novel itself)" (84). In *The Gothic Text* (Stanford: Stanford University Press, 2005), Marshall Brown offers an equally provocative explanation for the novel's curious inability to arrive at a resolution: "One of the book's commonest turns of phrase reflects the way a mass or heap can abruptly become an uncanny enemy. For both Frankenstein and his author have a counting problem. . . . The totality exceeds definition—not that the monster is measurably too big, but that it is somehow, unaccountably, too much to grasp. It can be made, perhaps even in a sense born, but it cannot be conceived" (191).

25. Viewing gothic fictions as thought experiments, Marshall Brown provides this philosophical explanation as to why Shelley's characters have so much difficulty looking at the monster: "Truth (in the definition used by Kant) is the coincidence of a perception with a judgment. But the monster cannot be properly perceived because it cannot be looked at without panic,

and it cannot be properly judged because it has no name with which to formulate an objective statement about it" (*The Gothic Text*, 198).

26. In *Cannibals and Philosophers: Bodies of Enlightenment* (Baltimore: Johns Hopkins University Press, 2001), Daniel Cottom explains the eighteenth-century preoccupation with cannibalism as offering a means of disavowing the possibility of polygenesis (which would justify consuming the other) and so maintaining the concept of universal humanity (which made consuming another an unimaginably heinous offense). This argument overrode attempts to recuperate the cannibal for universal humanity by leveling the eating of one's fellow humans with other forms of human violence and judging it on practical grounds. "In the eighteenth century," Cottom contends, "it become possible to see the fascination with cannibalism as a displacement and disavowal of the European consumption of human flesh that was most grievously carried out in the slave trade but also in myriad forms of exploitation, colonialism, enforced dependency, hierarchy, and, as William Blake would say, Christian mercy" (149).

3. Why a Good Man Is Hard to Find in Victorian Fiction

1. In "Representing Violence; or, How 'the West' Was Won," in *The Violence of Representation: Literature and the History of Violence*, ed. Nancy Armstrong and Leonard Tennenhouse (London: Routledge, 1989), Tennenhouse and I describe the protagonist's verbal authority as a form of aggression that allows her to overcome all rivals—indeed, virtually everyone who does not observe her domestic virtues—while, at the same time, appearing to be the victim of aggression at the hands of those same rivals (5–9).

2. In *The History of Sexuality*, vol. 1, *An Introduction*, trans. Robert Hurley (New York: Vintage, 1990), Foucault's explanation of the Victorian hystericization of the female body offers perhaps the most eloquent testimony to the sexual component of this psychological excess and the woman as its embodiment:

> Surrendering to fears, creating remedies, appealing for rescue by learned techniques, generating countless discourse, it was the first to commit itself to sexual erethism. The bourgeoisie began by considering that its own sex was something important, a fragile treasure, a secret that had to be discovered at all costs. It is worth remembering that the first figure to be invested by the deployment of sexuality, one of the first to be "sexualized," was the "idle" woman. She inhabited the outer edge of the "world," in which she always had to appear as a value, and of the family, where she was assigned a new destiny charged with conjugal and parental obligations. Thus there emerged the "nervous" woman,

the woman afflicted with "vapors"; in this figure, the hysterization of woman found its anchorage point. (121)

John Kucich tailors this concept for the subtler eroticism of the Victorian novel; he argues that

> although repression is often imagined by Victorian novelists as a form of social duty, explicitly presenting its anti-individualism as a surrender to collective will, it finally engenders an isolated subjectivity, through its silences and through the withdrawal implicit in its operation. Victorian repression, as a model of desire, promises an intense emotional upheaval, but it tries to deny the openness of that upheaval to anything that lies outside the self. In other words, the form within which self-negating libido is imagined in the nineteenth century is not a ritualistic or symbolic identification with others; this culturally organized form for desired death becomes, paradoxically, the boundary of individual consciousness and interiority. Through repression, characters in nineteenth-century fiction restrict self-negation to an internal, emotional consumption that scrupulously preserves individual will and emotional inviolability from penetration by others.
>
> (*Repression in Victorian Fiction*
> [Berkeley: University of California Press, 1987], 27)

3. The following statement is just one of Charles Darwin's several attempts to ground modern culture in primitive nature:

> I cannot doubt that language owes its origins to the imitation and modification of various natural sounds, the voices of other animals, and man's own instinctive cries, aided by signs and gestures. When we treat of sexual selection we shall see that primeval man, or rather some early progenitor of man, probably first used his voice in producing some true musical cadences, that is in singing, as do some of the gibbon-apes at the present day; and we must conclude from a widely-spread analogy, that this power would have been especially exerted during the courtship of the sexes—would have expressed the various emotions such as love, jealousy, triumph,—and would have served to challenge rivals. It is, therefore, probable that the imitation of musical cries by articulate sounds may have given rise to words expressive of various complex emotions.
>
> (Charles Darwin,
> *The Descent of Man, And Selection in Relation to Sex*
> [Princeton: Princeton University Press, 1981], 88)

All subsequent references are of this edition and will henceforth be provided in the text.

4. As Freud explains, "Our observations [on hysteria] throw a light on the contradiction between the dictum 'hysteria is a psychosis' and the fact that among hysterics may be found people of the clearest intellect, strongest will, greatest character and highest critical power. This characterization holds good of their waking thoughts; but in their hypnoid states they are insane, as we all are in dreams. Whereas, however, our dream-psychoses have no effect upon our waking state, the products of hypnoid states intrude into waking life in the form of hysterical symptoms" (Sigmund Freud and Josef Breuer, *Studies on Hysteria*, in *The Standard Edition of the Complete Psychological Works of Sigmund Freud*, trans. James Strachey [London: Hogarth, 1973–4], 1:13).

5. J. LaPlanche and J.-B. Pontalis, *The Language of Psycho-Analysis*, trans. Donald Nicholson-Smith (New York: Norton, 1973), 122–23.

6. Georg Lukács, *The Historical Novel*, trans. Hannah Mitchell and Stanley Mitchell (London: Merline, 1962).

7. Emily Brontë, *Wuthering Heights*, ed. Richard J. Dunn (New York: Norton, 2003), 20–21. All citations are of this edition and will henceforward be provided in the text.

8. For example, according to Glen Caveliero, *The Supernatural and English Fiction* (Oxford: Oxford University Press, 1995), "In *Wuthering Heights* preternatural elements coalesce with visionary ones. Whether Lockwood physically hears the ghost of Cathy crying at the window, or whether he only dreams about it, is secondary to the impression that in supernatural reality her spirit is there, as in her dying ravings she had predicted that it would be" (3–4).

9. For a full and sophisticated explanation of the uses to which masochism was put in Victorian culture, see John Kucich, "Olive Schreiner, Masochism, and Omnipotence: Strategies of a Preoedipal Politics," *Novel: A Forum on Fiction* 36, no. 1 (2002): 79–109.

10. In *Wuthering Heights: A Study* (Athens: University of Ohio Press, 1994), U. C. Knoepflmacher, for example, regards Emily Brontë as "one half of a divided authorial presence that is pitted against the other half, represented in the book as Catherine/Heathcliff.... [As the sibling] least willing to relinquish the childhood fantasy world all four children had shared, Emily is also very much a Catherine/Heathcliff. Despite her greater physical strength, she dies before Anne and Charlotte. And ... the circumstances of her death strangely mirrored Heathcliff's fictional self-consumption" (81).

11. Charles Dickens, *Dombey and Son*, ed. Alan Horsman (Oxford: Oxford University Press, 1999), 17. All subsequent references are of this edition and will henceforward be provided in the text.

12. In "Aggressiveness in Psychoanalysis," in *Écrits, a Selection*, trans. Bruce Fink (New York: Norton, 2002), Jacques Lacan uses Hegel to refute

Darwin's claim that aggression, along with genital desire, is natural in human beings: "The satisfaction of human desire is possible only when mediated by the other's desire and labor. While it is the recognition of man by man that is at stake in the conflict between Master and Slave, this recognition is based on a radical negation of natural values, whether expressed in the master's sterile tyranny or in work's productive tyranny" (27).

13. Andrew Elfenbein, "Managing the House in *Dombey and Son,*" *Studies in Philology* 92 (1995): 363.

14. See Claude Lévi-Strauss, *The Savage Mind* (Chicago: University of Chicago Press, 1966), 17, for a description of Dickens's use of *bricolage* in *Great Expectations* to convert the instruments of political aggression into objects that can be contained within the "suburban castle" known as Wemmick's castle.

15. F. R. Leavis describes the Conradian sensibility, for example, as "that of a writer so intimately experienced in the strains and starvations of the isolated consciousness, and so deeply aware of the sense in which reality is social, something established and sustained in a kind of collaboration" (*The Great Tradition* [New York: New York University Press, 1964], 209).

16. In "Desiring Difference: Sympathy and Sensibility in *Jane Eyre,*" *Novel* 37. nos. 1/2 (2003–2004), Lorri G. Nandrea explains that the Victorian novel inherited two different theories and literary traditions for representing feeling or emotion. Sensibility, she argues, manifests itself in *Jane Eyre* "by contaminating or subtly deranging sympathetic patterns" that complicate "the triumph of sympathy: the manner in which the attraction to difference and dissolution associated with sensibility has been repressed, or re-channeled into a desire for identity" (119). I found this problematic extremely useful in reading *The Mill on the Floss*, which, I believe, not only disguises sensibility as "natural desire" but also folds it into sympathy without transforming the self-enclosure of desiring subjects.

17. George Eliot, *The Mill on the Floss*, ed. Carol C. Christ (New York: Norton, 1994), 372. All subsequent citations are of this edition and will henceforward be provided in the text.

18. Of the letter as signifier, Lacan says, "the displacement of the signifier determines the subjects in their acts, in their destiny, in their refusals, in their blindnesses, in their end and in their fate, their innate gifts and social acquisitions notwithstanding, without regard for character of sex, [so that] willingly or not, everything that might be considered the stuff of psychology, kit and caboodle, will follow the path of the signifier" ("Seminar on 'The Purloined Letter,'" in *French Freud: Structural Studies in Psychoanalysis*, trans. and ed. Jeffrey Mehlman, special issue of *Yale French Studies* 48 [1972]: 60).

19. It is clear to me that the novel remains unresolved if one insists on evaluating the success of that resolution in relation to the story of an individual's growth and development. According to Gillian Beer, "the transgressions

that George Eliot liberates at the end of the novel are in that same moment suppressed and done away with" (*George Eliot* [Bloomington: Indiana University Press, 1986], 102). In "Superfluity and Suction: The Problem with Saving in *The Mill on the Floss*," *Novel* 35, no. 1 (2001), Deanna Kreisel offers a new economic reading of the novel that lends precision to this claim: Maggie "is not the victim so much of her self-denial or of her appetites alone, as of the confusion of the two; the economic imperatives of the novel require and bring about her elimination and that of her threatening desires and even more threatening self-abnegation. It is, after all, not the unrestrained, symbolically sexual waters of the flood that kill her, but rather the giant pieces of industrial machinery broken free of their moorings and rushing down the river" (99–100).

20. In *Waverley, or 'Tis Sixty Years Since* (Oxford: Oxford University Press, 1981), Scott locates the action of in these terms: "It is then sixty years since Edward Waverley, the hero of the following pages, took leave of his family to join the regiment of dragoons in which he had lately obtained a commission" (5). I find it too coincidental not to mention that in *The Voyage of the Beagle* (London: Dent, 1950), Charles Darwin uses this same novelistic trope to mark human progress: "From seeing the present state, it is impossible not to look forward with high expectations to the future progress of nearly an entire hemisphere. The march of improvement, consequent on the introduction of Christianity throughout the South Sea, probably stands by itself in the records of history. It is the more striking when we remember that only *sixty years since*, Cook, whose excellent judgment none will dispute, could foresee no prospect of a change. Yet these changes have now been effected by the philanthropic spirit of the British nation (486, my emphasis).

21. In *The Theory of the Moral Sentiments* (Amherst, N.Y.: Prometheus, 2000), Adam Smith worried about the issue of how a society of competitive individuals might ever achieve social harmony as a community:

> Mankind, though naturally sympathetic, never conceive, for what has befallen another, that degree of passion which naturally animates the person principally concerned.... What they feel will, indeed, always be in some respects different from what he feels, and compassion can never be exactly the same with original sorrow; because the secret consciousness that the change of situations, from which the sympathetic sentiments arise, is but imaginary, not only lowers it in degree, but in some measure varies it in kind, and gives it a quite different modification. These two sentiments, however, may, it is evident, have such a correspondence with one another, as is sufficient for the harmony of society. Though they will never be unisons, they may be concords, and this is all that is wanted or required. (22–23)

22. Immanuel Kant, "Perpetual Peace," in *Kant: Selections*, ed. and trans. Lewis White Beck (Englewood Cliffs, N.J.: Prentice-Hall, 1988), 439.

23. As H.L. Malchow has argued, the Victorian public did not in fact understand ruling-class masculinity in terms of a sharp contradiction between industrial capitalism and the privileges of inherited rank.

> Rather than developing an aggressive and separate class consciousness out of the grievances that oppressed them in the early nineteenth century, the divided world of successful commerce was won over by amelioration, enfranchisement, to co-optation of a minority in the political establishment, and the education of their heirs in public schools with their snobbery and service ethic. Not a new process by any means, but one which, it is said, proved surprisingly effective in transforming the crude provincial into the carefully dressed and spoken man or woman of polite society, in turning wealthy businessmen into subscribers of *Vanity Fair* and their sons into lawyers.
>   (*Gentlemen Capitalists: The Social and Political World of the Victorian Businessman* [Stanford: Stanford University Press, 1992], 364–65)

4. THE POLYGENETIC IMAGINATION

1. George W. Stocking Jr., *Victorian Anthropology* (New York: Macmillan, 1987), 173. All citations are of this edition and will henceforward be provided in the text. For an instructive reading of the ideological conflict enacted through the debate over monogenesis versus polygenesis, see Dana Nelson, *National Manhood: Capitalist Citizenship and the Imagined Fraternity of White Men* (Durham, N.C.: Duke University Press, 1998), 109–32. The implications of this argument seem especially clear in the United States under the circumstances leading up to and following from the Civil War. Abolitionist England had, on the other hand, learned to understand itself as exempt from the degeneracy of a United States that practiced slavery, only to face the problem of placing Englishmen in the same body of humanity with many of the Asian and African peoples incorporated within the British Empire.

2. John Locke, *Two Treatises of Government*, ed. Peter Laslett (Cambridge: Cambridge University Press, 1967).

> Is a Man under the Law of *England*? *What made him free* of that Law? That is, to have the Liberty to dispose if his Actions and Possessions according to his own Will, within the Permission of that Law? A capacity of knowing that Law. Which is supposed by that Law, at the Age of one and twenty years, and in some cases sooner. If this *made* the Father *free*, it shall *make* the Son *free* too. Till then we see the Law allows the

Son to have no Will, but he is to be guided by the Will of his Father or Guardian, who... must govern for him, and be a Will to him, till he hath *attained a state of Freedom*, and his Understanding be fit to take the Government of his Will. But after that, the Father and Son are equally *free* as much as Pupil and Tutor after Nonage; equally Subjects of the same Law together, without any Dominion left in the Father over the Life, Liberty, or Estate of his Son, whether they be only in the State and under the Law of Nature, or under the positive Laws of an Established Government. (II.LIX.13–32)

3. In *Darwin's Metaphor: Nature's Place in Victorian Culture* (Cambridge: Cambridge University Press, 1985), Robert M. Young points out that Darwin originally "seized on the image of nature as war and used Malthus's view of natural law ... as his authority for extending the principle of selection from the breeders' wishes to nature, that is, from artificial to natural selection" (54). Where the metaphor of natural struggle implies that nature selects the keenest competitor, cultural evolutionism implies that the wisest and most benevolent civilization trumps those where violence reigns. In *Darwin's Plots: Evolutionary Narrative in Darwin, George Eliot, and Nineteenth-Century Fiction* (London: Routledge and Kegan Paul, 1983), Gillian Beer calls attention to the discrepancy between the narrative of natural selection and the implications that those who drew on Darwin's theory would tease from that narrative: "Lying behind diversity [produced by natural selection] in Darwinian theory, slumbers the form of some remote progenitor, irrecoverable because precedent to history or anterior to consciousness. That idea of 'the single form' becomes itself a new and powerful source of nostalgia" (127–28).

4. I turn to Ann Laura Stoler's study of the relationship between desire and race in Foucault's notion of discipline for the best explanation of why I am not writing about race in this chapter, even though what I say can often be extrapolated and made to refer to that form of difference:

Scapegoat theories posit that under economic and social duress, particular sub-populations are cordoned off as intruders, invented to deflect anxieties, and conjured up precisely to nail blame. For Foucault, racism is more than an ad hoc response to crisis; it is a manifestation of preserved possibilities, the expression of an underlying discourse of a permanent social war, nurtured by the biopolitical technologies of 'incessant purification.' Racism ... is internal to the biopolitical state, woven into the weft of the social body, threaded through its fabric.

(*Racism and the Education of Desire: Foucault's History of Sexuality and the Colonial Order of Things* [Durham, N.C.: Duke University Press, 1995], 69)

5. Alfred Lord Tennyson, *In Memoriam*, in *The Oxford Authors: Alfred Tennyson*, ed. Adam Roberts (Oxford, Oxford University Press, 2000), 292, line 143.

6. Daniel C. Dennett, *Darwin's Dangerous Idea: Evolution and the Meanings of Life* (New York: Simon and Schuster, 1995), 59.

7. *Dracula* consequently entered literary critical consciousness as folklore, earning three pages in Montague Summers's *The Vampire: His Kith and Kin* (London: Routledge and Kegan Paul, 1928) and as many sentences in H. P. Lovecraft's *Supernatural Horror in Literature* (1939; reprint, New York: Dover, 1973).

8. Sigmund Freud, "The Uncanny," in *The Standard Edition of the Complete Psychological Works of Sigmund Freud*, trans. James Strachey (London: Hogarth, 1955), 2:237. All citations are of this edition and will henceforward be provided in the text.

9. Freud to Martha Bernays, August 18, 1883, in *Letters of Sigmund Freud*, ed. Ernst L. Freud, trans. Tania Stern and James Stern (New York: Basic, 1960), 51.

10. Freud to Minna Bernays, December 3, 1885, in *Letters of Sigmund Freud*, 189.

11. In *The Crowd: British Literature and Public Politics* (Berkeley: University of California Press, 2000), John Plotz shows that a number of exemplary literary texts from the Victorian period put "the crowd" in contention with other notions of the public sphere, such as the "privatizing ideology of the bourgeoisie," the "patriotic fervor of the Briton," and "the generalizing compassion of 'humanizing narratives.'" From this, he concludes that the notion of "the public" was itself an extremely mutable concept that could take any number of literary forms, even within a single text (12).

12. In "Desiring Difference: Sympathy and Sensibility in *Jane Eyre*," *Novel: A Forum on Fiction* 37, nos. 1–2 (2003–4), Lorri G. Nandrea argues that most Victorian novels invite us to read "sympathy's ideological function" as a way of "maintaining existing power structures." In following this lead, contemporary criticism generally fails to detect within "the discourse of feeling a submerged idea" that diverges "from the dialectical, individualistic, hierarchical properties of sympathy that do indeed support capitalist power structures" (118).

13. Gilles Deleuze and Felix Guattari, *A Thousand Plateaus: Capitalism and Schizophrenia* (Minneapolis: University of Minnesota Press, 1987), 25. All citations are of this edition and will henceforward be provided in the text.

14. Gilles Deleuze, *Repetition and Difference*, trans. Paul Patton (New York: Columbia University Press, 1994), 12–13.

15. Thomas Robert Malthus, *An Essay on the Principle of Population*, ed. Philip Appleman (New York: Norton, 2004), 16. All citations are of this

edition, unless otherwise indicated, and will henceforward be provided in the text.

16. It is worth noting that in the 1826 edition of *An Essay on the Principle of Population*, Malthus expanded the argument for culture as a negative, or cultural, check on population. As he compiled statistics for marriage, birth, and death in most of the great nations of the world, he evidently convinced himself that the marriage customs, hygienic practices, and practical attitude of the peasantry in such countries as Norway and Switzerland had all but eliminated the need for such positive checks as starvation or disease. He concludes his assessment of the checks to population in England on the hopeful note that "the increasing healthiness of a country will not only diminish the proportions of deaths, but the proportions of births and marriages" (*The Works of Thomas Robert Malthus, An Essay on the Principle of Population: The Sixth Edition (1826) with Variant Readings from the Second Edition (1803)*, ed. E. A. Wrigley and David Souden [London: William Pickering, 1986], 2:266. Robert Young contends that because Malthus so completely shifted his focus to the "doctrine of moral and prudential restraint from marriage until one could support a wife and family," he "was right to distinguish the second edition as 'a new work'" (*Darwin's Metaphor*, 31–32).

17. In *Modernism, Romance, and the Fin de Siècle* (Cambridge: Cambridge University Press, 1999), Nicholas Daly provides what is, to my mind, the most convincing explanation for the revival of romance fiction during the 1880s and 1890s. Arguing against the continuity of the gothic tradition from *Frankenstein* through *Dracula* and for what he calls "the modernity of the romance revival," he reads late Victorian romance as the "sibling of modernism," a robustly masculine form, "rather than as its unusually decrepit great uncle" (10). "Once we recognize the romance and modernism as part of the same moment," he continues, "we can begin to understand [that] the romance revival provided the narratives and the figures that enabled late Victorian middle-class culture to accommodate successfully certain historical changes, notably modernizing processes" (24).

18. For feminist readings, see Margaret Homans, *Bearing the Word: Language and Female Experience in Nineteenth-Century Women's Writing* (Chicago: University of Chicago Press, 1986); Mary Jacobus, "Is There a Woman in This Text," *New Literary History* 14 (1982): 117–54; and Mary Poovey, "'My Hideous Progeny': The Lady and the Monster," in *The Proper Lady and the Woman Writer* (Chicago: University of Chicago Press, 1984), 114–42. For sociological readings, see Franco Moretti, "Dialectic of Fear," in *Signs Taken for Wonders: Essays in the Sociology of Literary Forms*, trans. Susan Fischer, David Forgacs, and David Miller (New York: Verso, 1988), 83–108; and Paul O'Flinn, "Production and Reproduction: The Case of *Frankenstein*," Chris Baldick, "The Politics of Monstrosity," and Gayatri Chakravorty Spivak, "Three Women's

Texts and a Critique of Imperialism," in *Frankenstein: Mary Shelley*, ed. Fred Botting (New York: St. Martin's Press, 1995), 21–47, 48–67, and 235–60, respectively.

19. In *Romanticism and the Human Science: Poetry, Population, and the Discourse of the Species* (Cambridge: Cambridge University Press, 2000), Maureen McLane concisely explains the monster's perplexing relation to "the human": "The monster is not decisively human; nor, as his eventual fluency and rationality suggest, is he decisively not human. Victor inadvertently engineers not a human being but the monstrous critique of the very category" (88).

20. Mary W. Shelley, *Frankenstein*, ed. J. Paul Hunter (New York: Norton, 1996), 98. All citations are of this edition and will henceforward be provided in the text.

21. In his comparative analysis of the various nations of the world, Malthus reveals his aversion to the effects on humanity of the new urban environment. Not only do the industrial towns promote licentious sexual behavior among those who can least afford it, overcrowding also promotes filth and fosters contagion. It is important to note how his figure for "the population" changes abruptly here from a gendered peasantry to an angry mass: "A mob, which is generally the growth of a redundant population goaded by resentment for real sufferings, but totally ignorant of the quarter from which they originate, is of all monsters the most fatal to freedom . . . though, in its dreadful fits of resentment, it appears occasionally to devour its unsightly offspring; yet no sooner is the horrid deed committed, than, however unwilling it may be to propagate such a breed, it immediately groans with a new birth" (*The Works of Thomas Malthus*, 3:501).

22. Thomas Robert Malthus, *Principles of Political Economy, Considered with a View to Their Practical Application*, 2d ed. (London: William Pickering, 1836; reprint, New York: A. M. Kelley, 1964). Here, Malthus provides a new calculus wherein commodities outstrip demand and their price goes down, diminishing the share of profit that goes to the laborer (180). By making it possible for commodities to grow much faster than the number of consumers, machinery brings about this reversal in the relation of production to reproduction (209). All citations are of this edition and will henceforward be included in the text.

23. In his chapter titled "The Fetishism of Commodities and the Secret Thereof" in *Capital: A Critique of Political Economy*, ed. Frederick Engels (New York: International, 1992), Karl Marx famously explains how commodities effect a reversal of agency whereby what man produces comes to rule him: "The character of having value, when once impressed upon products, obtains fixity only by reason of their acting and re-acting upon each other as quantities of value. These quantities vary continually, independently of the will, foresight

and action of the producers. To them, their own social action takes the form of the action of objects, which rule the producers instead of being rules by them" (1:79).

24. Most notably, Patrick Brantlinger's classic study *Rule of Darkness: British Literature and Imperialism, 1830–1914* (Ithaca: Cornell University Press, 1988); David Glover, *Vampires, Mummies, and Liberals: Bram Stoker and Technology of Monsters* (Durham, N.C.: Duke University Press, 1996); and Stephen Arata, "The Occidental Tourist: Stoker and Reverse Colonization," in *Fictions of Loss in the Victorian Fin de Siècle* (Cambridge: Cambridge University Press, 1996), 107–32.

25. Bram Stoker, *Dracula* (New York: Penguin, 1993), 275. All citations are of this edition and will henceforward be provided in the text.

26. H. Rider Haggard, *She* (New York: Penguin, 2001), 283. All citations are of this edition and will henceforward be provided in the text.

27. The effects of Dracula's bite and Ayesha's mesmerism are faithful to the late-nineteenth-century model of addiction. For an account of that model and how it operates in *Dracula*, see Stacey Margolis, "Addiction and the Ends of Desire," in *High Anxieties: Cultural Studies in Addiction*, ed. Janet Farrell Brodie and Marc Redfield (Berkeley: University of California Press, 2002).

28. Robert Louis Stevenson, *The Strange Case of Dr. Jekyll and Mr. Hyde*, in *The Complete Stories of Robert Louis Stevenson*, ed. Barry Menikoff (New York: Modern Library, 2002), 307.

29. *Dracula* got off to an admittedly slow start in this respect. During the 1950s and 1960s, critical studies of vampires were still attempting to trace Stoker's source material through Eastern European myth (see n. 7, above). Most notable perhaps is Nandris Grigore's "The Historical Dracula: The Theme of His Legend in the Western and Eastern Literatures of Europe," *Comparative Literature Studies* 3 (1966): 367–96. Grigore makes the unsupported claim that *Dracula*, which has never been out of print since it was first published, is the second highest selling book of all time after the Bible, a claim that was picked up in several critical studies and made the basis for arguments concerning its cultural importance. Stoker was considered a hack. The 1970s saw the rise of literary criticism that brought *Dracula* into the novel canon, albeit in a peripheral position. During the 1980s, a number of critical studies, including Brantlinger's *Rule of Darkness* and Christopher Craft's "Kiss Me with Those Red Lips: Gender and Inversion in the *Fin de Siècle* in Bram Stoker's *Dracula*," *Representations* 8 (1984): 107–33, reclassified *Dracula* as a novel worthy of scholarly interest for its sophisticated response to late-nineteenth-century political issues.

30. See Nicholas Daly, *Modernism, Romance, and the Fin de Siècle*, 30–53, for a detailed discussion of the relationship between *Dracula* and the rise of professionalism.

31. Anita Levy, "Gendered Labor, the Woman Writer, and Dorothy Richardson," *Novel* 25 (1991): 50–71.

5. The Necessary Gothic

1. Naomi Schor, "The Writing of French Studies," in *Bad Objects: Essays Popular and Unpopular* (Durham, N.C.: Duke University Press, 1995), 72.

2. Carol Gilligan's *In a Different Voice: Psychological Theory and Women's Development* (Cambridge: Harvard University Press, 1982) offers what was one of the more influential applications of this novelistic move to actual women:

> As we have listened for centuries to the voices of men and the theories of development that their experience informs, so we have come more recently to notice not only the silence of women but the difficulty in hearing what they say when they speak. Yet in the different voice of women lies the truth of an ethic of care, the tie between relationship and responsibility, and the origins of aggression in the failure of connection. The failure to see the different reality of women's lives and to hear the differences in their voices stems in part from the assumption that there is a single mode of social experience and interpretation. By positing instead two different modes, we arrive at a more complex rendition of human experience which sees the truth of separation and attachment in the lives of women and men and recognizes how these truths are carried by different modes of language and thought. (173–74)

3. Sandra Gilbert and Susan Gubar, *The Madwoman in the Attic: The Woman Writer and the Nineteenth-Century Literary Imagination* (New Haven: Yale University Press, 1979), 78.

4. Wendy Brown, *States of Injury: Power and Freedom in Late Modernity* (Princeton: Princeton University Press, 1995), 45.

5. See, for example, Nancy Armstrong, *Desire and Domestic Fiction: A Political History of the Novel* (New York: Oxford University Press, 1987); Cathy N. Davidson, *Revolution and the Word: The Rise of the Novel in America* (New York: Oxford University Press, 1986); Doris Sommer, *Foundational Fictions: The National Romances of Latin America* (Berkeley: University of California Press, 1991).

6. See, for example, Shoshana Felman, ed., *Literature and Psychoanalysis: The Question of Reading, Otherwise* (Baltimore: Johns Hopkins University Press, 1982); and Naomi Schor, *Breaking the Chain: Women, Theory, and French Realist Fiction* (New York: Columbia University Press, 1985).

7. See, for example, Janet M. Todd, *Sensibility: An Introduction* (London: Methuen, 1986); Claudia Johnson, *Equivocal Beings: Politics, Gender, and*

Sentimentality in the 1790s (Chicago: University of Chicago Press, 1995); Jane Tompkins, *Sensational Designs: The Cultural Work of American Fiction, 1790–1860* (New York: Oxford University Press, 1985); Shirley Samuels, ed., *The Culture of Sentiment: Race, Gender, and Sentimentality in Nineteenth Century America* (New York: Oxford University Press, 1992); Julia A. Stern, *The Plight of Feeling: Sympathy and Dissent in the Early American Novel* (Chicago: University of Chicago Press, 1997); and Elizabeth Barnes, *States of Sympathy: Seduction and Democracy in the American Novel* (New York: Columbia University Press, 1997).

8. In *Gender Trouble: Feminism and the Subversion of Identity* (New York: Routledge, 1990), Judith Butler dismantles the fallacy of "agency," namely, the assumption that there is being behind doing. There is, she contends, "no gender identity behind the expressions of gender; that identity is performatively constituted by the very 'expressions' that are said to be its results" (25).

9. *Gender Trouble*, 31.

10. In his preface to *Studies in European Realism*, trans. Edith Bone (New York: Grosset and Dunlap, 1964), Lukács charges realism with the sacred duty of maintaining "the organic, indissoluble connection between man as a private individual and man as a social being, as a member of the community" (8). In *The Historical Novel*, trans. Hannah Mitchell and Stanley Mitchell (Lincoln: University of Nebraska Press, 1983), 171–250, Lukács argues that fiction abandoned this principle around 1848, even before realism had reached its peak in England and the United States.

11. Herbert Marcuse, "The Affirmative Character of Culture," in *Negations: Essays in Critical Theory*, trans. Jeremy J. Shapiro (Boston: Beacon, 1968), 95.

12. Ibid., 121.

13. Nancy Chodorow, *The Reproduction of Mothering: Psychoanalysis and the Sociology of Gender* (Berkeley: University of California Press, 1978).

14. Challenges to the exclusive naturalness of kinship based on the heterosexual couple and their biological offspring have proliferated in recent years thanks to the open formation of gay or "chosen" families and to new reproductive technologies. See, for example, Kath Weston, "Forever is a Long Time: Romancing the Real in Gay Kinship Ideologies," in *Naturalizing Power: Essays in Feminist Cultural Analysis*, ed. Sylvia Yanagisako and Carol Delaney (New York: Routledge, 1995), 87–110; Helena Ragoné, "Incontestable Motivations," and Corinne P. Hayden, "A Biodiversity Sampler for the Millennium," in *Reproducing Reproduction: Kinship, Power, and Technological Innovation*, ed. Sarah Franklin and Helena Ragoné (Philadelphia: University of Pennsylvania Press, 1998), 118–31 and 173–205, respectively.

15. Charlotte Brontë, *Jane Eyre* (New York: Penguin, 2003), 501.

16. A number of anthropologists credit Darwin for the narrowing down of kinship to this very restrictive notion of blood. See, for example Gilbert

Herdt, "Introduction: Third Sexes and Third Genders," in *Third Sex, Third Gender: Beyond Sexual Dimorphism in Culture and History*, ed. Gilbert Herdt (New York: Lane, 1994), 28–32; and Hayden, "A Biodiversity Sampler," 177. I would argue that the novel of the same period did more than science to transform theory into practice when it took the symbolic order of the so-called facts of life and recast them as many and various individual destinies, the success of which was realized in marriage and biological reproduction.

17. In *Profit and Pleasure: Sexual Identity and Late Capitalism* (New York: Routledge, 2000), Rosemary Hennessy claims, similarly, that alternative families do not alter the fact that primary goods and services continue to be distributed to most of the population through the family. Moreover, as she explains, the family ensures that despite "the recruitment of more women into the workforce, the division of labor in the home is not being dramatically affected" (63). "Domestic partnerships and gay marriages that redefine sexuality only in terms of rights for gays" leave unquestioned or even indirectly promote "capitalism's historical stake in the relationship among family, labor, and consumption" (67).

18. Judith Butler, "Is Kinship Always Already Heterosexual?" *differences: A Journal of Feminist Cultural Studies* 13, no.1 (2002):14–44.

19. In his essay "The Uncanny," in vol. 17 of *The Standard Edition of the Complete Psychological Works of Sigmund Freud*, ed. James Strachey (London: Hogarth, 1973), Sigmund Freud attempts to explain those moments in modern adults' lives when they abandon reason and understand their experience in terms of "the omnipotence of thoughts, with the prompt fulfillment of wishes, with secret injurious powers and with the return of the dead" (247). Such moments not only challenge the limits of individuated consciousness but also expose the fact that those limits are as much a cultural acquisition as the old belief in omnipotent thinking. As he explains, "We—or our primitive forefathers—once believed that these possibilities were realities, and were convinced that they actually happened. Nowadays we no longer believe in them, we have *surmounted* these modes of thought; but we do not feel quite sure of our new beliefs, and the old ones still exist within us ready to seize upon any confirmation. As soon as something *actually happens* in our lives which seems to confirm the old, discarded beliefs we get a feeling of the uncanny" (247–48). Freud mentions the possibility of collective regression as if to dismiss that possibility and get on with an argument in which "the distinction between the two" kinds of uncanny experience is "theoretically very important" (248). But the more he tries to differentiate the feeling we get when repressed material wells up within us from the feeling we get when only old collective thought modes can explain the world, the more Freud undermines the difference between the individual's internal nature and the culture external to that individual, until, he admits, his argument "no doubt extends the term 'repression' beyond its legitimate meaning" (249).

20. In *The Great Tradition: George Eliot, Henry James, Joseph Conrad* (New York: New York University Press, 1967), F. R. Leavis describes the Conradian sensibility, for example, as an internally divided one "so intimately experienced in the strains and starvations of the isolated consciousness, and so deeply aware of the sense in which reality is social, something established and sustained in a kind of collaboration" (209).

21. Bram Stoker, *Dracula* (New York: Penguin, 1993), 362–63. All citations are of this edition and will henceforward be included in the text.

22. In *Skin Shows: Gothic Horror and the Technology of Monsters* (Durham, N.C.: Duke University Press, 1995), Judith Halberstam links the figure of Dracula to those of the immigrant and Jew: "Dracula's need to 'consume as many lives as he can,' his feminized because nonphallic sexuality, and his ambulism that cause him to wander far from home in search of new blood mark him with all the signs of Jewish neurosis. Dracula, as the prototype of the wanderer, the 'stranger in a strange land,' also reflect the way that homelessness or rootlessness was seen to undermine nation" (98). In *Fictions of Loss in the Victorian Fin de Siècle* (Cambridge: Cambridge University Press, 1996), Stephen Arata identifies narratives of reverse colonization in which "problematic or disruptive figures come from the periphery of empire to threaten a troubled metropole" (107). Arata considers *Dracula* as a narrative that reflects imperial practices back to the British in monstrous form. In *Alien Nation: Nineteenth-Century Gothic Fictions and English Nationality* (Philadelphia: University of Pennsylvania Press, 1997), Cannon Schmidt reads *Dracula* through the lens of orientalism, contending that Stoker's purpose in having "the eastern vampire" threaten "the maternal" is to replace "multiple national identities with a single western one" (144).

23. In *Reproductive Urges: Popular Novel Reading, Sexuality, and the English Nation* (Philadelphia: University of Pennsylvania Press, 1999), Anita Levy resists a racialized reading of *Dracula* and instead asks the question, "what does the figure of the vampire make possible or facilitate?" (158). She responds to this question by reminding us that "the vampire makes possible ... a revised configuration of the household conjoining in and through the figures of the professional man and the literate woman labors of cultural reproduction with those of family formation and perpetuation. ... What is new in Stoker's representation of the privileged alliance between a middle-class woman and professional men is that the intellectual labor of cultural reproduction is no longer severed from the maternal labor of social and biological reproduction" (168). In *Modernism, Romance, and the Fin de Siècle* (Cambridge: Cambridge University Press, 1999), Nicholas Daly reads *Dracula* "as an origin-tale for a new professional class." The novel "represents the appearance of these new men as the necessary consequence of an external threat that then becomes embodied in the story's female characters. By the end of the narrative the vampire has been defeated, but the team of professional men lives on" (26).

24. For an illuminating explanation of the relation of such theories to *Dracula*, see Stacey Margolis, "Addiction and the Ends of Desire," in *High Anxieties: Cultural Studies in Addiction*, ed. Janet Farrell Brodie and Marc Redfield (Berkeley: University of California Press, 2002), 19–37.

25. The one exception to the rule of immediate and unrestrained consumption among the vampires in this novel stands out as a rather transparent device for letting Jonathan Harker know that he is soon to become the object rather than the subject of consumption, so prompting his escape from Dracula's castle. Eavesdropping at Dracula's door, Harker overhears him deliver this parodic endorsement of delayed gratification and respect for private property: "'Back, back, to your own place! Your time is not yet come. Wait. Have Patience. Tomorrow night, tomorrow night, is yours!' There was a low, sweet ripple of laughter, and in a rage I threw open the door, and saw without the three terrible women licking their lips" (70).

26. In *Vampires, Mummies, and Liberals: Bram Stoker and the Politics of Popular Fiction* (Durham, N.C.: Duke University Press, 1996), David Glover refers to Mina Harker as a "double-agent" on the rounds that the novel "temporarily recruits a woman into a man's place" only to abandon the parity of esteem accorded to phallic womanhood "for the overfeminized maternal" (96–97).

27. Brown, *States of Injury*, 158.

28. Melanie Klein's account of the early stages of the oedipal conflict includes a suggestive description of the confusion of penis and breast overinscribed in this bedroom scene and embodied anatomically in Stoker's vampire. Klein links such confusion to the fact that the formation of the gendered individual entails at once an irreparable separation from the mother's breast and the introjection of the father's penis, a situation giving rise to extraordinary ambivalence toward the mother. This ambivalence takes the form of the breast that can give complete gratification at one moment and withhold it at another, inspiring a deep and abiding destructive fantasy in which the child transforms its own rage outward at a world that provides a source of poison rather than nourishment. See *The Psycho-analysis of Children*, trans. Alix Strachey (London: Hogarth and Institute of Psycho-analysis, 1973), 268–325.

29. Immanuel Kant, "Perpetual Peace: A Philosophical Sketch," in *Kant: Selections*, ed. Lewis White Beck (Edgewood Cliffs, N.J.: Prentice-Hall, 1988), 436.

30. Ibid., 439.

31. Sigmund Freud, *The Interpretation of Dreams*, vol. 4 of *The Standard Edition of the Complete Psychological Works of Sigmund Freud*, ed. James Strachey (London: Hogarth, 1973), 165–87.

32. Claude Lévi-Strauss, "How Myths Die," *New Literary History* 5 (1974): 269–81.

33. Michel Foucault, *Discipline and Punish: The Birth of the Prison*, trans. Alan Sheridan (New York: Vintage, 1995).

34. In "Anne Frank and Hannah Arendt: Universalism and Pathos," in *Cosmopolitan Geographies*, ed. Vinay Dharwadker (New York: Routledge, 2000), Sharon Marcus effectively uses Arendt to challenge the opposition of universal to particular as it inflects Holocaust studies. Arendt, according to Marcus, "offers a definition of humanity that is universal, but frees universality from its troubling antipathy to particularity." As she explains, "Arendt defines universal humanity as the conditions of plurality and natality.... What human beings have in common is the world, which can only exist between people and thus requires, rather than denies, the difference and distance between them; and what each human being represents is natality, the possibility of beginning something new and initiating the unforeseen" (112). Indeed, Marcus maintains, Arendt understands the Holocaust as "an attack on human diversity as such, that is, upon a characteristic of the *human status* without which the very words *mankind* or *humanity* would be devoid of meaning" (269).

INDEX

Althusser, Louis, 29–31, 50, 162n5,
   162n9
ambivalence, 56–58, 61, 75
Anderson, Benedict, 50
Arata, Stephen, 184n22
Austen, Jane, 6, 7, 16, 18, 20, 22,
   43, 51, 52, 53, 54, 59, 81, 144;
   Emma, 16–18, 43, 53, 140; *Mans-
   field Park*, 139; *Northanger Abbey*,
   18–21; *Persuasion*, 44; *Pride and
   Prejudice*, 46–48, 49

bad subject, 29, 31, 37, 48–49, 51,
   54, 56, 63, 81; in Austen,
   43–48; in *Frankenstein*, 70; in
   Moll Flanders, 39, 40; in *Robinson
   Crusoe*, 32, 35; in *Roxana*,
   39–40
Balibar, Étienne, 54–58, 60
Barbauld, Anna Laetitia, 6, 21
Beattie, Dr. James, 2
Beer, Gillian, 173–74n19, 176n3
Bentham, Jeremy, 50–51
Bernays, Martha, 112

bourgeois morality, 27–28, 33, 48–49,
   50, 51, 161n1
Brontë, Charlotte, 86, 140; *Jane
   Eyre*, 22, 79, 80, 109, 113, 124,
   139, 140, 143–44, 150, 173n16;
   Villette, 22
Brontë, Emily, 86, 92; *Wuthering
   Heights*, 22, 80, 81, 84–87,
   89, 103, 124, 146, 172n8,
   172n10
Brown, Homer O., 7, 21, 156n9
Brown, Marshall, 169n24, 169–
   70n25
Brown, Wendy, 140–41, 150, 164n17
Burghardt, Andrew, 168n19
Burnett Tylor, Edward, 106
Burton, Thomas, 161n2
Butler, Judith, 141–42, 144–45,
   167n15, 182n8

Caveliero, Glen, 172n8
Chodorow, Nancy, 143
citizenship, 30, 33, 56, 58, 102; limits
   of, 58, 75; and the social contract,

35; versus sexual contract, 38, 41, 164n17. *See also* subject, the

Stevenson, Robert Louis: *Dr. Jekyll and Mr. Hyde*, 124–25, 146

Stocking, George, 106, 107–8

Stoker, Bram, 110, 125, 152; *Dracula*, 23, 24, 101–2, 105, 108, 110, 114, 116, 120–34, 138, 146–50, 151, 153, 177n7, 178n17, 180n27, 180n29

Stoler, Ann Laura, 176n4

subject, the, 1, 3, 43, 54–56, 63–64, 76–77, 82, 152–53; in the eighteenth-century novel, 3–10, 15–22, 25, 48–52, 59, 61, 79–81, 134–35; hegemony of, 10–11; in Hume, 12; limits of, 111–12, 114, 134–35; in Locke, 11–12, 15; mobility of, 5, 27–28, 37; and morality, 27–28; and polygenesis, 129–30, 132; relation to property, 11–12, 33–35, 39; relation to the social contract, 30–32; 60–61; in Rousseau, 12–15; in Smith, 13–15; in utopian thinking, 137–39, 153; in Victorian fiction 8, 22–23, 105, 108–10. *See also* novel, the; individualism

supplement, the, 4–6, 28, 40, 41–42, 44–45, 52, 58, 95

sympathy, 12–15, 19–20, 99, 157–58n16, 158n19

Tennenhouse, Leonard, 156n5, 161n2, 163n15, 170n1

Tennyson, Alfred, 109

terra nullius, 68, 168n19

Thackeray, William Makepeace: *Vanity Fair*, 80

Trollope, Anthony: *The Eustace Diamonds*, 80, 81

Trumpener, Katie, 166–67n12

uncanny, the, 22, 110–13, 130, 145, 183n19. *See also* Freud, Sigmund

utopian thinking, 137–39, 145, 153

Wahrman, Dror, 155n1

Walpole, Horace, 2, 16; *The Castle of Otranto*, 15, 17

Watt, Ian, 23

Weber, Max: *The Protestant Ethic and the Spirit of Capitalism*, 161n1

Wilde, Oscar: *The Picture of Dorian Gray*, 102, 134

Woolf, Virginia, 139; *A Room of One's Own*, 110; *Orlando*, 110

Young, Robert, 176n3, 178n16